Suffering in Worship

How does the universal experience of suffering relate to the experience of worship? Questioning how Anglican liturgy welcomes people who are suffering, *Suffering in Worship* uniquely applies a narrative–ritual model for the analysis of both the liturgical text and worship services themselves.

In this book, van Ommen draws on interviews with participants in worship as well as clergy. Highlighting several elements in the liturgy which address suffering, including the Eucharist, songs, sermons and prayers of intercession, he shows the significance of a warm and safe liturgical community as a necessary context for suffering people to find consolation. This book also uses the concept of remembrance to plead for liturgy that attends to the suffering of both God and people. As such, it will be of interest to scholars of pastoral theology as well as clergy.

Armand Léon van Ommen is Christ's College Teaching Fellow in Practical Theology at the University of Aberdeen, UK. He completed his Ph.D. studies in 2015 at the Evangelische Theologische Faculteit (Leuven, Belgium) where he is also involved in teaching practical theology and liturgical studies. After growing up in a Reformed church in the Netherlands, and having been part of evangelical churches during his studies, Léon became a member of the Church of England in 2011.

Liturgy, Worship and Society

Series Editors:
Dave Leal Brasenose College, Oxford, UK
Bryan Spinks and Teresa Berger Yale Divinity School, USA
Paul Bradshaw University of Notre Dame, USA
Phillip Tovey Ripon College Cuddesdon, UK

For a full list of titles in this series, please visit www.routledge.com/Liturgy-Worship-and-Society-Series/book-series/ALITWORSOC

Towards Liturgies that Reconcile
Race and Ritual among African-American and European-American Protestants
Scott Haldeman

Gender Differences and the Making of Liturgical History
Lifting a Veil on Liturgy's Past
Teresa Berger

The Rite of Christian Initiation
Adult Rituals and Roman Catholic Ecclesiology
Peter McGrail

Liturgy and Society in Early Medieval Rome
John F. Romano

Richard Baxter's Reformed Liturgy
A Puritan Alternative to the Book of Common Prayer
Glen J. Segger

Evangelicals, Worship and Participation
Taking a Twenty-First Century Reading
Alan Rathe

Eucharist Shaping and Hebert's *Liturgy and Society*
Church, Mission and Personhood
Andrew Bishop

Suffering in Worship
Anglican Liturgy in Relation to Stories of Suffering People
Armand Léon van Ommen

Suffering in Worship
Anglican Liturgy in Relation to Stories of Suffering People

Armand Léon van Ommen

LONDON AND NEW YORK

First published 2017
by Routledge
2 Park Square, Milton Park, Abingdon, Oxon OX14 4RN

and by Routledge
711 Third Avenue, New York, NY 10017

Routledge is an imprint of the Taylor & Francis Group, an informa business

© 2017 Armand Léon van Ommen

The right of Armand Léon van Ommen to be identified as author of this work has been asserted by him in accordance with sections 77 and 78 of the Copyright, Designs and Patents Act 1988.

All rights reserved. No part of this book may be reprinted or reproduced or utilized in any form or by any electronic, mechanical, or other means, now known or hereafter invented, including photocopying and recording, or in any information storage or retrieval system, without permission in writing from the publishers.

Trademark notice: Product or corporate names may be trademarks or registered trademarks, and are used only for identification and explanation without intent to infringe.

British Library Cataloguing in Publication Data
A catalogue record for this book is available from the British Library

Library of Congress Cataloging in Publication Data
A catalog entry for this book has been requested

ISBN: 978-1-4724-7540-4 (hbk)
ISBN: 978-1-315-61128-0 (ebk)

Typeset in Bembo Std
by Cenveo Publisher Services

Contents

Foreword by Bruce T. Morrill, S.J.   vii
Acknowledgements   ix

1   Introduction   1

PART I
A narrative and liturgical–ritual analysis of liturgy and stories of suffering   21

2   A narrative analysis of liturgy   23

3   Liturgy through the lens of narrative–ritual polarities   46

4   Themes in addressing suffering through liturgy   57

5   Suffering in worship: empirical perspectives   69

PART II
Liturgical theology: human tears and divine tears   83

6   Connections: human tears and divine tears   85

7   Remembering   95

8   Remembering suffering   103

9   When stories meet: liturgy as transformation and healing   117

10 A communal and liturgical spirituality of reconciliation	132
11 Conclusion	146
Bibliography	157
Index	165

Foreword

For several decades now theologians have been working hard at developing methodologies adequate to the simple fact that Christianity only exists in practice. Professional circles of practical theologians have formed and expanded, often finding themselves obliged to justify the scientific rigour and relevance of their work amid their academic faculties. In the field of liturgical theology the relationship between practice and theory has come to be conceptualized in terms of "primary theology" and "secondary theology." The former refers to the actual practised faith of people symbolically performed in liturgy, while the latter entails the analytical arguments and normative claims for what liturgy is and means. "Secondary theology" is the work of academic theologians, one step removed from the Church's primary theological work – namely, the people's ritually enacting Christian worship.

In the best efforts, the goal is for the two types of theological work – the theoretical and the practical – to inform one another. This has proved difficult for numerous reasons, not the least of which is the nature of liturgy as ritual, for ritual entails all the powerful yet discursively evasive dimensions of human bodily existence – physical, social, interpersonal, traditional. We ritualize what we cannot sufficiently or satisfyingly discuss or explain. Yet as both scholarly and ecclesial endeavour, theology has strived for understanding the faith – completely. In that endeavour, as J. B. Metz has so trenchantly pointed out, Christian churches have fashioned themselves possessors of far too many answers and too few questions. The problem resides not only in theological scholarship. The language and deportment of Sunday liturgy largely silences the cries of human suffering. Narrative performances of suffering, if allowed, would disturb the claims of an overly realized eschatology that, ironically, is proving powerless in its promises to contemporary souls who cannot find satisfaction (redemption, salvation) apart from the stories of their bodily lives. Across the North Atlantic world the Christian message, as both ritually enacted in liturgy and theologically explained, has come to fall largely on deaf ears.

The hope for faithful service to the Gospel in this moment lies in Church leaders, pastoral and academic, opening their ears to listen to the people. Therein lies the key to Christian renewal, both in practice and in theological argumentation. If liturgy's power has waned in a secularized Europe and a rapidly secularizing America, one reason may well be that those controlling it misread the true power of its performed content – namely, the Gospel mystery of Jesus' life, passion, death, and resurrection. The mystery is the revelation of God's power at work precisely where humans – ever seeking control – do not expect to hear of it – namely, in narratives of compassion with and for the suffering.

Stories of suffering, I have found over twenty years as a theology professor, are our younger generations' point of encounter with religion and, ultimately, the Divine. In this highly original work of practical–theological scholarship one of their number, Léon van Ommen has courageously taken this key to his generation's (often unarticulated) yearning in faith to open up a crucial dimension of experience so pervasive yet suppressed across the bodies assembling for worship today. In his characteristically direct style, van Ommen encapsulates the relevance of his topic and method at the outset: "Suffering is universal; liturgy is at the core of faith communities. With this book we hope to contribute to the life and liturgy of the Church, seeking ways to address the universal reality of suffering in the central acts of the Church." The scholarly method apposite to such a meeting of liturgy and (uncontrolled) life is narrative analysis, an approach essayed by a few pastoral–liturgical theologians that van Ommen takes up and advances through qualitative empirical work coupled with theological treatments of memory and healing.

In the end, van Ommen returns to the story from which his entire theological itinerary unfolded, two teenagers struggling at liturgy to grieve freely over a friend's tragic death. "The [Anglican] Liturgical Commission has drafted the script and the General Synod has approved it," he writes. "But Anna and Kate have not come to meet with the Liturgical Commission or the members of synod, but with God and their fellow believers. As a matter of fact, God and the people are the primary narrators in the liturgical performance." Readers who treat themselves to the theoretically insightful and pastorally passionate chapters leading to that conclusion will arrive with a wealth of knowledge of what is humanly at stake and divinely on offer behind that deceptively simple, if not arresting assertion.

Bruce T. Morrill, S.J.
Vanderbilt University

Acknowledgements

Writing this first page marks, in a real sense, the end of the story of writing this book. Looking back, I see the truth of the statement that research and writing are communal acts. The research and the writing have been done by myself, but not without the support of many who accompanied me on my journey. I am grateful for all who were part of this story.

In particular, I would like to thank Professor Dr Helge Stadelmann, who accompanied the first stages of my writing. He challenged me time and again to argue for every point I make. If there is still anything not argued well, it is certainly not because of him. I would like to thank Dr René Erwich. This project has benefited greatly from his methodological sharpness. I am grateful for the many hours we discussed the project, which were always helpful and greatly encouraging. Many thanks also to Professor Dr Paul F. Bradshaw. His inside knowledge and understanding of (Anglican) liturgy is phenomenal. Moreover, he challenged me particularly with regard to the narrative method, which helped me to point out clearly the contribution of such a method for liturgical studies.

When writing this boook, I had the privilege to work in the stimulating and friendly atmosphere of the Evangelical Theological Faculty. I now work at the University of Aberdeen. Thanks to all my colleagues for their support and interest in my research. During the greater part of writing this book I shared an office with Jelle Creemers and Maria Verhoeff. Thanks to them for the numerous conversations we had, for their critical questions, friendship and cakes. Huge thanks also to Jack Barentsen, colleague in the Department of Practical Theology and friend. I also would like to thank Rinke van Hell for our stimulating conversations about practical theology, narrative theology and empirical research, and Simon van der Lugt for his passion for the topic.

Special thanks go to the people who were willing to be interviewed. Often I drove home after an interview feeling privileged that people who did not know me shared their painful and vulnerable stories with me. Also, thanks to the churches and clergy who allowed me to do research in their communities, and to the clergy and readers whom I interviewed. I hope this book will make a modest contribution to the liturgical life of these churches in return.

Many thanks to Eleanor Childs who proofread the first draft of the entire manuscript and corrected my Dutch English. I am also grateful to Trevor Childs who has been a great support to me. Thanks to Harm and Berdien Wijnalda for their interest in my project. Many thanks also to Wouter Biesbrouck, Phil Lane and Niels Vandereyken for their friendship and encouragement.

I would like to thank my wife, Nele Beutels, and my children Hannelore and Jonathan. They are truly home. Hannelore and Jonathan will be glad that daddy has finally finished writing his book. The support Nele has given to this project, in so many ways, is simply beyond words. Love and thanks to her.

Finally, thanks be to God, in narrative terms, the (co-)author and audience of my life.

1 Introduction

Several years ago a friend told me the story of Anna and Kate, whom she knew from church.[1] A group of teenagers from their church in Belgium were on holiday in an African country. On their way from one place to another the driver lost control of the car. The car crashed and two teenagers died in that terrible accident. Back home they had a funeral and the funeral service expressed the Christian message of hope. But no words of pain. No words of mourning. No words of grief. Two weeks later my friend saw Anna and Kate after a church service. These girls had lost two of their friends. My friend looked at Anna and Kate and said: "You mourn, don't you?" All of a sudden the girls burst out in tears and my friend just embraced them and let them cry. That evening Kate's mother rang my friend and said: "Thank you." Rather surprised, my friend answered: "Why do you say thanks?" Kate's mother replied: "Because no one has given my daughter the opportunity to express her grief. You are the first one."

The story of Anna and Kate is one of many which I have come across and which has stimulated my interest to write this book. It is a story about grief and a church community that was not able to give room for Anna's and Kate's stories of suffering, neither as a community nor in their worship services. Even in the funeral service the pain was not dealt with. In the face of tragedy, the tragedy itself was not faced. The grand story of divine hope was communicated at the expense of the small stories of human suffering.[2] But how can liturgy acknowledge stories of suffering? How do the story of God and the stories of people come together in public worship? These are the kinds of questions this book raises.

In the present chapter we will discuss a number of issues that set the parameters for our research. First, we bring out the tension between liturgy and suffering, which leads to the primary research question for this book. We then briefly review the treatment of the topic in contemporary research and the relevance of the topic. We then discuss some keywords and reflect on our specific research interests and on our own position. In the following section we introduce the narrative–ritual liturgical approach to our topic. Finally, we introduce the churches and people who participated in this project.

The tension between liturgy and suffering

The story of Anna and Kate is not an isolated one. Many people struggle with finding a place for their grief and sorrows in church. A number of theologians who study suffering, and lament as an expression of suffering, testify to the limited space for suffering in the liturgy and the community of believers.[3] Furthermore, some of the participants in this research who shared their stories of suffering testified that the church did not provide the space to express their grief and struggles. Apparently, it is not easy for churches to address suffering and connect with people who go through difficult times. Nevertheless, not all church communities and not all worship services lack the sensitivity to deal with suffering. Some communities and some liturgies do comfort those who go through a bad patch. As a matter of fact, the church has a rich tradition and resources to address suffering in its pastoral care, its community of believers and its worship. After all, the central story of the Christian faith is that of God's love expressed in the suffering and death of Jesus Christ and of resurrection life that still shows scars of wounds.

These stories and witnesses demonstrate that the relationship between liturgy and suffering is ambiguous. The ambiguity is highlighted by some participants in our project who say that liturgy addresses suffering and at the same time "I feel I cannot express my own suffering." In this book we want to explore and evaluate what is going on between liturgy and narratives of suffering, asking how liturgy can do justice to people who experience significant negative life events.[4]

The complaints about the lack of attention to suffering in liturgy are not limited to only one denomination. The scholars and participants referred to so far, and the stories they refer to in their publications, come from a huge variety of Church backgrounds, including Free Church Evangelical, Baptist, Lutheran, Presbyterian, Anglican, Pentecostal and Roman Catholic. These Churches vary in style, in theology and in atmosphere within the community (and sometimes these variations are found even within one denomination), and yet the observed tense relationship between liturgy and suffering runs across these Churches.

In this book we will focus on the Anglican community, more specifically, on the Church of England. This Church has explicit resources in its liturgy to address stories of suffering. At the same time, it will be interesting to discover whether a difference can be found between 'high' and 'low' churches. Anglicans have a rich tradition of worship for which the *Book of Common Prayer* has been, and still is, foundational. Throughout the twentieth century the Church of England (and other churches within and outside the Anglican Communion) has seen much liturgical revision, the latest being a range of worship books in the series of *Common Worship*. For our project, to study worship in this church is most interesting because most churches within the Church of England make use of *Common Worship*, while great differences of style and (theological) emphasis can be found, ranging from Anglo-Catholic to frontier 'Fresh

Expressions.' Apart from these reasons to study Anglican liturgy, the choice is informed by being Anglican myself and my own appreciation of its worship. Given the fact that I live in Belgium and know the Church of England in the Benelux best, the focus will be on this geographical area.[5]

The above observations lead to the following main question that we hope to answer in this book: How does or can Anglican liturgy (in the archdeaconry of North West Europe in the Church of England's Diocese in Europe) address and connect to people with regard to their narratives of serious negative life events?

Status quaestionis

The relationship between liturgy and suffering is not much reflected upon from a practical theological perspective or in liturgical studies, at least not with regard to the regular worship services (the literature on the so-called *casualia* is rich). The topic does not find its way easily into general introductions of liturgy, and the number of monographs or articles discussing it is limited. A thorough exploration of how people appropriate liturgy when experiencing negative life circumstances is lacking, especially from an empirical point of view.

In the field of liturgical studies, *Rachel's Cry: Prayer of Lament and Rebirth of Hope* by Kathleen Billman and Daniel Migliore is one of the few monographs devoted to the subject of lament and therefore of suffering.[6] The topic of suffering is addressed by James Farwell from the perspective of Holy Week.[7] Gail Ramshaw proposes five "Theses for Discussion," which seek room for lament in the Eucharistic liturgy and place lament within the typological framework of praise and grace.[8] Don Saliers is one of the few liturgical scholars who takes the human plight very seriously throughout their books. Saliers also writes one chapter specifically on lament.[9] Together with Nancy L. Eiesland he has edited a volume on human disability, which contains several essays on disability and liturgy.[10] Taking into account insights from trauma theory, Dirk Lange rereads Luther's theology and rethinks liturgy.[11] John Witvliet provides biblical underpinnings for the recovery of lament in liturgy in his *Worship Seeking Understanding*.[12] Finally, the work of David Power needs mentioning, as he engages with the topic of suffering and liturgy extensively in his *Eucharistic Mystery*. His work includes a narrative perspective on liturgy.[13]

Some other books on worship take up the theme of suffering (often more specifically the theme of lament), but seldom devote more than one chapter to the topic. Furthermore, these chapters often draw on Old Testament studies, thereby not taking liturgy as point of departure, let alone empirical research on worship.[14] One exception to this is the collection of essays in *Worship That Changes Lives*, edited by Alexis Abernethy. Some of these essays are based on empirical research. The focus of that particular project is on transformation and the topic of suffering is included. However, at the end of the book Abernethy urges that "future research will need to consider more fully the important role of pain, suffering, and sadness."[15] From a practical theological perspective comes *Lament: Reclaiming Practices in Pulpit, Pew, and Public Square*.[16] This book contains a collection of essays that aim at rediscovering lament as a valid and much needed expression of suffering and brokenness. Finally, the collection of essays in *Evoking Lament*, edited by Eva Harasta and Brian Brock, should be mentioned here, although most essays in this collection deal with lament from a systematic theological perspective.[17]

It should be mentioned here that feminist liturgical scholars have asked attention for the suffering of women.[18] In a sense the feminist liturgical movement(s) can be seen as one group that thoroughly reflects on suffering and liturgy. The suffering often mentioned is the silencing of female voices throughout the Scriptures, tradition and in contemporary liturgy, especially by male dominated language, rituals and power.

In sum, few monographs or articles are directed to the specific topic of suffering and liturgy in regular worship services. Some books pay attention to the topic, but do not have it as their main focus. What is often lacking is a thorough treatment of what is happening when liturgy and the human experience of suffering meet, whether or not lament is part of that. Such a treatment asks for grounding in the empirical reality or worship. Even when books on worship assume that lament should be part of worship, the points of connection or disconnection between the liturgical act or text and situations of suffering are hardly reflected upon. That is the gap which this book addresses.

Relevance

Suffering is part of life. Many times during the research for this book I have heard people saying that suffering is inherent to life. The stories above and the brief overview of literature in the field make clear that the topic is not one that gets much attention in relation to liturgy. Yet it is in the liturgy that God and people meet. It is in the public liturgy, often on Sundays, that the Christian community gathers to bring their lives before God. Here it is that people worship and hope to be inspired anew to face the challenges of life. Suffering is universal; liturgy is at the core of faith communities. With this book we hope to contribute to the life and liturgy of the Church, seeking ways to address the universal reality of suffering in the central acts of the Church.

The present study also contributes to the academic liturgical theological discourse on the relationship between liturgy and suffering, both from the perspective of the liturgical text and from people who experience negative life events. The study focuses on the area that is most often absent in the reflections on this relationship – i.e. the area of connection or disconnection between liturgy and suffering. Moreover, by taking the perspective of people who suffer as starting point, the study contributes to the discourse by providing much needed empirical underpinnings for it. The theoretical and methodological approach to this study is a narrative one, for reasons which we will discuss below. For now it is important to note that detailed narrative analysis of liturgy is still in its infancy. To approach both participants in worship and the worship itself narratively is rather unique. This book will show the value of such an approach for liturgical studies and thus further contributes to the liturgical and practical–theological (academic) discourse.

Keywords

The keywords in this book are suffering, (Anglican) liturgy and narrative. It will be helpful to discuss these terms before moving on. We will first briefly discuss what we mean by suffering in the context of this book. Second, we will briefly comment on liturgy and worship. The third section discusses liturgy in the Anglican tradition. Since the research happens within the context of Anglican liturgy, both at the empirical and academic level, it will be helpful to establish an initial Anglican liturgical framework. Therefore, the third section is necessarily longer.

Suffering

The question of this book is how liturgy can address or connect with people who are suffering. The question deliberately does not specify what type of suffering. The interest is in the more general plight of suffering, which can be anything. The Oxford online dictionary defines suffering as "the state of undergoing pain, distress, or hardship."[19] This definition makes clear that suffering involves a state in which someone is, but at the same time the word 'undergoing' shows that it is dynamic. 'State' and 'undergoing' relate closely to two aspects that will come back in the analytical method that we use – i.e. moment and process (see pp. 52–53). Furthermore, the definition makes clear that the semantic field of suffering contains words that are usually associated with negative things: pain, distress or hardship.

Still, suffering is a word that can mean different things to different people. It is an elusive concept. A situation can mean suffering for one person, while it does not for another. Whether something is experienced as suffering or not has a lot to do with the meaning that someone gives to circumstances and events, and also with one's ability or disability to cope with these circumstances and events.[20] For example, in one church a British couple was about to move from Belgium to Uganda. The man was delighted and looked forward to it very much, while his wife dreaded the move. For the woman, this move meant suffering, for the man obviously not. In order to make the concept of suffering operational for this project, it is helpful to turn to the field of psychology in religion. In the context of coping strategies suffering is sometimes defined as a significant negative life event. Another term that is frequently used is 'major life stressor.'[21] In this book, the following indicators are used to determine suffering:[22]

1 the circumstances or event are experienced as negative;
2 the circumstances or event have major impact on the lives of those involved – i.e. (a part of) life is uprooted;

3 it can be physical or mental;
4 it might have happened in the past or is still happening now.

Throughout the book it will become clear that suffering is not easily defined and many aspects can be commented upon. As some of the results of the research will show, the answer to the research questions sometimes even depend on the definition of suffering (see pp. 65–67). The working definition which we will start with is suffering as a major negative life event or issue.

Liturgy and worship

Liturgy has several meanings and is not always sharply distinguished from 'worship.'[23] Given the focus on Anglican liturgy and worship in this research project, the definition of these terms by the Liturgical Commission of the Church of England in its report *Transforming Worship* provides a helpful starting point for our discussion:

> In this report, the words *worship* and *liturgy* are used in precisely distinct senses. If *worship* is the deepest response of redeemed humankind to God's loving purpose, then *liturgy* is the set of particular structured actions in which worship is expressed and by which worship is released. Liturgy is the occasion of worship.
>
> It will be helpful to keep the term 'liturgy' free from connotations of formality or church style, as if it were a starchier or high-church synonym for 'worship.' In our use of the terms, 'café worship' will be just as much a liturgy as a solemn Eucharist in the catholic tradition: the pattern and order may be quite different in the two, but both of them depend on *a* pattern and *an* order of some kind so that worship may happen. Liturgies are much more than texts: although words are an important part of liturgy, so too are movement and silence and music, and the way in which they are all articulated in space.[24]

The word 'liturgy' emphasizes the pattern and order of the occasion; 'worship' emphasizes the actions. The definition of terms is also helpful in pointing out that texts are only part of the occasion, and that many other factors have an influence on the worship experience. However, the definition does not make clear that liturgy is more than the pattern and order of the (usually) Sunday worship service. The rhythm of liturgy includes daily prayer, the church's calendar, and some would even claim the whole of life.[25] In our research we focus on the regular weekly worship services and liturgy is then the pattern provided for that. Still, we leave open the uses of the term 'liturgy' in a broader sense to include those other meanings.[26]

Anglican liturgy

The area of liturgical studies is vast. In this study we will take an Anglican perspective on liturgy. In order to establish such a perspective for the purpose of this book we will primarily – but not only – consult liturgical literature from within the Anglican Communion, and more specifically, from within the Church of England. In this way a kind of self-understanding of Anglican liturgy comes to the fore. The reason for limiting the liturgical perspective to an Anglican one is twofold. First, a certain delineation is called for in the wide field of liturgy. Since this book deals with Anglican liturgy, it follows logically that one should base the research on an Anglican perspective. Second, Anglicans are keen on their worship (at least at the official level). Therefore, any study that seeks to contribute to (the understanding of) Anglican liturgical practice will only be able to do so if working within the parameters of Anglican liturgical principles. That is not to say that another perspective cannot shed light on Anglican practices, nor do we suggest that Anglicans do not want to listen to other voices. However, in order to understand Anglican liturgy one needs to know their self-understanding of liturgy. Moreover, any suggestions for the amelioration of liturgical practices will need to be in line with Anglican liturgical principles. Therefore, the question that will help to delineate the research and that will guide the present paragraph is: What is Anglican liturgy?[27]

For a long time, Anglican worship has been inspired and dominated by the *Book of Common Prayer*. First issued in 1549 by Archbishop Thomas Cranmer, soon followed by a revision in 1552 and 1559, and more than a century later in 1662, the *Book of Common Prayer* has been *the* worship book of the Church of England and of many provinces in the Anglican Communion.[28] Indeed, as J. Barrington Bates calls it, the *Book of Common Prayer* is the "icon of denominational unity."[29] In 1927/1928 a major revision of the prayer book failed to pass the English House of Commons, although it had passed the Church Assembly. However, since the 1960s onwards liturgical revision could not be stopped any longer, and from that time onwards until 2000 much work has been done and is still being done.[30] For our discussion most notable are the issuing of the *Alternative Service Book* in 1980, the report *Patterns for Worship* in 1989 and finally *Common Worship* in 2000.[31]

The contemporary discussion of liturgical identity and liturgical renewal centres on the tension between uniformity or unity and diversity.[32] The *Book of Common Prayer* introduced uniformity in the structure and text of worship 'in this realm of England.' The aim was social-political as much as religious, but whatever the motives were, uniformity in worship was established, the most revolutionary element being the use of the vernacular, and the prayer book was to make its stamp on worship in the Church of England until well into the twentieth century. The need for liturgical renewal was widely felt in the twentieth century, partly due to the international Liturgical Movement.[33] The 1960s and 1970s saw a range of new liturgies and experimental services. Some of those received final approval in the 1980 *Alternative Service Book*. With this new liturgical prayer book the pendulum swung to the side of diversity officially. The texts were authorized for a period of ten years, which was extended another ten years until 31 December 2000. During the first period of experimentation it was felt that more flexibility was needed as it did not respond well enough to two recent developments. The first development was the phenomenon of family services, also called all-age worship. In many places these (non-Eucharistic) worship services were the most well attended services in the parish. The liturgical resources could not adequately provide for this new development. The second development was the need for greater flexibility in liturgy for parishes in Urban Priority Areas, as the report *Faith in the City* called for. As a response to these two developments the Liturgical Commission drafted *Patterns for Worship*. It appeared in the form of a report to the General Synod in 1989. This report marked "the final unravelling of uniformity."[34] Most of it was authorized by 1995. The hallmark of *Patterns for Worship* is that it provides a Service of the Word which contains only rubrics and no texts. It has then a large resource section to give flesh and bones to the structure.[35] The huge flexibility which allows each parish to compile its own liturgy feels like a loss to some within the church. Can Anglicans still recognize each other by their worship, as it has been the case for centuries? It is therefore interesting to see that the latest renewal of liturgies, in *Common Worship*, returns to a common text, although the emphasis is on structure rather than on text.

Given the liturgical renewal and the different responses to the question of unity (and sometimes uniformity) and diversity, the question what Anglican liturgy is comes to the fore. This question is reinforced by the pressure on the unity within the Anglican Communion in the early years of the twenty-first century. So, if we talk about Anglican liturgy, what are we talking about? Several authors have dealt with this question, including several liturgical scholars who contributed to the Prague meeting of the International Anglican Liturgical Consultation in 2005.[36]

A good starting point for the search for what constitutes Anglican liturgy is the titles of the earliest and the latest prayer books of the Church of England: the *Book of Common Prayer* and *Common Worship*. The emphasis falls upon 'common.' Michael Perham reflects on the question why *common* worship is important. His answer is threefold. First, in the liturgy the Church of England expresses its doctrine.[37] Second, worship is a major source of unity in this church. Wherever one attends worship, Perham holds, it is recognizably Church of England worship. Third, liturgy provides spiritual memory.[38] Note that, again, the unity of the Church is of great concern in its liturgical expression.

The two key elements of Anglican worship are 'Word' and 'Sacrament,' Christopher Irvine states. He continues by saying that the core principles or tendencies of Anglican worship are the following:

- worship is liturgical, has an ordered shape and a common structure;
- it holds in unity prayer and social action;
- the Bible has an important place.[39]

Irvine briefly lists some other features of Anglican worship: corporate confession, public confession and absolution; the role of the bishop as chief liturgical minister; baptism and Eucharist; aesthetic sensibility; time (Church Year and daily prayer); liturgical Psalter, and worship concludes with a blessing. Irvine comments that "These principles are neither prescriptive, nor intended as a checklist to exclude, but an attempt to map out some general defining qualities."[40]

In the same booklet, which contains some papers in preparation of the meeting of the International Anglican Liturgical Consultation in Prague 2005, in search of the Anglican liturgical identity Trevor Lloyd quotes from *Patterns for Worship*, a report in which he was deeply involved himself. Anglican worship is marked on one hand by the common features, shared experiences, language and patterns or tradition, and on the other hand by the recognition of a variety of forms as locally appropriate. Lloyd quotes also the further marks the report gives:

- A recognizable structure for worship.
- An emphasis on reading the word and on using psalms.
- Liturgical words repeated by the congregation, some of which, like the creed, would be known by heart.
- Using a collect, the Lord's Prayer, and some responsive forms in prayer.
- A recognition of the centrality of the Eucharist.
- A concern for form, dignity, and economy of words ... [41]

The report itself continues by clarifying another mark of liturgy, which Lloyd does not quote in his paper – i.e. that it should not be divisive in terms of doctrine. So there is no allowance for 'party' texts by which other 'parties' feel excluded. Phrased more positively: "Another mark of Anglican worship is a willingness to use forms and prayers which can be used across a broad spectrum of Christian belief."[42] In Lloyd's own words, the 'evolving core' of the liturgy contains "both clear and familiar structures, and some texts which everyone knew."[43]

Common Worship marks the return to a common core of texts, after the unrivalled (and 'unravelling' as Botha has it) liturgical diversity allowed for by *Patterns for Worship*. As Perham notes, in the light of the growing diversity in liturgical texts it is remarkable that *Common Worship* seems less permissive.[44] *Common Worship* still allows a great deal of freedom, yet it is clear where uniformity is desirable. Because the focus in our research project is on *Common Worship*, it is worthwhile to quote Perham at length when he compares *Common Worship* to the *Alternative Service Book* of 1980:

> *Common Worship* tries to ask much more clearly at which points this freedom is desirable and helpful – and where it is to encourage it all the more – and at which points commonality is much more desirable and helpful – and where it is to signal its importance. Thus *Common Worship* is stronger, less permissive than the ASB [= *Alternative Service Book*], on order and shape.

There is, in almost every case where the ASB gave options of shape, one clear, preferred structure to the service. It is also clear where only authorized texts are permitted, such as prayers of penitence and Eucharistic prayers, and where there are almost unlimited freedoms. It is clear at what points in the year the Church is to unite around a common lectionary celebrating the central events of our salvation and at what points local decision making might lead to a different lectionary track. For those ready to follow there is a clear message: common prayer is good, liturgical diversity is good, finding the proper balance is important.[45]

Perham points out the (new?) hallmark of Anglican liturgical identity: a common structure, shape and pattern, a small core of fixed texts and a great deal of freedom in other matters.

Thirty-eight churches from all over the world together make up the Anglican Communion. The issue of finding unity and at the same time allowing for local expressions of worship is inherent to such a Communion. Perham points out the importance of *common* worship, as we saw above. Yet local diversity and inculturation is important as well. Leonel Mitchell, in an article in which he searches for the essence of Christian and Anglican worship, quotes Indian theologian Amalorpavadass who says that "the church cannot be truly catholic or universal until it is truly incarnated in a people and inculturated according to various cultures."[46] Susan Mary Smith stresses the importance of indigenization when she reflects on principles for liturgical renewal. First, she notes that indigenization is part and parcel of Anglican liturgical renewal: "The 'Church of the English' was born of indigenized liturgy."[47] Smith's point is underlined by the report *Patterns for Worship*, which says: "To accept a variety of forms, dictated by local culture, is part of our Anglican heritage, spelt out by Archbishop Thomas Cranmer in his 1549 Preface: 'it often chanceth diversely in diverse countries.'"[48] However, Smith is aware of the tension that diversity brings to the unity in the Anglican Communion. In order to evaluate this tension, Smith helpfully introduces the metaphor of the tides. Neither ebb nor flow is to be evaluated positively or negatively; they should rather be interpreted in terms of rhythm. "Yet as in tides, so in liturgy: the stakes for balance are high."[49] These are the stakes: "Worship must be recognizably Christian, across ever-changing cultures, across 2,000 years of history. Worship must be recognizably human to the diverse peoples worshiping in these various societies and centuries."[50]

In conclusion, several authors use the metaphor of family likeness to describe liturgy that is recognisably Anglican.[51] It has to do with Anglican style, which is an elusive concept.[52] This style has to do with the tone set by Thomas Cranmer in the *Book of Common Prayer*. Gail Ramshaw observes that nearly all newly written Eucharistic prayers in the Anglican Communion between 1985 and 2010 are very similar in style.[53] Yet a tension between unity and diversity will remain.[54] Smith's metaphor of ebb and flow is a reminder that the tension need not be evaluated negatively, but that it constitutes a rhythm to be used.

Perham would agree: "common prayer is good, liturgical diversity is good, finding the proper balance is important."[55] *Common Worship* tries to find this balance in a clear structure and encourages sticking to that structure, while at the same time allowing for great textual variety and creativity. Within the framework or structure is seemingly endless room for diversity. In this book we will take the text of *Common Worship, Order One* as the main liturgical text for analysis.

Research interests and own position

Behind every book and every research project are the writer's motivations and aims – in other words, knowledge interests. The present research is built around an empirical, an emancipatory and a pastoral knowledge interest. The first interest of this project is to build an empirical basis for the scholarly debate about the relationship between liturgy and suffering. Another is a clearly emancipatory interest. I do not intend to take a militant stance here. I mean rather that if people who suffer are not addressed by the liturgy, or feel that there is no connection between the worship service and their lives, then liturgy, as the pulse of the Christian community, might do well to listen to these people. As David Power notes in his impressive work on the Eucharist, "the weak, the suffering, the underprivileged, the children, are always the privileged to whom Christ wants to be particularly present in the liturgy of the table ritual and of the ethics of foot-washing."[56] Related to this is the pastoral interest of this project. Joyce Ann Zimmerman writes, referring to the development of newer methods in liturgical studies: "A marriage of methodological advancements with pastoral issues could prove beneficial as well as interesting."[57] The expectation for this book is as such.

The pastoral and emancipatory interests of this project beg to take the experience of those who suffer seriously. Anton Boisen has given impetus to study people as 'living human documents.' According to Charles Gerkin, when Anton Boisen coined this phrase, one of his concerns was to give the experience of the suffering person the same weight as hermeneutics does to texts. "To the living human document he [Boisen] assigned the same authority and right to speak on its own terms as hermeneutical scholarship had learned to assign to the historical text, be that a New Testament text or any other written record of the human experience left by a writer of another time and place."[58] Therefore, the experience of suffering people is foundational for this book. Recently, Pamela Cooper-White argued again for taking suffering as the starting point for doing theology. It is telling that her article on suffering is first in a vast companion to practical theology.[59] Also, Don Saliers claims, in his influential book *Worship as Theology*, that "the study of liturgy is everywhere and always the study of what real men and women do and suffer in their lives."[60] Again, Power asserts: "With the event of the pasch, it is impossible to know and love God except from within the divine embrace of humanity's suffering. It is impossible to speak of God except from this starting-point."[61] In this book we want to listen to those who suffer and give them a voice in the liturgical and theological discourse.

The presupposition is that suffering needs to be addressed in liturgy and that liturgy is about meeting with God. In narrative terms, the liturgy is a place where the stories of human beings are connected to the story of God. All of these stories contain glory and happiness, but also suffering. The need to address suffering in liturgy is testified by several scholars. For example, Michael Perham writes in his handbook of pastoral liturgy: "The Church's worship is never an escape from the realities of the world. People come to a service weighted down (or sometimes uplifted) by the world's concerns, and the Church must be able to respond to this."[62] He holds that what people bring in the liturgy, God takes, touches and gives back. Thus people are healed.[63] As long as suffering is part of human life and as long people are in need for healing, it remains necessary for liturgy to address suffering. The impressive report to the Church of England's House of Bishops, entitled *A Time to Heal*, points out that Christ overcame suffering and death. But it continues by stating: "That story, however, is not yet complete. The world still suffers. The Church still proclaims healing to the sick. The Holy Spirit still empowers people to embrace that proclamation. But the end has not yet been reached. We are still in the midst of the ministry."[64] It is necessary to keep addressing the topics of suffering and healing in the context of liturgy, for "the world still suffers."

A final note on my own position is in place, because willingly or not, my background as a researcher influences the research.[65] When I started doing research my wife and I had recently found our spiritual home in an Anglican church in Belgium. After a couple of years my wife and I became Anglicans ourselves. My own upbringing was in a Reformed church in the Netherlands and my wife was raised in a nominal Roman Catholic family in Belgium. During my student years I was involved in Evangelical free churches in Belgium. In our Anglican church I became one of the archdeaconry representatives, which has helped me to get well acquainted with the archdeaconry of North West Europe, which is the geographical area in which I have conducted the empirical research. My involvement in the Church and studying Anglican liturgy often have happily coincided. My knowledge about Anglican liturgy is not limited to liturgy in the archdeaconry of North West Europe. Part of broadening my scope has been through participating in several conferences and membership of liturgical societies in England and beyond. Studying Anglican liturgy has been a wonderful journey on which I have become very appreciative of Anglican liturgy.

An empirical, practical–theological, narrative approach to liturgy

Thomas Schattauer distinguishes three disciplines within the area of liturgical studies: liturgical history, liturgical theology and liturgy as ritual and symbolic event. Empirical research falls within the third discipline, as does the present research.[66]

This book finds itself in the discipline of practical theology and employs a practical-theological method. In our understanding of practical theology, research does not stop at the descriptive or interpretive level, but contains normative reflection as well.[67] The normative reflection is liturgical–theological. Moreover, within practical theology this book positions itself in that branch which argues that the point of departure for doing theology is the reality of suffering. The basic practical theological method that we follow is explained by Richard Osmer and consists of four 'tasks.'[68] The first task is to describe the situation empirically, the second to interpret it, the third to reflect on the situation normatively and the fourth task is to develop a strategy for dealing with the situation. Chapters 2 through 5 deal with the first two tasks, using a narrative–ritual lens to study liturgy in relation to suffering. Chapters 6 through 10 are liturgical–theological and deal primarily with Osmer's third task, but make also some suggestions for the strategic or pragmatic task.

To study liturgy from a narrative point of view is not common. Nevertheless, the liturgy lends itself, and, as we will argue, calls for a narrative approach. Several arguments lead to this position. First, human beings are surrounded by stories. In the words of cultural philosopher James Smith: "We tell ourselves stories in order to live."[69] This is no less true for the liturgy. We tell ourselves the story of the liturgy in order to live with the divine. Or more precise: in the liturgical performance we rehearse the Christian story which the liturgy tells. In the liturgy, as a centrepiece of Christian communal living, the human stories and the divine story are woven together.[70] As Don Saliers notes: "When worship occurs, people are characterized, given their life and their fundamental location and orientation in the world. Worship characterizes human beings who recall and give expression to a story about the world."[71] By telling the human and the divine stories, (suffering) people find meaning for their lives – at least, that is what liturgy potentially offers. Second, the nature of the liturgy itself is narrative, as several scholars argue. John Gibaut has extensively and convincingly argued for this claim by showing how different aspects of the liturgy are inherently narrative.[72] Gibaut sees narrative as the "fundamental nature of all Christian liturgy."[73] The narrative nature can be seen in the reading of the lectionary, the preaching of the Gospel, the narrative parts of the Eucharist and the content of hymns. Moreover, the way the whole of the rite is constructed bears a narrative character.[74] A key concept in Eucharistic theology, *anamnesis*, has a narrative structure by invoking the biblical story of the Last Supper. Note its central place in the Eucharist and therefore in the liturgy, its bringing together of past, present and future, and that it is a central concept for quite a few scholars who argue for a narrative approach to the liturgy. A third reason to approach liturgy narratively is that the different 'parties' involved are storied. The different parties of liturgists, participants, text and context, are all storied themselves. The storied nature of different parties has been explored at length in homiletical literature. Particularly helpful is the work of Kees van

Dusseldorp. Working on narrative homiletics, and building upon the narrative practical–theological theory of Ruard Ganzevoort, he distinguishes between several narratives that are at play in the homiletical situation: the story of the sermon; the story of the preacher; the story of the listener; the story of the (biblical) text.[75] This applies *mutatis mutandis* to the liturgical situation as well: the story of the liturgy; the story of the liturgist; the story of the participant; the story of the (liturgical) text. All this happens within a certain place and time, the context, which is storied in itself as well.

We see liturgy as a ritual or set of rituals. Recently, the study of liturgy has been strongly informed by ritual studies.[76] Liturgy is perceived as essentially a ritual. Such a perspective does not conflict with a narrative approach. On the contrary, an important part of the ritual is the telling of stories. John Gibaut even speaks of a "symbiotic relationship."[77] Mark Allman, exploring the narrative dimension of the Eucharist, states that the Eucharist is a ritualized narrative or a narrative ritual.[78] The strong relationship between ritual and narrative is also seen when one recalls that storytelling is a performative activity. The reciprocal relationship between ritual and narrative is also confirmed by speech act theory.[79] Joseph Schaller explains:

> the ritual not only forms the context for the text, but the text also reciprocally 'informs' the ritual, allowing the participants to come to a more profound understanding of the meaning of the actions they are performing. Thus text and ritual performance are mutually and circularly dependent for their intelligibility, not merely in the manner in which they communicate information, but in the way in which both accomplish something, which, as ritual, 'not only communicates something of value but is taken by those performing it to be 'doing something' as well.'[80]

So much is clear, that narrative and ritual cannot be separated, although they are distinct.[81] The focus in the present book is on narrative, but set within the framework of liturgy and therefore of ritual.[82] The ritual/liturgy will be analysed and interpreted via the narrative inherent in it.

Churches and participants

In this book we will look at the liturgical text *Common Worship*. Nevertheless, liturgy and worship are much more than a text; liturgy is performed by real people in real places. Therefore, we ground our study in empirical reality of four real churches. We looked at four churches which are all in the archdeaconry of North West Europe in the Church of England's Diocese in Europe (geographically this coincides with Belgium, the Netherlands and Luxembourg). They all have a main service in which *Common Worship, Order One* is used as 'default' liturgical text. The churches range from high church to low church. They were selected in order to be able to make meaningful comparisons within the total of the data set where methodologically appropriate. In this book we will call the churches St Stephan's, All Saints, St Peter's and St Alcuin's.

We did not only observe the liturgical performance of these churches, but we also interviewed twenty-two participants in worship. The stories of suffering that the participants told were diverse. Six participants told their story of feeling called to ordained priesthood and the difficult, or even failed, process towards it. Five women told their story of divorce or otherwise broken relationships with their partner. This included sometimes stories of adultery on the part of the husband. Four participants told their story of bereavement, sometimes of parents, sometimes of children, sometimes of friends. Three women told about difficulties with conception or, in the case of one women, how she was under a lot of pressure from her environment to abort her child. Two persons told of their mental or physical illness. Two men told how they had to come to terms with their homosexuality. Other stories were about the loss of a job (the issue of jobs was prominent in a couple of other stories as well), strained family relationships, having to deal with being single and there was one story about an attempted suicide within the family.

Table 1.1 gives an overview of the stories that were told, the number of participants that told similar stories and their (fictive) names, how many female or male narrators told a particular story and in which church these people are at the moment. Note that some stories did not happen while the narrators were in the church they are now. Often the church they are part of now does play a part in the development of the story, but not always. For example, some participants ended up in the church they are now as a result of the negative life event they experienced (and often of how their previous church dealt badly with it).

Table 1.1 Stories of suffering

Suffering	Number	Names	Female	Male	Church
Ordination	6	Olivia, Tim, Alice, Matt, Kayleigh, Patrick	3	3	SST, SPE, SAL (2), ASA (2)
Divorce / broken relationship	5	Betty, Diana, Katrina, Catherine, Rebecca	5		SST (3), SAL (2)
Bereavement	4	Judith, Tim, Mary, Katrina	3	2	SST, SPE (2), ASA, SAL
Conception and birth	3	Abigail, Hannah, Betty	3		SST (2), SPE
Illness	2	Keith, Grace	1	1	SST, SPE
Sexual identity	2	Peter, Patrick		2	ASA, SAL
Loss of job	1	Rachel	1		ASA
Strained family relationships	1	Kayleigh	1		SAL
Attempt to suicide in family	1	Alex		1	ASA

Note: Church names are abbreviated as follows: SPE = St Peter's; SST = St Stephan's; SAL = St Alcuin's; ASA = All Saints. These are fictive names of the churches in order to warrant the anonymity of churches and participants.

The sample for the participants in worship is relatively balanced. The participants come from four different churches, between four and six participants for each church. The age of the participants ranged from around 20 to 80 and spread quite equally among the churches. Two-thirds of the participants are between the age of 40 and 69. This does not surprise as this reflects both the demography of the expat churches and also because people with more life experience are likely to have experienced more suffering. Also, some participants tell about negative life events which they have now peace with or that are healed. In every age group there is at least one man, except for the group aged 20–29. In total, one-third of the participants are male and two-thirds are female.

We also interviewed seven liturgists, five clergy and two lay ministers. Six of them are working within these four churches. One priest had served in one of the four churches in the past and now serves somewhere else. Confidentiality was also promised to these liturgists. We call the liturgists Ron and Gerald (All Saints), Ross and Al (St Alcuin's), Brett (St Stephan's), Donald and Finn (St Peter's). Finally, in each of the four churches one worship services was videotaped for analysis, for which consent was given beforehand.

Notes

1 Anna and Kate are fictive names.
2 Gerard Lukken, *Rituals in Abundance: Critical Reflections on the Place, Form and Identity of Christian Ritual in Our Culture* (Leuven and Dudley: Peeters, 2005), 333ff. esp. 337–338.
3 For example, John Swinton, *Raging with Compassion: Pastoral Responses to the Problem of Evil* (Grand Rapids, MI: William B. Eerdmans, 2007), 90–93; Don E. Saliers, *Worship as Theology: Foretaste of Glory Divine* (Nashville, TN: Abingdon Press, 1994), 120–121; Kathleen D. Billman and Daniel L. Migliore, *Rachel's Cry: Prayer of Lament and Rebirth of Hope* (Eugene, OR: Wipf and Stock Publishers, 1999), 7.
4 The term 'significant negative life event' is used in coping literature, as well as other terms like 'major life stressor' – for example, Kenneth I. Pargament, G. Koenig, and Lisa M. Perez, "The Many Methods of Religious Coping: Development and Initial Validation of the RCOPE," *Journal of Clinical Psychology*, 56(4) (2000): 519–543; Kenneth I. Pargament, "Patterns of Positive and Negative Religious Coping with Major Life Stressors," *Journal for the Scientific Study of Religion*, 37(4) (December 1998): 710–724.
5 In terms of the Church of England, this geographical area is called the archdeaconry of North-West Europe, which is in the Diocese in Europe. See http://europe.anglican.org/where-we-are/archdeaconries, accessed on 7 July 2014.
6 Billman and Migliore, *Rachel's Cry*.
7 James W. Farwell, *This is the Night: Suffering, Salvation, and the Liturgies of Holy Week* (New York and London: T&T Clark, 2004).
8 Gail Ramshaw, "The Place of Lament Within Praise: Theses for Discussion," *Worship*, 61 (1987): 317–322.
9 Saliers, *Worship as Theology*.
10 Nancy L. Eiesland and Don E. Saliers, eds, *Human Disability and the Service of God: Reassessing Religious Practice* (Nashville, TN: Abingdon Press, 1998).
11 Dirk G. Lange, *Trauma Recalled: Liturgy, Disruption, and Theology* (Minneapolis, MN: Fortress Press, 2010).
12 John D. Witvliet, *Worship Seeking Understanding: Windows into Christian Practice* (Grand Rapids, MI: Baker Academic, 2003).

13 David N. Power, *The Eucharistic Mystery: Revitalizing the Tradition* (New York: Crossroad Publishing Company, 1992).
14 For example, Debra Rienstra and Ron Rienstra, *Worship Words: Discipling Language for Faithful Ministry* (Grand Rapids, MI: Baker Academic, 2009); Witvliet, *Worship Seeking Understanding*.
15 Alexis D. Abernethy, ed., *Worship that Changes Lives: Multidisciplinary and Congregational Perspectives on Spiritual Transformation* (Grand Rapids, MI: Baker Academic, 2008), 273.
16 Sally A. Brown and Patrick D. Miller, *Lament: Reclaiming Practices in Pulpit, Pew, and Public Square* (Louisville, KY: Westminster John Knox Press, 2005).
17 Eva Harasta and Brian Brock, eds, *Evoking Lament: A Theological Discussion* (London: T&T Clark, 2009).
18 For example, Gail Ramshaw, *Reviving Sacred Speech: The Meaning of Liturgical Language: Second Thoughts on Christ in Sacred Speech* (Order of Saint Luke Pub., 2000); Marjorie Procter-Smith, *Praying with Our Eyes Open: Engendering Feminist Liturgical Prayer* (Nashville, TN: Abingdon Press, 1995); Marjorie Procter-Smith, *In Her Own Rite: Constructing Feminist Liturgical Tradition* (Order of Saint Luke Pub., 2000); Janet R. Walton, "The Missing Element of Women's Experience," in *Changing Face of Jewish and Christian Worship in North America*, ed. Paul F. Bradshaw and Lawrence A. Hoffman (Notre Dame, IN: University of Notre Dame Press, 1991), 199–217.
19 Available at: http://oxforddictionaries.com/definition/english/suffering?q=suffering, accessed on 12 December 2012.
20 Pamela Cooper-White, "Suffering," in *The Wiley-Blackwell Companion to Practical Theology*, ed. Bonnie J. Miller-McLemore, 1st edn (Malden: Wiley-Blackwell, 2012), 25; cf. C.L. Park and S. Folkman, "Meaning in the Context of Stress and Coping," *Review of General Psychology* 1(2) (1997): 115–144; R. Ruard Ganzevoort, "Religious Coping Reconsidered. Part Two: A Narrative Reformulation," *Journal of Psychology and Theology* 26(3) (1998): 276–286.
21 See for both terms Pargament, Koenig, and Perez, "The Many Methods"; Pargament, "Patterns of Positive and Negative Religious Coping with Major Life Stressors."
22 Concepts (like 'suffering') are 'unpacked' by indicators. As Tom Wengraf notes, "an 'empirical indicator' (EI) is a measurement, an observation, a datum, which is taken to be 'evidence' for a particular theoretical concept (TC) being in one 'state' or another (such as information overload or its opposite, high medium or low alienation, increasing or decreasing rates of social polarization, etc.)." This process might also be called 'operationalization.' Wengraf warns that in qualitative research this process is a complex one, moving "between concepts and material, between theory-language and empirical indications." Tom Wengraf, *Qualitative Research Interviewing: Biographic Narrative and Semi-Structured Methods* (London, Thousand Oaks, CA, New Delhi: SAGE Publications, 2001), 53, 56.
23 The many uses of the term 'liturgy' are testified to, for example, by Benjamin Gordon-Taylor in the recent collection of essays in *The Study of Liturgy and Worship*: "The nature and definition of liturgy has been extensively studied, yet, while many discussions of definition can be found, no single definition can do justice to its many aspects." "Liturgy," in *The Study of Liturgy and Worship: An Alcuin Guide*, ed. Juliette Day and Benjamin Gordon-Taylor (London: SPCK, 2013), 12.
24 "Transforming Worship: Living the New Creation. A Report by the Liturgical Commission," 2007, 1. The document is freely available on: www.transformingworship.org.uk/about-us/, accessed on July 7, 2014.
25 Joyce Ann Zimmerman, *Liturgy as Living Faith: A Liturgical Spirituality* (Scranton, PA: University of Scranton Press, 1993).
26 Note in methodology that in the interviews the terms were often used interchangeably; the distinctions are rather academic and not always relevant in talking with people who do not have a specific interest in the study of liturgy and

18 Introduction

   worship. Moreover, because liturgy and worship are intertwined, it is sometimes not even possible to distinguish one from the other. Therefore, in this book the use of both terms is not always clearly distinguished.
27 I am aware that this emic perspective has its limits. An etic perspective on Anglican liturgy can reveal different elements and blind spots. However, the aim of this research project is not to come up with a phenomenological understanding of what Anglican liturgy is. The present paragraph serves to establish a liturgical perspective that provides a reference point or framework in which to discuss the research questions.
28 Cynthia Botha notes how carefully the *Book of Common Prayer* was translated into other languages, often hardly deviating from the original English version. "Worship and Anglican Identity – a Résumé," in *Anglican Liturgical Identity: Papers from the Prague Meeting of the International Anglican Liturgical Consultation*, ed. Christopher Irvine, Joint Liturgical Studies, 65 (Norwich: SCM-Canterbury Press, 2008), 15ff.
29 J. Barrington Bates, "Expressing What Christians Believe: Anglican Principles for Liturgical Revision," *Anglican Theological Review*, 92(3) (June 1, 2010): 474.
30 It is not necessary to review the history of liturgical revisions in detail here. For a detailed overview, see Paul Bradshaw, "Services and Service Books," in *Companion to Common Worship*, ed. Paul Bradshaw, Vol. 1, Alcuin Club Collections 78 (SPCK, 2001), 1–21; Michael Perham, "Liturgical Revision 1981–2000," in *Companion to Common Worship*, ed. Paul Bradshaw, Vol. 1, Alcuin Club Collections 78 (SPCK, 2001), 22–37.
31 Liturgical diversity has been present since the time of Thomas Cranmer himself, as the chapter by Paul Bradshaw in *Companion to Common Worship* points out. Moreover, the liturgical revisions mentioned in the present text only include those in the Church of England. In other provinces, similar work has been done; see, for example, the overview of Eucharistic prayers from 1985 to 2010 in Colin Buchanan, ed., *Anglican Eucharistic Liturgies 1985–2010: The Authorized Rites of the Anglican Communion* (London: Canterbury Press Norwich, 2011).
32 Louis Weil, "'Remembering the Future': Reflections on Liturgy and Ecclesiology," in *Anglican Liturgical Identity: Papers from the Prague Meeting of the International Anglican Liturgical Consultation*, ed. Christopher Irvine, Joint Liturgical Studies, 65 (Norwich: SCM-Canterbury Press, 2008), 32. The need to address this question also becomes clear in the publication of a number of essays written by members of the Liturgical Commission in Michael Perham, ed., *The Renewal of Common Prayer: Unity and Diversity in Church of England Worship* (London: SPCK and Church House Publishing, 1993).
33 See, for example, Frank C. Senn, *The People's Work: A Social History of the Liturgy* (Minneapolis, MN: Fortress Press, 2006), Chap. 18.
34 Botha, "Worship," 15.
35 This imagery is used by the report itself; see "Patterns for Worship: A Report by the Liturgical Commission of the General Synod of the Church of England" (Church House Publishing, 1989), 15.
36 Christopher Irvine, ed., *Anglican Liturgical Identity: Papers from the Prague Meeting of the International Anglican Liturgical Consultation*, Joint Liturgical Studies, 65 (Norwich: SCM-Canterbury Press, 2008).
37 Cf. Gordon-Taylor, "Liturgy," 14–15.
38 Michael Perham, *New Handbook of Pastoral Liturgy* (London: SPCK, 2000), 13–15.
39 Christopher Irvine, "Introduction: Anglican Liturgical Identity," in *Anglican Liturgical Identity: Papers from the Prague Meeting of the International Anglican Liturgical Consultation*, ed. Christopher Irvine, Joint Liturgical Studies 65 (Norwich: SCM-Canterbury Press, 2008), 8. Note that the discussion here concerns the Anglican Communion as a whole, not only the Church of England.
40 Ibid., 11.

41 Trevor Lloyd, "Liturgy Unbound by the Book," in *Anglican Liturgical Identity: Papers from the Prague Meeting of the International Anglican Liturgical Consultation*, ed. Christopher Irvine, Joint Liturgical Studies 65 (Norwich: SCM-Canterbury Press, 2008), 28.
42 "Patterns for Worship," 5.
43 Lloyd, "Liturgy Unbound," 29.
44 Perham, *New Handbook of Pastoral Liturgy*, 12–13, 16.
45 Ibid., 16.
46 Leonel L. Mitchell, "Essential Worship," *Anglican Theological Review*, 79(4) (1 September 1997): 504.
47 Susan Marie Smith, "The Scandal of Particularity Writ Small: Principles for Indigenizing Liturgy in the Local Context," *Anglican Theological Review*, 88(3) (June 1, 2006): 376.
48 "Patterns for Worship," 5.
49 Smith, "The Scandal," 377–378.
50 Ibid., 378.
51 For example, Mark Earey and Gilly Myers, eds, *Common Worship Today: An Illustrated Guide to Common Worship* (London: HarperCollins Publishers, 2001); Perham, *New Handbook of Pastoral Liturgy*; Irvine, "Introduction."
52 Mitchell, "Essential Worship," 503.
53 Gail Ramshaw, "A Look at New Anglican Eucharistic Prayers," *Worship*, 86(2) (1 March 2012): 161–167.
54 Cf. Bates, "Expressing what Christians Believe: Anglican Principles for Liturgical Revision," 475.
55 Perham, *New Handbook of Pastoral Liturgy*, 16.
56 Power, *The Eucharistic Mystery*, 313.
57 Zimmerman, *Liturgy as Living Faith: A Liturgical Spirituality*, 36.
58 Charles V. Gerkin, *The Living Human Document: Re-Visioning Pastoral Counseling in a Hermeneutical Mode* (Nashville, TN: Abingdon Press, 1984), 38–39.
59 Cooper-White, Pamela, "Suffering."
60 Saliers, *Worship as Theology*, 26.
61 Power, *The Eucharistic Mystery*, 313.
62 Perham, *New Handbook of Pastoral Liturgy*, 8.
63 Ibid., 9.
64 *A Time to Heal : A Report for the House of Bishops on the Healing Ministry* (London: Church House Publishing, 2000), 21.
65 Cf. Johnny Saldana, *Thinking Qualitatively: Methods of Mind* (Thousand Oaks, CA: SAGE Publications, 2015), 6.
66 Thomas H. Schattauer, "Liturgical Studies: Disciplines, Perspectives, Teaching," *International Journal of Practical Theology* 11(1) (April 2007): 106–137.
67 Cf. Richard Osmer, *Practical Theology: An Introduction* (Grand Rapids, MI: William B. Eerdmans, 2008). See also the epilogue in his *The Teaching Ministry of Congregations* (Louisville, KY: Westminster John Knox Press, 2005).
68 Osmer, *Practical Theology*.
69 James K.A. Smith, *Imagining the Kingdom: How Worship Works*, Vol. 2, Cultural Liturgies (Grand Rapids, MI: Baker Academic, 2013), Chap. 3. This phrase is part of the chapter title.
70 Cf. Herbert Anderson and Edward Foley, *Mighty Stories, Dangerous Rituals: Weaving Together the Human and Divine* (San Francisco, CA: Jossey-Bass, 1998).
71 Don E. Saliers, "Liturgy and Ethics: Some New Beginnings," in *Liturgy and the Moral Self: Humanity at Full Stretch Before God*, ed. E. Byron Anderson and Bruce T. Morrill (Collegeville, PA: The Liturgical Press, 1998), 17.
72 Other scholars include Mark J. Allman, "Eucharist, Ritual & Narrative: Formation of Individual and Communal Moral Character," *Journal of Ritual Studies*, 14(1)

(January 1, 2000): 60–68; Anderson and Foley, *Mighty Stories*; Ronald O. Bearden and Richard K. Olsen, "Narrative Prayer, Identity and Community," *Asbury Theological Journal*, 60(1) (March 1, 2005): 55–66; Farwell, *This is the Night*; Bruce T. Morrill, *Divine Worship and Human Healing: Liturgical Theology at the Margins of Life and Death* (Collegeville, PA: Liturgical Press, 2009). If one accepts the claim that the whole nature of understanding and human being is narrative, then the narrative nature of liturgy is a matter of fact.

73 John St H. Gibaut, "The Narrative Nature of Liturgy," *Theoforum*, 32(3) (1 October 2001): 343.

74 David A. Stosur, "Liturgy and (post) Modernity: A Narrative Response to Guardini's Challenge," *Worship*, 77(1) (January 1, 2003): 35; Joyce Ann Zimmerman, *Liturgy and Hermeneutics*, American Essays in Liturgy (Collegeville, PA: The Liturgical Press, 1999), 76.

75 Kees Van Dusseldorp, *Preken Tussen de Verhalen: Een Homiletische Doordenking van Narrativiteit* (Kampen: Kok, 2012), 112.

76 This is especially true for the Netherlands (e.g. Gerard Lukken, Paul Post, Marcel Barnard) but less so in the United States, where the focus is more on historical liturgical research (e.g. Paul Bradshaw).

77 Gibaut, "The Narrative Nature of Liturgy," 344.

78 Allman, "Eucharist, Ritual & Narrative: Formation of Individual and Communal Moral Character," 60–61.

79 For example, Ronald L. Grimes, "Infelicitious Performances and Ritual Criticism," *Semeia*, 41 (1 January 1988): 103–122; Jean Ladrière, "The Performativity of Liturgical Language," *Concilium*, New Series 2(9) (1973): 50–62.

80 Joseph J. Schaller, "Performative Language Theory: An Exercise in the Analysis of Ritual," *Worship*, 62 (5) (1 September 1988): 420. Schaller quotes Roy A. Rappaport.

81 Cf. Anderson and Foley, *Mighty Stories*, 25.

82 For the relationship between liturgy and ritual, see, e.g., Barnard, Cilliers and Wepener, who speak about 'liturgical ritual.' Marcel Barnard, Johan Cilliers, and Cas Wepener, "Worship in the Network Culture: Liturgical Ritual Studies. Fields and Methods, Concepts and Metaphors, " *Liturgia Condenda*, 28 (Leuven: Peeters, 2014).

Part I

A narrative and liturgical-ritual analysis of liturgy and stories of suffering

In this first part of the book the question how suffering can find a voice in liturgy will be answered from an empirical perspective. In terms of Osmer's practical theological model, which underlies this work, this part presents the first two tasks of the model. These tasks comprehend describing the situation and interpreting it. To this end we start by analysing our four data sources (liturgical text, interviews with participants and with liturgists, and observations of worship services) based on Ruard Ganzevoort's narrative analytical model. The second lens through which we explore these sources is through a narrative-ritual lens, based on the theory of Herbert Anderson and Edward Foley (Chapter 3). The analysis of text, interviews, and observations yields a number of themes to discuss (Chapter 4). The last chapter of this part answers the research question and concludes the research from an empirical perspective. Part II will follow up the empirical findings by reflecting on the question and the empirical findings from a liturgical-theological perspective.

2 A narrative analysis of liturgy

This chapter presents a narrative analysis of the various data sources: the liturgical text, participants, liturgists and the worship services. The method that was applied consistently to all data was the narrative method designed by Ruard Ganzevoort. The method consists of both a structured way of reading the data sources and of distinguishing six narrative elements. Before applying the reading method we will first comment on the various authors and audiences in the liturgy. The reading method will be introduced when discussing the storylines of the liturgical text. How the six narrative elements function in the liturgy will then be discussed, but first we will explain the elements in general now.

Ganzevoort defines narrative as "the story-like structure in and through which the author (from his or her own perspective) experiences and understands life, assigns parts and roles, positions him- or herself relationally, and accounts for him- or herself before the audience."[1] Six dimensions or elements constitute his narrative model: structure, perspective, experience, role assignment, relational positioning and audience. We will comment briefly on these.

Every story has a *structure*. The dimension 'structure' includes at least three aspects. First is the time sequencing of events. By creating a certain time order, the narrator invites the reader into the world of the story. Second, structure also means that a certain meaning is created by ordering the events and experiences in the way the narrator does. The ordering may be according to processes of cause and effect, or contrast, or thematic, or otherwise. In this way the plot of the story emerges. The third aspect of structure is its valued endpoint.[2] Every story wants to 'get somewhere,' or to 'arrive' at a certain point. In the story the valued endpoint can be reached, or the narrator can get further away from it. The whole process of structuring the story is called emplotment.

A narrator can only speak from her own *perspective*. This perspective determines which events and experiences are included in the stories, and which not. Moreover, the perspective determines the value attached to each part of the story. A narrative approach does not consider this a distortion of reality, but is exactly interested in the diverse perspectives represented by different authors. A negotiation of perspectives is called for. A second aspect of perspective is horizon or scope. To which extent does the author take into account the broader context? For example, it is sometimes said that elderly or ill people have a narrow horizon – their perspective is sometimes limited to the close relatives and their own direct environment. The third aspect has to do with the needs and interests of a person. Finally, the issue of power needs to be mentioned as a possible aspect of perspective. What power does the narrator have in relation to others? The dimension of perspective is closely related to the *cui bono* question: who tells what, with which purpose, and to whom?[3]

The element of *experience* includes the tone in which the story is told. Ganzevoort uses the element of tone to describe the attitude or pose of the narrator. Is she a hero, or a victim, or an accuser? Tone determines, together with the plot, the genre of the story. Ganzevoort distinguishes between four genres: comedy, novel, tragedy, irony. In the *comedy*, the hero is often an outsider. In the end, all turns out well for the hero, "because the establishment and the narrow-minded society needs to surrender to the purity and authenticity which the hero represents."[4] Ganzevoort calls the genre of comedy 'spring stories.' Also in the *novel* it turns out well for the hero. But here the hero comes from within the society. In this genre the hero "save[s] the society, of which the norms and values need protection."[5] This is the genre of 'summer stories.' The next genre, the *tragedy*, ends less positively. In the end everybody, including the hero, loses. This is the genre of 'autumn stories.' The last genre is that of *irony*. In this genre everything is hopeless, pointless, absurd. The hero does even not try to change things. All that is left is the folly of life. Here one just laughs to keep from crying. These are the dark stories of winter. In a life story the various genres are represented by different episodes. Taken together, the life story expresses a fundamental tone which connects the stories into a whole.

The narrator ascribes roles to himself and to other characters in the story: the element of *role assignment*. These characters can be other people, God or even other forces. The kernel of this dimension of narrative is that through role assignment, the narrator "construes a constellation of roles deemed useful for the maintenance or enhancement of the narrative structure and identity of the author."[6] Through the different roles of the characters in the story in relation to the author, the identity of the latter takes shape. Also the structure is to a great extent fleshed out by the roles of the characters. Different storylines can exist next to each other, and the characters can have different roles in the various storylines.

With *relational positioning* we move from the elements *within* the story (the previous four elements) to the elements that deal with *the telling of* the story, and how this narrating is used in relation to the audience. Whereas role assignment deals with the roles within the story and with maintaining the identity of the author, relational positioning has to do with the maintenance, establishment, shape or conclusion of relationships. The relationships meant here are the relationships the author has with those to whom he narrates his story (e.g. in interviews this is primarily the interviewer/researcher). How does the author want to be seen by the listener, and how do the author and the listener see their relationship (and their relationship to others)?[7] In our project, in the interviews the interviewer is the only explicit listener, and therefore one can argue that the negotiation is limited. But in the total constellation of the liturgical drama different narrators are present: the liturgy as written, the liturgy as performed, the liturgists and the participants of the liturgy (interviewees). Is any negotiation or relational positioning going on between these 'authors?'

In one publication Ganzevoort calls the dimension of *audience* 'justification for an audience,' and indeed adding the words 'justification for' is important in this element.[8] This dimension starts from the view that every person is a 'summoned self.'[9] This means that a person is spoken to, or summoned, before he speaks himself. That starts already at the birth of the child. The child is given a name, and it grows up in certain structures of family, society and culture. The child is positioned in relationships by all these people and structures, before it can even begin to position itself.[10] According to Ganzevoort, "the summoned author now justifies him- or herself before an audience of significant others."[11] The author "accounts for his or her life in front of these significant others. This account or justification is judged by criteria for legitimacy and plausibility which the audience holds."[12] This means also, in a sense, that the audience determines how many and which storylines are needed for justification. In general, the more heterogeneous the audience is, the more storylines are needed, and vice versa. Note that the audience is not only the explicit audience of the listener, but that more than one audience can be implied.

Against the background of these narrative elements we can now turn to an analysis of the liturgy. First we turn to the characters of the liturgy: the authors and the audiences.

The authors and the audiences

Stories can only exist by virtue of their authors. The author and the audience are inherent in the way Ganzevoort formulates the goal of storytelling: to begin, enhance, change or end relationships.[13] Storytelling is inherently relational. However, in the liturgy several stories come together: the story of the liturgical text, the story of each participant, the story of the liturgists and the story of the liturgical performance itself. As noted when introducing a narrative approach to liturgical studies, all of this happens within a particular context which is storied itself. In other words, in the liturgical performance many authors, narrators, participants and audiences are involved.[14] Because so many stories come together we need to ask: who are the authors of the stories and who are the audiences?

The authors

An author is someone who tells a story. Which story is told in the liturgy? Most obviously, the story that is being told is dominated by the liturgical text or script. The words that sound and the texts that are rehearsed are the words from the liturgical resources, in our case from *Common Worship*. The main author, therefore, is the liturgical text.[15] Of course, it is odd to speak of a text as an author, because a text is not an author but is authored itself. However, in the case of the liturgy it is the text, quite apart from its author, that provides the main or dominant story to be told. In that sense from a narrative perspective on liturgy the text can be viewed as author.

Even when liturgies follow the liturgical script as outlined by the liturgical text, still the liturgy contains many instances at which choices need to be made and at which extempore words are used. In most cases it is the liturgist who makes these choices and speaks these words. Therefore, the second author, in order of influence on the story, is the liturgical presider. He is not only dominant in the liturgical action, he is also the 'professional' who selects texts and songs, and makes a number of other choices (the rubrics of the liturgical text leaves many decisions up to the presider).[16] In many cases, and indeed in all four liturgies observed in our project, the liturgical presider is also the preacher, making him even more dominant in the liturgical performance. On one hand, this balances the power of the liturgical text to enforce itself upon the story; on the other hand, a lot of power is invested into the hands of the liturgists. The liturgist's own story, perspective, background, theology, liturgical preferences, etc. gain a huge place in the liturgy.

The participants come with their own stories. If the liturgical text and the presider have such dominant positions in shaping the liturgical story, what is the position of the participants? What is the narrative space that the liturgy opens up for them? In Webb Keane's words this is the problem of agency, which "becomes especially acute ... in circumstances that are supposed to involve otherworldly agents, and in practices that impose severe constraints on the human practitioner."[17] The answer is sobering, for the participants have very limited control over the story of the liturgy. They have hardly any power in the explicit shaping of the story. Yet they have an important role in the performance of the script – i.e. in telling the story – as the observation of worship services shows. For example, the participants say many texts, like the confession and the creed, as well as many responses, like the *sursum corda*. Furthermore, they sing songs, which is an important aspect of their participation as the interviews with participants revealed. Physically, the worshipers are drawn into the liturgical action most obviously in going up to the altar rail to receive communion. So, on one hand the significant role the participants have is limited in terms of their influence in shaping the story: the worshipers narrate a story they have not authored. On the other hand, the participants' role can be viewed more positively.

Here the words 'explicit' and 'implicit' are important. While participants have no explicit role in shaping the liturgy, they will implicitly exercise a lot of control over what happens in the liturgy to them individually. Analysis of the interviews with participants in worship shows that the connection between the story of the liturgy and the participants' own stories is made by the participants themselves, and therefore not explicitly by the liturgy but implicitly by each individual. The liturgy may enable this connection to happen, and the liturgists have an important role in this regard, but the connection itself is made by the participants. Mark Allman states that "At any celebration of Eucharist there is a myriad stories (sic) being proclaimed ... All of these stories intersect and parallel *the* story, the story of salvation through Jesus Christ memorialized in the Eucharist."[18] How the individual stories "intersect and parallel *the* story" is a matter for the individual worshipper.

The chaplain from St Alcuin's uses a very similar image. In the liturgy we all cut our own plant and graft it on to the plant which is Jesus Christ, he says. The grafting is a process encouraged and facilitated by the liturgy, but the actual grafting is done by the individual worshipper. From a faith perspective, one can say that it is the work of the Holy Spirit. Thus, it is fair to say that the worshippers do not actively shape the story, but they are actively involved in the telling of the story, and implicitly they are the ones who appropriate the story. Michael Perham warns that "the most active and crucial contribution may be the one that, to the outsider, may seem a passive non-role."[19] The image of grafting gets further support by Louis Weil, although in different words. Full participation in liturgy

> is far more than saying the responses and singing the hymns. Listening to the reading of scripture at the liturgy together with other believers becomes a weekly occasion to hear the great story of salvation history and to unite to it our own personal story in thanksgiving for God's gracious presence in our own lives, as in the lives of our ancestors in faith who have gone before us. The linking of our own story to the great story of salvation is central to the purpose and meaning of our assemblies as God's people.[20]

Thus, the description of the liturgical text and the liturgical ministers as dominating the liturgical action, thereby leaving a more passive role to the participants, is questionable. Moreover, an important theme in the experience of liturgy in light of suffering is the experience of community (see pp. 57–58). The participants in worship are the very people who make up the community, and therefore they mutually influence each other. This has as much to do with the story of the context as with the story of the liturgy.[21] The participants are not without influence.

Finally, there is the story of the liturgical performance itself. This story is made up by the stories of the liturgical text, the choices and words of the liturgical presider who is influenced by his own stories and also by the stories of the participants. Even if the liturgical performance is not an author per se, as a mixture of all other stories it is a new story in itself, different from all others yet without annihilating them. Moreover, it is necessary to regard the liturgical performance as a story in itself for, as the observation of worship services shows, no one liturgical performance is identical to another. The story changes according to the time of the liturgical year, the choices that are made, the words being said, the songs being sung, etc.

All this is viewed from an empirical stance. Theologically, the question arises to what extent God is an author as well. God is a character in the liturgy, even though not in the same way as other characters. The liturgical text makes God a character – for example, in the greeting, the absolution and Eucharist. One can argue that God is author in the sense that the Scriptures are read.[22] But apart from the Scriptures, God is not the author of the liturgy, even if he is a character in the liturgy, and even if one says from a faith perspective that God is active in the liturgy and the liturgy itself asks for God's activity (e.g. "cleanse the thoughts of our hearts"; "receive our prayer"; "Send us out in the power of your Spirit").

So who is the author of the liturgy? The overview shows that there are multiple authors who shape the story of the liturgy. Dominant are the written liturgical resources and the liturgical presider. But also the participants exercise a certain amount of influence, even if not explicitly. All these authors and narrators come with their own backgrounds and stories, together telling a new and unique story, which is appropriated by the participants and liturgists in their own individual ways.

The audiences

As well as having multiple authors the liturgy has multiple audiences. In Ganzevoort's definition "narrative is the story-like structure in and through which the author (from his or her own perspective) experiences and understands life, assigns parts and roles, positions him- or herself relationally, and accounts for him- or herself before the audience."[23] The audience summons the author and judges the author's story by criteria of legitimacy and plausibility. Important for our discussion is that the "constellation of the audience determines the number and consistency of stories needed for justification."[24] This is important because in the liturgy a number of stories come together, although not from one author. The question in light of the just quoted statement by Ganzevoort is how consistent these stories are with each other.

If the liturgical text provides the script and the ministers are the main actors, then the participants are the main audience. It is arguable that the liturgical action is directed towards them, sometimes on behalf of them, sometimes addressing them directly. The participants as audience summon the authors of the liturgy most explicitly in the elements of the liturgy that are more extempore, such as the sermon, and in the many choices that need to be made, such as the selection of songs. These words and choices are as much as possible tailored to the audience. It is less obvious how the liturgical text as a standard provision is summoned by the audience, although here is a process of summoning and responding at work as well. Ganzevoort gives the example of how a child is summoned just by being born and growing up in a particular family and context. The child constructs its own life story accordingly. In a similar way the liturgy is 'born' in a particular context and a particular Church family, which both bear on how the text is constructed.

The second audience are the liturgical ministers. When all stories come together, the ministers are at times not only storytellers but also recipients of the story, and therefore audience. At certain points in the liturgy a dialogue is going on between the presider and the participants – for example, in the greeting. Here the presider is directly addressed by the participants. Moreover, the participants come with their own stories, and the interviews with both participants and liturgists show that the ministers know their flock well. The dynamic of the author–audience is a bit different here, because the participants as authors of their story do not tell their own story explicitly in the liturgy. Yet these stories are present, and therefore they influence how the liturgical ministers respond and shape the liturgy.[25] The liturgical ministers are also addressed by the story of the liturgical text, in two ways. First, in preparing the liturgy the text comes to them. Before the liturgists select which storylines will be emphasized, which songs will be sung, etc., they listen to the liturgical text themselves. Only after that they become co-authors in making all these choices. Second, the liturgists are addressed by the liturgical text in the liturgical performance. Until now we have spoken about liturgists and participants, but the liturgists are participants themselves in the first place, and therefore they are audience as well.[26]

The liturgical text is not a person. As we argued above, insofar as the text tells a story or provides a story to tell, it can be regarded as an author. However, since the text is not a person, it is not an audience. It does summon the other authors, but rather as narrator than as audience itself. The same is true for the liturgical performance. In sum, the audiences in the liturgy are the participants and the liturgists.

As with the authors, theologically we must say that God is audience in the liturgy as well. Indeed, together with the participants, God is the main audience. First of all, the prayers in the liturgy are directed towards God. The liturgy can be viewed as a dialogue between God and people. They are the two protagonists of the liturgical story. Second, the goal of storytelling is beginning, enhancing, changing or ending relationships. The relationship that is under negotiation in the liturgy is that between God and people. So God and the participants are the main audiences, and the liturgists are an additional audience.

A complementary view on the various roles in the liturgy, including participant roles, comes from Erving Goffman, summarized by Webb Keane as follows:

> Speech events [include] the *principal* who bears responsibility for what is said, the *author* who formulates the actual words, the *animator* who utters them, the proximal *addressee* of the utterance, the *target* to whom the words are ultimately directed, and the *overhearer*.[27]

Distinguishing these roles helps to gain further insight in what is going on between the various partners in the liturgical action. Day applies several of these roles to the liturgy:

> These roles are not fixed, but shift and merge between the human participants who are present in the liturgical event and God as the

liturgy unfolds. Thus the congregation are clearly the proximal addressee and the target when called to confess their sins, but are overhearers when the priest recites the Eucharistic prayer which is directed to God; they are the target of the prayer of absolution even though this is addressed to God, but the proximal addressees of blessings which are only indirectly addressed to God.[28]

This application by Day demonstrates why it is not straightforward to determine who the authors and who the audiences are. The roles shift and at different moments in the liturgy author can become audience, audience can become narrator, and addressee can become author. The changing roles and the limited narrative space that is accorded to some authors make it all the more important to analyse the narrative elements of role assignment and relational positioning (see pp. 38–42). But before analysing these elements, we turn to the storylines within the liturgical text.

Storylines in the liturgical text

In order to discern the storylines of a text, the first two steps of Ganzevoort's narrative reading method need to be applied.[29] In the first step, the reader writes down a summary of the text and formulates the central themes or storylines[30] of the text after the first reading. The storylines need to be both sufficiently distinguished from each other (which does not mean that they cannot interrelate) and sufficiently broad to encompass the whole of the story within just about three storylines. What follows now is a summary and the tentative formulation of central themes.

> *The general picture that emerges from a global reading of the text, is one of a high deity in relation to an assembly of people who are meeting to rehearse and enact a part (the core?) of the Christian story, faith and belief. In this picture the Christian story is that of a people not living up to the expectations of the high deity – who is called God, Father, Son/Lord/Jesus, and Holy Spirit – but who is ready to forgive. This God even sent his own son to save the people. A couple of times the son is pictured as a Lamb. The people are supposed to give glory to God, to love him and their neighbour, in their daily lives. This picture is explicit in the first and third part of the meeting, the Gathering and the Liturgy of the Sacrament. In the third part the story is enacted in taking bread and wine as the body and blood of Jesus Christ. The other parts do support this picture. The central themes in the liturgical text are sin and forgiveness/salvation, glorifying God/God's glory, living a particular lifestyle.*

The task of the second reading step now is to validate (or correct) the central themes/storylines of the story. Whereas the first reading step is intuitive, now the conclusions of that step will be put to analytical tests. The themes that came up after the global reading in the first step were: (1) sin and forgiveness/salvation;

(2) glorifying God/God's glory; and (3) living a particular lifestyle. For the sake of coding and readability these themes are shortened to single words: (1) salvation; (2) glory; and (3) living. All of the liturgical text is assigned to one or more storylines. The rubrics are left out in this step, since these contain instructions for the president and are not the content of the liturgy as such. Ganzevoort suggests two checks for knowing whether these themes are indeed the central storylines. First, it is expected that in the opening statements of the interview all central themes will be mentioned. Second, it should be possible to code all meaningful text of the interview (in this case all the text of the liturgy) with one of the three themes. If not, it may be necessary to formulate other central themes.

We start with the second check. Is it possible to code the liturgical text in its entirety with these three themes? Most of the text fits very well into one or more of the three themes. In order to illustrate how these themes present itself in the text, the prayer for forgiveness may serve as an example. The prayer is said by all people, and is the first of the two options *Common Worship* gives.[31]

<u>Almighty God, our heavenly Father,</u>
we have sinned against you
and against our neighbour
in thought and word and deed,
through negligence, through weakness,
through our own deliberate fault.
We are truly sorry
and repent of all our sins.
For the sake of your Son Jesus Christ,
who died for us,
forgive us all that is past
AND GRANT THAT WE MAY SERVE YOU IN NEWNESS OF LIFE
<u>to the glory of your name.</u>
<u>Amen.</u>

This example shows how the three codes present themselves in the prayer. It could be argued that some parts should have more than one code. Especially the part of admitting one's sin is closely related to living. Here we code this part with 'sin and forgiveness/salvation' because sin and forgiveness are prominent.

Applying the test of whether the whole of the text can be coded with these storylines reveals that a couple of lines prove hard to code with these themes. These are:

- Greeting/opening in the beginning.
- Exchange of peace at the start of Eucharist.
- Parts of the Lord's Prayer (difficult to code "Your kingdom come, your will be done, on earth as it is in heaven" and "Give us today our daily bread").
- Some lines of the peace and blessing at the dismissal.

Because a few lines in the liturgical text prove to be difficult to code with the three themes, further reflection is needed. The lines not yet coded have to do with peace, with a state of *shalom*. This comes close to the first theme we identified – i.e. sin and forgiveness/salvation. This theme expresses the process towards wholeness. Redefining the theme of "sin and forgiveness/salvation" to "(restoring) wholeness/*shalom*/peace," which includes the theme of salvation, is helpful. The code expresses both the process towards wholeness – i.e. the process of forgiveness for sins – and the 'state' of wholeness. With this theme it is possible to code those parts that could not yet be coded. The greeting is related to wholeness. The peace at the start of the Eucharist and at the end of the service is related to wholeness as well, as are the petitions of the Lord's Prayer "Your kingdom come, your will be done, on earth as it is in heaven" and "give us today our daily bread." For the sake of readability the code will be named 'wholeness.'

The only part that is still difficult to code is the very opening where the minister says: "In the name of the Father, and of the Son, and of the Holy Spirit." And the people respond: "**Amen**."[32] This opening should be read as a setting of the scene rather than as expressing a certain theme. The gathering of the people is in the name of the Trinity. By these opening sentences the main characters are presented: the Father, Son and Holy Spirit, and the people because they are the address of the opening and they respond to it.

The second test we apply is the mentioning of the themes in the opening statements of the interview, here the beginning of the liturgical text. Indeed, one does not have to go far into the text in order to find all three themes present. The greeting rite and first prayer are given here including their codes. After the opening in the name of Father, Son and Spirit, the president greets the people with either of two options:

The Lord be with you
and also with you.
(or)
Grace, mercy and peace
From God our Father
and the Lord Jesus Christ
be with you
and also with you.

From Easter Day to Pentecost this acclamation follows:

<u>Alleluia. Christ is risen.</u>
He is risen indeed. Alleluia.
Words of welcome or introduction may be said.
Almighty God,
to whom all hearts are open,
all desires known,
and from whom no secrets are hidden:
cleanse the thoughts of our hearts

by the inspiration of your Holy Spirit,
THAT WE MAY PERFECTLY LOVE YOU,
<u>and worthily magnify your holy name;</u>
<u>through Christ our Lord.</u>
Amen.

The themes of glory and wholeness are present from the very beginning. Wholeness or peace is expressed in the greeting: "The Lord be with you: **and also with you.**" Even clearer is the alternative greeting: "Grace, mercy and peace from God our Father and the Lord Jesus Christ be with you: **and also with you.**" The theme of glory is evident in what follows (from Easter to Pentecost): "Alleluia. Christ is risen: **He is risen indeed. Alleluia.**" That Christ is risen fits under both the theme of glory and (restoration to) wholeness. Of course, this acclamation is only said from Easter to Pentecost. But also the following prayer (the Prayer of Preparation, traditionally called 'The collect for purity') has the theme of the glory of God in both its address ("Almighty God") and its conclusion ("and worthily magnify your holy name"). The theme of living is present in this prayer as well ("that we may perfectly love you"), when loving God is taken as having influence on the lives of the believers. Even if this is not taken as such, the theme comes up in the next element of the text, where Jesus' summary of the law is read.

The two checks indicate that the themes of wholeness, glory and living are indeed the main themes of the liturgical text. All the text can be coded with these three themes. 'Wholeness' and 'Glory' are present from the beginning, and living comes in only a little bit later, still at the beginning of the liturgical text. That living comes in a little later parallels the observation that the other themes are more dominant in the whole of the text.[33]

One more check at the analytical level is to see whether the alternative texts, given at several points, contain the same themes.[34] If yes, the central place of the themes is confirmed. Indeed, analysis shows that most alternatives have the same codes, so the conclusion is warranted that the third check generally affirms the central themes.

Finally, after having established the three storylines of the text and having applied the analytical tests, one still may wonder whether other storylines are possible. For example, one can think of sacrifice, praise, death and life and other. However, applying the tests to these storylines make clear that these are already included in or less convincing than the ones we have established above. For example, praise is included in the code 'glory.' The theme of 'death and life' is present in the code 'wholeness,' in which sin and forgiveness are prominent. Death and life make up for a good part of text coded 'wholeness,' but the word 'wholeness' is able to capture more text than 'death and life' and passes the tests more easily. A similar argument applies to 'sacrifice.' No doubt sacrifice is an important (theological) theme in the liturgical text. Yet it has less potential as a storyline to code all of the text, together with the other themes.

In conclusion, the codes 'wholeness/peace/*shalom*,' 'glorifying God/God's glory,' and 'living a particular lifestyle,' pass the two tests proposed by Ganzevoort. A third check on top of those two tests affirmed the appropriateness of these themes. Trying some other storylines shows that the three storylines as established here are more convincing than some alternatives.

Comparison of narrative elements

In this section we will take the next step in Ganzevoort's reading method, which is the analysis of narrative elements in the liturgy. This section draws on all data sources – i.e. the liturgical text, the participants, the liturgists and the observation of worship services. All data sources and every interview was analysed individually. However, within the limits of the present work we can only present a more general analysis.

Structure

The narrative analysis of the liturgical text and of worship services showed that the storylines of the liturgy are wholeness, glory and living. Wholeness is synonymous with *shalom* and peace, or, in theological terms, salvation, and includes both the process towards wholeness and the state of being whole. Glory includes both the glory of God and ascribing glory to God. Living is the shorthand for living a particular lifestyle. In some liturgies one storyline is emphasized more than in others, and storylines may be added or set within a particular context, often according to the liturgical season or day.

In her narrative approach to the liturgy, Juliette Day comes close to the same storylines when she says that the "role of the liturgy is to insert ourselves into salvation history such that we might appropriate and participate in salvation history in an acute and predetermined fashion and consequently live out our lives as part of that history."[35] The roles of the liturgy she mentions are similar to our storylines of wholeness and living. The storyline glory is absent from her description, whereas this is fundamental to the liturgy according to Louis Weil. "The gathered community, united in Christ through baptism, is joined with Christ in praise and thanksgiving to God, which is the basis of all liturgical prayer in Christian tradition."[36] Weil warns that the role of the liturgy is not didactic, "for that would distort its purpose of praise and thanksgiving to God for all the mighty acts of God from creation on through human history."[37] The purpose of the liturgy, then, is glorifying God; it is centered around the mighty acts of God which are all characterized by life in abundance – i.e. wholeness; and the liturgy draws people into God's mission in this world which means a particular lifestyle. In the liturgy people confess the broken state of this world, including their sinfulness, which brings us back to the storyline of wholeness.

How do these storylines, as coming up from the liturgical text and confirmed by the observation of worship services, compare with the stories of the participants? The question in itself is an interesting one, but the answer is not straightforward. For each story of the participants the themes of the story, and thus the storylines, were established anew. Therefore, it is impossible to bring all stories together with the help of the storylines for they are unique to each story. It would be artificial to relate all these storylines to the storylines of the liturgy, since the participants do not relate their stories to the storylines of the liturgy necessarily. However, the question how the storylines relate is answered indirectly by the list of issues and themes that have come up from the interviews (see Chapter 4).

Perspective

If one thing becomes clear from a narrative approach to liturgy and suffering, it is that everything depends on perspective. Take, for example, a candidate for ordination and the chaplain who turns her down, as in one story actually happened. Next Sunday they come to the liturgy with a very different view on things. The chaplain might recognize that it must be hard for the turned-down candidate, but has the responsibility of leading the whole congregation into worship. The turned-down candidate comes to the worship service (if she fancies coming at all!) shattered, and distrusting people.

The example is to the point, because the biggest difference in perspective that can be observed is between the participants and the chaplains. This does not surprise since both groups of people have different roles and therefore alone different perspectives. In terms of Anderson and Foley's polarity of individual and public meaning (see pp. 50–51), to which they add official meaning, each participant holds an individual meaning of the liturgical celebration, and the participants together make up the public meaning. The liturgists, on the other hand, represent the official meaning, being officially appointed in their roles of lay ministers or ordained priests. That is not to say that they do not hold an individual meaning themselves or that they may not share the public meaning of the liturgy, but they are first associated with the official meaning.

Often the perspectives of the liturgists and participants conflate. The liturgists believe in the power of the liturgy to transform lives, and this power is attested to by the participants. The liturgists point to specific points in the liturgy to address suffering, and the participants point to the same, most notably music, the sermon, prayers of intercession and the Eucharist. The liturgists do not point to the Eucharist as often as the participants, but they point more often to the liturgical year. Nevertheless, as the example of the candidate turned down and the chaplain shows, the perspectives can be quite different as well. And even in less conflictual situations perspectives are person-specific. Someone reared in the Church of England tradition with the *Book of Common Prayer* will experience the liturgy very different from a local, non-native English speaker, participant.

When different perspectives come together a negotiation of perspectives takes place. Perspective is about the needs and interests of each narrator but also about the power of each one. In the liturgy the participants have only very limited power to change the story towards their own ends. Of course, they can do this for themselves in how they appropriate the liturgy (cf. the individual meaning), but the script is given, and the liturgists chooses what will be included and what not. The power, therefore, rests with the authors of the script (the Liturgical Commission and General Synod[38]), and the power to adopt and adapt the script rests with the liturgical presider. This might sound conflictual but it does not need to be, for two reasons. First, in the contemporary Western society it is an individual's choice to come to the worship gathering. Second, as the interviews with the liturgists show, the ministers know the people in the congregation well, and they are very much aware of the pastoral needs and try to fit the liturgy according to those needs as far as possible and appropriate. Moreover, in general the participants speak positively about the clergy in their current parish.

Experience, genre, tone, atmosphere

The narrative element of experience includes the tone and genre of the story. When it comes to the observation of the liturgical performances we add 'atmosphere' to make the most out of this element for analysing worship services.

In his narrative theory, Ganzevoort distinguishes four genres: comedy, novel, tragedy and irony. The liturgical text is a genre *sui generis*. Nevertheless, the text resembles the genre of comedy. The designation of comedy here has nothing to do with comedy in the popular sense of the word. It rather describes a plot along the lines of a young hero who needs to overcome severe difficulties, challenges the values and norms of society, and in the end overcomes the evil in society. Also, the liturgy starts with a problem that needs to be overcome (the alienation between God and people, in the first place overcome by the rite of confession and absolution). In the liturgy, the hero who solves the conflict is the Son, or the Father through the Son.

The observed liturgies followed the main story of the liturgical text and therefore are in the same genre. The interviews with participants show that most of their stories fall into either the category of comedy or of novel. In both genres a serious conflict arises, but in the end all is well that ends well. Is it possible that participants relate well to the story of the liturgy because both are similar in genre? There is no correlation between the genre of the participant's story and their negative or positive experience of liturgy. Some stories fall into the genre of novel but still have had a hard time with the experience of liturgy, and some stories fall into the genre of tragedy and yet the experience of liturgy was positive.

The general tone or atmosphere of the liturgical celebrations is closely connected with the genre. A deepening of the just sketched general picture is given by Juliette Day. She explains that the liturgy combines several genres in its story. For example, a prayer of confession is of a different genre from a collect. Some genres within the liturgy follow a highly stylized pattern, whereas other genres are more flexible.[39] The tone at which something is said is strongly related to the genre. Therefore, as the liturgy deploys various genres, the tone is different in various parts of the liturgy. The prayer of humble access, before the distribution of the Eucharistic elements, sounds different from a doxology such as the Sanctus earlier in the Eucharistic prayer.

Which genres connect with people who suffer differs from person to person. It makes quite a difference whether someone has just been diagnosed with cancer or whether someone is starting to benefit from the treatment of it. One can imagine that for the first person the frailty of human life pops out from words of the creed ("for us and our salvation he came down from heaven"), whereas the second person can joyfully say a little further in the same creed "We believe in the Holy Spirit, the Lord, the giver of life." So even within the same genre people might relate quite differently to the words. Moreover, even the same words might be appropriated differently. The acclamation "Dying you destroyed our death, rising you restored our life: Lord Jesus: come in glory" will be heard differently by someone who benefits from the cancer treatment or by someone who is terminal because of the same illness.

Furthermore, how the words are heard by the participants depends also on where the person is within their story of suffering, and also on how they relate their faith to their suffering.[40] For example, one of the participants said he has a "shaky faith," and it is hard for him to relate his faith to his suffering. Another participant commented on the laments of David, in the Psalms, and said that she thought it was inappropriate to use such bold language towards God and wondered at which stage in his faith David was when he wrote these Psalms. The discussion shows that the connection with suffering people is not necessarily related to the genre of the particular elements of the liturgy, but rather to their own place within their story and how they include their faith in the way they cope with their suffering.

Here it needs to be said that it is quite hard to find examples in the liturgical text that explicitly address the frailty of human life. What is mentioned in terms of human brokenness and the need for salvation is all set within the context of sin, thereby focusing on sin as trespassing, not sin as a general state of living in a fallen and broken world. The participants in worship do not point to liturgical texts when they talk about the points of connection between their stories and the liturgy. They point rather to those parts of the liturgy which change from week to week: music and songs, the sermon, the readings and prayers of intercession. The exception is the Eucharist, which almost all participants refer to. Yet even there they do not necessarily point to the words of the liturgy, but some rather point to the act of going up to the altar rail, of receiving the body and blood of Christ and the sense of community it gives. The comparison of the liturgical text with the participants' experiences shows that the liturgical celebration connects mostly to suffering people in the bits that are not prewritten in the liturgical text.

Role assignment

The narrative element of role assignment is particularly helpful in the analysis of liturgy. A narrative perspective explicitly focuses on the characters, and the particular method deployed in this project even distinguishes between the roles assigned by the author within the story, and the roles taken by authors and audiences in the telling of the story (the latter is called relational positioning, see pp. 40–42 below). Moreover, the method allows a detailed analysis of the roles in that it helps to see how roles can change even within the story itself – i.e. within the various storylines. It furthermore helps to see who is actually involved and the relative weight of each role.

Narrative is concerned with the identity of people. One of the basic assumptions in narrative theory is that people understand themselves narratively and thus form their identity narratively. The process of meaning-making that is going on whenever suffering is experienced serves to integrate this experience into one's life story – in other words, into one's identity.[41] The way the author of a story assigns roles to the various characters serves to maintain or enhance her identity. The question arises how the difference between author and narrator bears upon the identity and meaning-making process going on in storytelling.

From this theory a number of questions arise for the comparison of the various data sources. Who are the characters in the story of the liturgy? How do they vary according to different storylines? What is the identity of the various authors? Do they go well together or do they clash instead? In the liturgical text the main characters are God and people. The liturgical dialogue is between them, facilitated by the liturgical ministers. The role of God is to receive glory and it is the role of the people to give glory to God (storyline glory). However, this does not happen and therefore a conflict arises between the protagonists. The roles are extended. In the storyline of wholeness, in which the conflict is overcome, the role of the people is to ask for forgiveness for not giving glory to God by having sinned against God and their neighbour. The role of God is to pronounce forgiveness, but also to make it possible to forgive. Forgiveness is pronounced in the absolution,[42] but the price God paid to enable forgiveness to happen is high: it cost his own Son. The role of the people is to receive forgiveness which they do in the absolution. Both the giving role of God and the receiving role of the people are more elaborated and stronger in the sacrament of the Eucharist. The storyline of living brings the protagonists back to the beginning, although the image is one of an upward spiral rather than of a full circle. Empowered by the self-giving of God the people are to live a particular lifestyle, which glorifies God.

The analysis of the stories of the participants showed that the protagonists vary from story to story. It is outside the space limits of this book to show the characters for all stories and how they differ within the stories according to the storylines, nor is it necessary to do so. In sum, in all cases one of the main characters is the narrator herself and sometimes God is the other protagonist, sometimes it is the clergy, sometimes even others. About half of the participants talked about their experience of God, although in different ways. Some hold to the view that God is in control, others that He is present in the suffering but not necessarily in control. The participants hold a variety of perspectives with regard to the question of theodicy. All arrive finally at the point of having a positive view of God. It is hard to see how the roles of God attributed by the participants in their stories relate to the roles of God in the liturgy. One similarity is that in both the liturgical text and the stories of participants God is seen as the greater party (cf. 'relational positioning' below).

The observation of the liturgical action in four churches demonstrates a different and more complex assignment of roles. At face value the main characters are the liturgical ministers: they do the action. The people in the pew seem to be spectators. However, the analysis of their roles shows that they are not spectators but throughout the worship service they are participants. Furthermore, the parts of the liturgical action in which they are seemingly not involved are still done to them or on behalf of them. While they have hardly any role in writing the script, they are involved in telling the story. The liturgical text shows that they are no less than protagonists in the liturgical story, bringing their own stories with them in which they are protagonists as well. Above we said that God is a character in the liturgy as well, although different from all other, more visible, characters. Since the liturgical action is the performance of the liturgical text, the roles of God as established by the liturgical text are the same in the performance.

The chaplains confirm the liturgical text. For example, the analysis of the liturgical text showed that the liturgy makes clear to the people that their identity is not as they would like to have it ideally. Brett, chaplain of St. Stephan's, makes a very similar comment: "The liturgy presents us with the people who we are and the people who we ideally would be."[43] One aspect of the people's identity and that of God remains the same: from beginning to end they relate to each other as greater and lesser party, and their roles remain accordingly as those of giving and receiving glory respectively. From beginning to end God is benevolent towards the people. Nevertheless, another aspect is transformed in the liturgy. Whereas the liturgy starts out by creating a distance between the protagonists, the distance is soon overcome by the people seeking forgiveness and by God giving forgiveness. This is repeated, elaborated and deepened in the sacrament of the Eucharist. The liturgy starts by presenting the people with who they are, as Brett says, but it works towards the renewal of this identity – from brokenness towards wholeness, from sinners to saints.

Having discussed the main characters in the various liturgical data sources, we now come back to the question: who are the protagonists of the liturgy? According to the liturgical text it is God and the people. His identity is being almighty, glorious and he wants to receive glory. The people are the lesser party and they have not given glory because of having sinned against God and their neighbour. Yet the people's identity is changed through the story of the liturgy and the relationship with God is restored. In the stories of the participants it becomes clear that for them the liturgy is indeed about the relationship between God and themselves, while God is perceived as one who is with them in their situations of suffering. In the stories of the participants the role of the clergy comes also to the fore. In the liturgical celebration the role of the clergy is to be presider of the liturgy. The interviews with participants make clear that this role is not separate from their role as pastors. Here liturgy and pastoral care are intertwined. The liturgists themselves affirm this connection. They recognize the need to be aware of the pastoral situation of their congregation and to take this into account in the liturgy where possible and appropriate. Furthermore, they affirm the centrality of God in the liturgy and the importance of connecting the stories of the participants with the story of God as told in the liturgy. The observation of the liturgies in turn shows the importance of the liturgists in the celebration. They are the liturgical actors, although the whole congregation participates in the celebration, and the identity of God as receiving and giving is confirmed. In sum, God is the greater party, connecting with the participants in liturgy, and this connection is liturgically mediated by the liturgical ministers.[44]

Relational positioning

Closely connected with role assignment is relational positioning. Indeed, when the narrator is also the protagonist in the story, the distinction is blurred.[45] Nevertheless it is helpful to distinguish between role assignment which happens within the story, and relational positioning, which has to do with how the story is used to begin, enhance, change or end relationships. This is particularly important because, as we have seen, the story is told by several narrators, especially liturgists and the participants, who are not the primary authors of the script. They are main characters in a story they have not written. Yet by retelling the story, they become co-authors. The liturgists, and also the participants to a certain extent, exercise a huge influence on how the story is told (just ask the question why one liturgy is experienced as boring whereas another one is experienced as exciting, while using exactly the same script, and the influence of the narrators on the script and performance of the script becomes clear).

The previous section made clear that the liturgical script assigns to God the role of greater party who is asking to be glorified, whereas the role of the people is being the lesser party, and they come to the liturgy in a state of sinfulness. The question of relational positioning is whether the participants in the worship services agree with these roles. For example, they will join in with the words in bold type, confessing their sinfulness, but at the same time they might not say it from the heart. They will pray for the gift of the Holy Spirit in the post-communion prayer, to "give light to the world," but they might wonder what that actually means.

So how do the participants relate to God? Do they question the words of the liturgy, do they speak them wholeheartedly? In the focus groups during the first phase of this project the topic of sin came up quite regularly and spontaneously. People see the need for confessing their sins and the confessional rite was pointed to as a place where brokenness is dealt with. In the interviews with the participants the topic was raised less often. Some participants still point to the confession as a point where liturgy connects with their suffering, although it is not clear if they mean their own particular suffering. The remarks about the confession are more general. However, it seems that none of the participants has a problem with the relationship between God and people as the scripts put forward.

The experience of God revolves nonetheless around a different relationship with God. The question for the participants is not so much in terms of sin as in terms of God's involvement in the situation. In the end nearly all participants have a positive view of God. God is with them in their situation whether or not he is in control, and whether or not this involvement is positive. The positive view of God is fostered by the liturgical script in the sense that God is benevolent towards his people. Furthermore, the view and experience of God being with the people in their situation resonates with many parts of the liturgy. Interestingly the resonance starts at the beginning of the liturgy with the greeting and is there at the end as well in the blessing. Many other places can be mentioned here. The climax of God's presence with his people might said to be in the Eucharist, in the epiclesis and in the consummation of the elements of bread and wine.

Whether the observation of the liturgies confirms the presence of God with the people is another matter. Here we are reminded of Annie Dillard's exclamation:

> Does anyone have the foggiest idea what sort of power we so blindly invoke? Or, as I suspect, does no one believe a word of it? The churches are children, playing on the floor with their chemistry sets, mixing up a batch of TNT to kill a Sunday morning. It is madness to wear ladies' straw hats and velvet hats to church; we should all be wearing crash helmets. Ushers should issue life preservers and signal flares; they should lash us to our pews. For the sleeping god may wake some day and take offence, or the waking God may draw us out to where we can never return.[46]

Of course, the presence of God is rather invisible, although made visible in various ways and especially in bread and wine. Whether people feel God present or not is hard to say from the observation of worship services. The people in the churches wear neither velvet hats nor crash helmets. The intercessions observed in St Peter's were extempore and passionate. Especially the passion might point to a sense of God's presence or at least of a relationship with God. From the interviews with both liturgists and participants, though, it should be concluded that the people do believe God to be present in the worship services.

We began this section by pointing to the influence that the narrators have on the liturgical script and performance, and we commented on the participant's influence. The liturgist's influence on telling the story is even stronger.

Coming to the liturgy with his own personal story and relation to God, this all bears on the selection. In previous sections we saw already the responsibility of the liturgist, and this is once more highlighted, because the liturgist does not preside in the liturgy for himself, but for the whole congregation. The minister's relational positioning vis-à-vis God and the people has also to do with the view of his role as priest or reader. Does the liturgist represent God – for example, in declaring the blessing? Does the liturgist represent the people – for example, in parts of the Eucharistic prayer? Is the liturgist one of and with the people, or does she have a status that is distinguished from the people? These questions open up the area of the theology of ministry, and it is outside the scope of this book to discuss this in detail. But at least the element of relational positioning shows the questions that arise from the relation the liturgist has with regard to God and the congregation.

Liturgical analysis in narrative approach of Ganzevoort is less concerned with ultimate truths and more with ultimate relationships.[47] This point bears specifically on relational positioning for in telling stories relationships are negotiated. Or the other way around, relational positions are negotiated by storytelling. In the liturgy the people 'negotiate' with God about their relationship. Throughout the liturgy and in all data sources God is the greater party. The people realize they are sinners but ask for forgiveness, which God gives, and the relationship is restored. Furthermore, the participants experience God as present in their stories, and that resonates well with the liturgy, although it cannot be concluded from a purely empirical point of view. The relationship between liturgists and the participants varies but is often positive. How the clergy deal pastorally with the participants in their time of suffering influences also the participants' experience of liturgy. We also saw that the relationship between the liturgist and God has a certain influence on the liturgical celebration – hence the responsibility of the liturgists.

Audience

An important question in our search for narrative space for suffering people to tell their story in the liturgy concerns the matter of narrative competence. If authors are summoned by their audience, as was said in the introduction of this chapter, then how competent are they to author and narrate their story? The analysis of the liturgical text yields an ambiguous answer. On one hand, the fact of having a pre-given liturgical script means that not much room is allowed for authoring one's own story. On the other hand, that same script gives a plethora of possibilities to shape and give content to the liturgical story. The observation of the worship services shows a similar ambiguity concerning narrative competence: on one hand, the storylines of the liturgical text remain intact, at the same time each liturgical performance has its own emphasis, sometimes even adding storylines, or setting it in a particular framework (usually the framework is the theme proposed by the liturgical calendar). So yes, creativity is called for, leaving room for creative use of narrative competence. But whose competence?

For most parts of the liturgy it is the narrative competence of the liturgical ministers that is called for, because she makes decisions and choices about what will be the final script. Moreover, in our research the liturgists also preach and in one case even lead the intercessions. Except for the prayers of intercession little room is left for the participants in liturgy to shape the story. The narrative competence for the participants is very limited indeed.

Conclusion

In this chapter we have applied the narrative theory and method of Ganzevoort to the study of liturgy. The four data sources – i.e. the liturgical text – the participants in worship, the liturgists and the observation of worship services, were compared with each other. First, we argued that we cannot speak of just one author and one audience. In the liturgical performance and even in the text itself, multiple authors and audiences play their part. We then established three storylines that are central to the liturgical narrative: wholeness/peace/ *shalom*, glorifying God/God's glory and living a particular lifestyle. In short: wholeness, glory and living. Third, we analysed the data sources with the six narrative elements that constitute Ganzevoort's narrative theory. To present a detailed analysis of all data sources and of each and every participant would require much more space than we have in this volume. Yet the strength of the narrative approach to liturgy lies in bringing together the data sources, which gives then many important insights for addressing the question how liturgy does or can make space for stories of suffering. Chapter 5 will show the implications of the analyses in this chapter.

Notes

1 R. Ruard Ganzevoort, "Reading by the Lines: Proposal for a Narrative Analytical Technique in Empirical Theology," *Journal of Empirical Theology*, 11(2) (1998): 25. Ganzevoort develops his method in a number of publications, of which we mention the most important here: Ganzevoort, "Religious Coping Reconsidered, I"; Ruard Ganzevoort, "De Praxis Als Verhaal: Introductie Op Een Narratief Perspectief," in *De Praxis Als Verhaal: Narrativiteit En Praktische Theologie*, ed. Reinder Ruard Ganzevoort, Kampen Studies (Kampen: Kok, 1998), 7–27; R. Ruard Ganzevoort and Jan Visser, *Zorg Voor Het Verhaal: Achtergrond, Methode En Inhoud van Pastorale Begeleiding* (Zoetermeer: Meinema, 2007); R. Ruard Ganzevoort, "Narrative Approaches," in *The Wiley-Blackwell Companion to Practical Theology*, ed. B. Miller-McLemore, 1st edn (Malden: Wiley-Blackwell, 2012), 214–223. See also my article "A Narrative Understanding of Anglican Liturgy in Times of Suffering: The Narrative Approach of Ruard Ganzevoort Applied to Common Worship," *Questions Liturgiques / Studies in Liturgy* 1–2(96) (2015): 64–81.

2 This term comes from Kenneth Gergen: "An acceptable story must first establish a goal, an event to be explained, a state to be reached or avoided, an outcome of significance or, more informally, a 'point.' … The selected endpoint is typically saturated with value: it is understood to be desirable or undesirable." Kenneth J. Gergen, *Realities and Relationships: Soundings in Social Construction*, Reprint edn (Cambridge, MA: Harvard University Press, 1997), 190.

44 *Analysis of liturgy and stories of suffering*

3 Ganzevoort, Ruard, "Hoe Leest Gij? Een Narratief Model," in *De Praxis Als Verhaal: Narrativiteit En Praktische Theologie*, ed. Reinder Ruard Ganzevoort, Kampen Studies (Kampen: Kok, 1998), 78.
4 Ibid., 173, translation mine.
5 Ibid., 174, translation mine.
6 Ganzevoort, "Reading by the Lines," 26.
7 Ganzevoort gives the example of two children negotiating about the question whether a third child is the best friend of the one or of the other. "Hoe Leest Gij? Een Narratief Model," 83.
8 Ganzevoort, "Narrative Approaches," 221.
9 The term is Ricoeur's, see Ganzevoort, "Hoe Leest Gij? Een Narratief Model," 84.
10 This point is also vividly made by Gerard Lukken: "No person enters the world like Adam on the day of his creation. There are already very many previous givens. These begin with one's name: one does not choose it oneself, but it is given by one's parents, and they in turn were dependent on certain customs or trends in doing so. What is true of one's name is also true for one's actions and speech." *Rituals in Abundance*, 38–39.
11 Ganzevoort, "Hoe Leest Gij? Een Narratief Model," 85, translation mine.
12 Ganzevoort, "Reading by the Lines," 26.
13 Ibid.
14 Cf. Webb Keane, "Religious Language," *Annual Review of Anthropology*, 26 (1997): 60.
15 The liturgical text has in turn its own authors. It is beyond the scope of the research interests of the present book to go into detail about this point. Note that the text of *Common Worship* reveals great continuity with traditional and ecumenical liturgical texts, not the least with the *Book of Common Prayer*. An analysis of the continuity of liturgical prayers throughout the Anglican Communion can be found in Ramshaw, "A Look at New Anglican Eucharistic Prayers." For a discussion of the author behind the liturgical text, see Juliette J. Day, *Reading the Liturgy: An Exploration of Texts in Christian Worship* (London and New York: Bloomsbury, 2014), Chap. 2.
16 Cf. Day, *Reading the Liturgy*, 154.
17 Keane, "Religious Language," 65.
18 Allman, "Eucharist, Ritual & Narrative: Formation of Individual and Communal Moral Character," 60.
19 Perham, *New Handbook of Pastoral Liturgy*, 21.
20 Louis Weil, *A Theology of Worship* (Lanham, MD: Cowley, 2002), 51–52.
21 Cf. Van Dusseldorp, *Preken*, 112–113.
22 This view presupposes the inspiration of the Scriptures by God.
23 Ganzevoort, "Reading by the Lines," 25.
24 Ibid., 26.
25 Also Alastair Daniel notes the dynamic between actors, audience and context: "even the high-end performance of classical theatre is dependent on more than the abilities of the actors – on a shared communal response to the performance event." Daniel writes in the context of classroom storytelling, and adds: "In the classroom community of storytellers, a sense of communal competence lies at the core of storytelling." While his context is admittedly different, his statements apply *mutatis mutandis* to the context of liturgy as well, for the dynamic to which he points is pretty much the same. Alastair K. Daniel, *Storytelling across the Primary Curriculum* (London: Routledge, 2012), 8.
26 Cf. Perham, *New Handbook of Pastoral Liturgy*, 19, 30–34.
27 Keane, "Religious Language," 58; cf. Erving Goffman, "Footing," in *Forms of Talk* (Oxford: Basil Blackwell, 1981), 124–159.
28 Day, *Reading the Liturgy*, 154–155.

29 Ganzevoort, "Reading by the Lines"; cf. van Ommen, "A Narrative Understanding."
30 In this chapter the words 'central theme' and 'storyline' are used interchangeably.
31 The differing types of the font reflect the different codes. Italics: *salvation*; underlined: glory; small capital: LIVING. The bold type indicates that the prayer is said by all.
32 Bold type in the text means that these words are said by all.
33 Also in the interviews the third storyline often comes in later.
34 Further evidence is given by Mark Allman, who states in his article on narrative and ritual in the Eucharist that "The theme of the narrative ritual is the rescue of humankind from the destructive power of sin and death." This theme is included in our code 'wholeness.' Allman, "Eucharist, Ritual & Narrative: Formation of Individual and Communal Moral Character," 64.
35 Day, *Reading the Liturgy*, 68.
36 Weil, *A Theology of Worship*, 38.
37 Ibid.
38 The Liturgical Commission produces draft material which the General Synod revises and eventually authorizes.
39 Day, *Reading the Liturgy*, 51–54.
40 Park and Folkman, "Meaning in the Context of Stress and Coping"; see also Ganzevoort and Visser, *Zorg Voor Het Verhaal*, 299ff.
41 Ganzevoort, "Religious Coping Reconsidered, I."
42 Grammatically, the text of the absolution does not make clear whether the absolution is actually pronounced and declared or rather wished for. The commentaries on this text do not speak about the issue. One commentator says that if the president uses the absolution in the declaratory form the sign of the cross may be made when saying the words "pardon and deliver you." The sign should be bold as it refers to the power of the cross. This comment reveals that the absolution can be used in different ways indeed, and the context of the comment suggests that the issue is that if 'you' and 'yours' is used, it is a declaration of absolution; if instead 'us' and 'our' is used, even by the priest or bishop, it is rather the form of a prayer. See Perham, *New Handbook of Pastoral Liturgy*, 116–117.
43 Brett, I, 151.
44 Designating to the liturgists the role of mediating between God and people is done from an observational point of view. Theologically, Christ is the supreme mediator.
45 Ruard Ganzevoort affirmed this in a personal conversation.
46 Annie Dillard, *Teaching a Stone to Talk: Expeditions and Encounters* (New York: HarperCollins, 1982), 40; cited in Saliers, *Worship as Theology*, 21; and Constance M. Cherry, *The Worship Architect: A Blueprint for Designing Culturally Relevant and Biblically Faithful Services* (Grand Rapids, MI: Baker Academic, 2010), 270.
47 Ganzevoort, "Narrative Approaches," 216–217.

3 Liturgy through the lens of narrative–ritual polarities

In addition to the narrative theory and method of Ruard Ganzevoort, we analysed the liturgical text, interviews and observations through the lens of several polarities, as proposed by Anderson and Foley. The main concern of Anderson and Foley is the connection between the human and divine story – in other words, between the story of the liturgy and the stories of human beings. Together with their pastoral interest, their concern runs parallel with the concerns of the present book. Their narrative–ritual theory informs both the method used in this book and the liturgical–theological reflections in Part II. An important part of Anderson and Foley's theory is formed by several polarities. We will now introduce these polarities, before applying them to our data sources.

Myth and parable. Most important is the polarity of *myth and parable*, based on John Dominic Crossan's theory of story.[1] For a clear understanding of the term 'myth' it is perhaps best to state what it is not. In his introduction to Crossan's *The Dark Interval*, Robert Funk states it most helpfully:

> The term myth is misleading in popular parlance. Myth does not mean a story that is not true, or a story that is about gods and goddesses; myths order the world in which we live by turning randomness into pattern, by replacing appearances with some ultimate reality, by reconciling the frustrations produced by contradictory experience in some higher unity. The basic function of myth is not the particular reconciliation established by individual myths; rather, its purpose is to establish that reconciliation is possible.[2]

Myth points to the ideal picture human beings have. For example, a wedding day has a mythic outlook; everything should be perfect on that day. But we need the parable, which points to contrast in life.

> Human beings are inclined toward the mythic, and because of that we need to keep the parabolic perspective alive, lest we believe that mythic weddings will make happy marriages, lest we become trapped in mythic expectations of perfection … Parabolic stories invite transformation by

opening us to the possibility of something new. The Jesus story is the ultimate parable – it challenges our mythic dreams of a life without suffering or contradictions.[3]

Myth and parable both have double functions. Myth serves "to resolve particular contradictions and, more importantly, to create a belief in the permanent possibility of reconciliation."[4] An example is the fairy tale *Beauty and the Beast*, in which many opposites are reconciled: beauty and beast, poor and rich, commoner and royalty, woman and man, captive and free. Parable, by way of contrast, introduces contradiction and undermines the belief in reconciliation. Parables point to ambiguity and tension, they are agents of change and sometimes of disruption, especially when things seem stable and secure.[5] Both narrative and ritual can be perceived from the duality of myth and parable.

Individual and communal. While every person has her own narrative, no one authors her story all by herself, as the polarity *individual and communal* shows. Many different factors play a part in the making of a narrative. In other words, the personal narrative is always co-authored. People who believe in God will point to God as one of the co-authors.[6] Under the influence of the therapeutic paradigm in pastoral care, the individual narrative is emphasized, often at the expense of the interplay between individuals and the community. When the individual is disconnected from the larger faith community, she is increasingly disconnected from the faith story of the community.[7] It is the ritual aspect of faith and community that stresses the divine narrative. Therefore, the individual needs to be in community and its rituals.[8] At the same time, Anderson and Foley recognize that the community and its rituals should not overlook the individual narratives.

Concealing and revealing. Both story and ritual can reveal or conceal. The following quote about storytelling is true for rituals as well:

> When the stories we tell conceal rather than reveal our understanding of ourselves and our world, they isolate us from others. When, however, the aim of storytelling is to interact with others and identify common ground, stories have the potential to build authentic communities of shared meaning and values.[9]

Not only do stories and rituals build community or isolate, if they are revealing they are life-giving and connecting the storyteller to the divine. The life-giving quality of story and ritual is closely connected to the idea of ritual honesty.

Ritual honesty is another way to think of rituals and storytelling as revealing or concealing.[10] Rituals are revealing when ritual honesty occurs – i.e. where rituals are authentic. Often rituals are authentic when the public, official and private meaning converge. The public meaning is the interpretation most participants of the ritual attach to it; the official meaning corresponds with the intention of the originators of the ritual; the private meaning is the meaning individuals give to it.[11] When these meanings correlate and the rituals and storytelling are honest, story and ritual have transformative power.[12]

Moment and process. The polarity of moment and process is best seen in the so-called *rites de passage*. These rites are the subject of the second part of Anderson and Foley's book. The authors point to the meaning of this polarity already by the chapter titles in this part of their book. They do not entitle the chapters simply 'Baptism,' 'Wedding,' and 'Burial,' but 'Welcoming the Child,' 'Preparing for Marriage,' and 'Encountering Death.' These titles show the need to attend not only to the specific rituals that surround these moments in life, but also to the processes towards these moments – processes filled with narrative and rituals.

Public and private. In the paragraph on concealing and revealing above, it was already noted that rituals have a public, official and private meaning. Both individual and community play a part in most rituals and stories. A telling example is a wedding. The decision to marry is a couple's individual decision. Yet when the couple announces their intention to marry, the decision is made public. The individual decision is finally celebrated publicly and the vows are made in public on the wedding day.[13]

This summary of Anderson and Foley's polarities brings out two important points for the present book. First, narrative and ritual are intimately connected: distinct, but not separated. Therefore it is possible, if not necessary, to make use of ritual categories when developing a narrative analysis model for liturgy (even though in this book the focus remains on narrative). Second, the brief overview of the several polarities at work in narrative and ritual provides a helpful lens and heuristic value through which to see liturgy and the experience thereof by participants and liturgists. However, as Anderson and Foley remind their readers, more important than looking at these polarities themselves, is to take into account the underlying structure: the paradox of faithful living. Human beings are easily inclined to emphasize one pole over the other – often the myth over the parable. If the paradoxical nature of the narrative and ritual is more important than each polarity in itself, then this structure is open for the inclusion of other polarities. Therefore, the analysis of the data may yield additional polarities as well.

Having introduced the polarities, we will now analyse the liturgy and interviews through this lens.

Myth and parable

Both the liturgical text and most of the participants' stories contain elements of both myth and parable. The hope of reconciliation, the character of myth, is also one of the main themes of the liturgy. At the same time in the liturgical story reconciliation is only possible through Jesus Christ. His "story is the ultimate parable – it challenges our mythic dreams of a life without suffering or contradictions."[14] Therefore, the story of the liturgy is not characterized by such a mythic dream, although the basic assumption with which people participate in worship is that reconciliation is possible. The relationship between God and people is one of inequality and a conflict is to be overcome, but God is benevolent towards the people.

The statement that "the Jesus story is the ultimate parable" opens up possibilities for liturgy to address suffering and connect to people who are suffering. Jesus' story involves suffering itself, and it is at the heart of the liturgy in the Eucharistic sacrament where his body is broken and his blood poured out. This story opens up the possibility to set out hope in the face of suffering, for Jesus rose from the dead. The acclamation from Easter Day to Pentecost, right at the beginning of the liturgy, at once testifies to this hope.

Most stories of the participants are told within the genre of the novel. The liturgical text bears many traces of the comedy. In both genres the hero wins, but in the novel the hero comes from inside the society, in the comedy he comes from outside. Both genres are at the mythic end of the continuum of myth to parable. This reveals that both the participants and the liturgical script are committed to the possibility of reconciliation, of a world in which all is well that ends well. It is clear that neither the liturgy nor the participants live with a cheap, Disneyfied, version of myth – too much suffering and too much of the parabolic is involved. But the parable opens up new possibilities for living, thus leading to a new belief in reconciliation, albeit through suffering. The fact that the genres are so close makes it easier for the stories of the participants to connect with the story of the liturgy, or vice versa.

Concealing and revealing

Often it is difficult to say whether stories are concealing or revealing, because to know this, one needs more information than only the story told by this one person in this particular interview. Only in a few cases elements of concealing might be assumed. The clearest examples are when people do not tell about their plight in church. Most stories sound like they are revealing. In these stories there is no sense of trying to hide anything that might be judged negatively by the audience (see relational positioning and audience, Chapter 2, pp. 40–43).

The question with regard to the participants in relation to the liturgical text is whether the liturgical text helps them to tell their stories honestly in the liturgy. In other words, is a connection taking place between the participants and the liturgical script? Virtually all of the participants are able to point to elements in the liturgy that connect to them in their situation. Those are points at which they recognize their own story in the story of the liturgy. These elements are places where the narrative space is opened up for the participants and where the narrative-competent participant can creatively weave his or her own story with that of the liturgy. Thus, the liturgy might be said to be revealing.

However, if the participants need to make connections by themselves, it places a huge demand on their narrative competence. Therefore, the task of making the connection cannot rest on the shoulders of suffering people alone. In order to address suffering and foster the connection between liturgy and the stories of the participants, the liturgical text needs to give as good and as many possibilities as possible, and also the liturgical presider has an important role. The interviews with participants make clear that the text does give opportunities, and the liturgists are aware of the need to address suffering and they try to do so. Thus, whether stories are revealing or concealing depends on the narrative competence of all authors involved.

Private, public and official

The liturgical text expresses the official meaning of the liturgy as the authors (Liturgical Commission and General Synod) intended. The official meaning is further represented by the clergy, although it must be said that they come with their own private meanings as well. But as 'liturgical professionals,' one may expect them at least to understand the official meaning and to represent that. The participants have their own individual meaning or understanding of the liturgy.

Private, public and official meaning of stories and rituals has a lot to do with 'ritual honesty.' The more similar the various meanings are, the more likely it is that the story or ritual is honest, which means that it is authentic and therefore revealing. The question is whether the meanings do converge or not. With regard to the liturgical text and the appropriation thereof by the liturgists, it must be said that most of the liturgical ministers show both their acquaintance with the provisions in *Common Worship* (as well as other resources) and the need for crafting the liturgy. The meanings of the official liturgy and the official representatives of it converge.

It is different with the participants. The interviews make clear that in some cases official, public and individual meanings differ – in other cases, they are similar. The individuals have their own understanding of liturgy, church, dogma and moral issues. That does not mean that their interpretation is necessarily invalid. Anglican liturgy deliberately allows for different understandings of theological issues. The point of interest for this book is whether the understandings of liturgy are in line with the participant's understanding of their own stories in light of the liturgy. In other words, the connections the participants see between the story of the liturgy and the stories of their lives, are they authentic in light of all these stories? Is the connection or interpretation a participant makes true to the liturgy and true to one's own situation?

By way of example, we pose these questions to the story of Abigail. Her story is one of many failed pregnancies and therefore of loss of life. After twelve years of not going to church, she finally goes again, driven by other problems in her life and because she "missed the good old Anglican way of actually having to get out of your seat and walk to the front."[15] When the moment of Communion comes and she actually walks to the front,

> all of a sudden, all those little bits of life, that were um, that were the result of the IVF, it was just as if there were all these just little kids that were sort of bumbling around by my legs etcetera, like I was a parent ... And as I went up to communion they came up, and then they just continued on, and it was as if the grief finally was done.[16]

It is clear that the official meaning of the liturgical text does not envisage necessarily these kinds of visions. In terms of liturgical performance, the story testifies to the power of ritual – 'the good old Anglican way.' It is also clear that a vision like this does not converge with the public meaning of getting up and walking to the altar rail.[17] Yet the private meaning is revealing. The vision is authentic to Abigail's own story of loss and grief. This is finally done with. At face value the public and official meaning are different, but that still does not mean that the private meaning contradicts these meanings. When the meanings do conflict, they are concealing and not life-giving. But none of this is present here. The connection between the stories are life-giving, they reveal both the grief that had not been dealt with entirely yet and God's healing through the liturgy. Moreover, the experience is in line with the storyline 'wholeness' of the liturgical text and it sets Abigail free to move on with her life in a new way (storyline 'living'). The ritual of the 'good old Anglican way' and the connection with Abigail's story is revealing indeed, albeit unintended.

One example alone does not suffice to conclude that the meaning of the ritual and story of the liturgy in relation to the stories to the participants is authentic and revealing, and that ritual honesty takes place. It does show that it can and does happen, even in unexpected ways. Ritual honesty does not always happen, as the interviews show. For example, at the lowest point in Matt's story, the official, public and individual meaning conflict to such an extent that Matt decides to leave the church and give up on what he at first felt was his calling to ordination. Yet for most people, the official and public meaning of the liturgy are such that they can relate their own stories to the liturgy and appropriate it for themselves, thereby converging their private meaning with the other meanings.

Individual and communal

Individuals have stories and the community tells a story. What is the role of the individual in the community and of the community in the story of the individual? Liturgy is first and foremost a communal act. Individuals gather together and become the worshiping community while performing the liturgy. The text emphasizes the communal nature of the liturgy by the consequent use of the plural. The only place where the worshipers use the first person singular is at the invitation to communion in one of the three options. There the text has: "Lord, I am not worthy to receive you, but only say the word, and I shall be healed." Almost ironically, these words are said by everyone.

Anderson and Foley are concerned that the communal nature of the liturgy is emphasized to the extent of almost neglecting the individual story. The liturgical text stresses the communal nature of the liturgical act. Yet as part of the community, the individual stories do not need to be left at home when coming to church. They are included in the gathering of the community. The interviews show that most participants do find their individual stories recognized by the liturgy, or at least they find points at which they can connect their story to the story of the liturgy.

Moment and process

The liturgy is performed at a particular moment, but involves processes as well. The liturgy tells a story and moves from one point to the other. Most notably in the liturgy the process of being made whole again happens. It is a miniature retelling of the grand 'metanarrative which is characterized by wholeness, the glory of God and a particular lifestyle. The liturgy furthermore has the element of a process in the series of celebrations throughout the liturgical year. Each liturgy is different, and Juliette Day points out that, for example, the proper prefaces in the Eucharist alter the story.[18] Nevertheless, Bridget Nichols states that all prefaces taken together throughout the Church's year tell the whole Christian story.[19] So every liturgy is at once a self-standing unity in its own right as well as part of a bigger picture or process. Storytelling is a process itself, involving the weaving of a plot, assigning roles, and in the case of the liturgy involving and negotiating with co-authors and audiences.

Anderson and Foley introduce the polarity of moment and process to highlight the pastoral context around worship services, especially around the *rites de passage*. Liturgy happens in the context of the whole of church life. Similarly, a participant's experience of liturgy and connection (or not) with his own life in the liturgy happens within the context of his whole life. So, even when liturgy is viewed as a moment, as in the context of Anderson and Foley's discussion, that moment takes place in the wider context of church life and personal lives: processes. For our discussion of addressing suffering in liturgy, that means that liturgy and pastoral work are interrelated. Not only are they interrelated, by integrating ritual and narrative, and therefore by integrating liturgy and pastoral work, human stories and God's story get connected, according to Anderson and Foley.[20]

This sheds new light on the question of narrative competence and on the role of the liturgist (who is often also involved in pastoral work) to enable people to make the connection between liturgy and suffering. By integrating pastoral work and worship service they can start to resonate with each other. On one hand, in pastoral conversations the meaning of the liturgy can be brought to the fore. Storytelling is about identity and meaning-making. Pastoral conversations are moments at which identities as found in the liturgy can be explored further. This might also be the place to see how official, public and private meanings of the liturgy and of one's situation or story interact. On the other hand, the meaning-making going on in pastoral conversations continues in the act of worship. Thus, the integration of pastoral conversations and liturgy can enhance the narrative competence of the suffering participant. At the same time the pastorally and liturgically aware minister brings the understanding of both parts of her work to the liturgical performance and her preparation of the liturgy. Therefore, the integration of pastoral work and presiding in liturgy fosters her role of enabling people to make the connection between liturgy and their situations.

Other polarities

Underlying all these polarities is the paradox of living faithfully, according to Anderson and Foley. The paradox is more important than the polarities themselves. It implies that other polarities might be found. In our research we have come across a number of other issues for which it is helpful to regard them as polarities. These are: liturgy and community, individual story and liturgical story, sin and suffering, text and context, and Word and Table.

The polarity *liturgy and community* is related to the polarity individual and communal but gives it a different twist. The polarity comes to the fore in all data sources. The analysis of the liturgical text makes clear that the liturgy is written and to be performed in the community. Only once the individual pronoun 'I' is used. All the participants in worship mention the theme of community, whether negatively or positively. Here we find a correlation between the experience of the liturgy and the experience of community. When one is positive, the other is as well. When one is negative, the other is negative as well (see pp. 57–58).[21] Also the liturgists mention the theme of community most often. The observation of worship services confirmed the importance of community. The liturgy is embedded in the community, even though written by a liturgical commission which does not write in the same sort of community. Moreover, the liturgical action draws people into the community, and fosters and sustains the community. This becomes even clearer in the fact that the liturgical community stays after the liturgical performance for refreshments. One chaplain calls this even the liturgical fellowship after the liturgy. Anderson and Foley write that all poles of the polarities are worth attention in themselves, but "what is more important is an awareness and willingness to hold as valuable the paradox of faithful living that these juxtaposed pairs highlight."[22] One element is not to be valued over the other and certainly should not be compartmentalized. Liturgy and community are both important. Both have their own place, but become even more valuable in the interplay with the other. The "paradox of faithful living" requires both.

Another polarity that might be added is *individual story and liturgical story*. This polarity is related to others but highlights the fact that in the liturgical performance many stories come together. There is the story of the liturgical script. There is the story of the liturgical presider, often also the compiler of the specific liturgical script on this specific occasion. There are the many stories of the participants. There is the metanarrative of God's story with his people. Day writes that "participation in the liturgy permits me to embed my narrative in the narrative of salvation."[23] But what is the narrative space for each story and each author? How do the various stories relate to each other? By highlighting this polarity these questions are brought to the fore, which is relevant to our question how liturgy addresses and connects to stories of suffering. What is the narrative space for stories of suffering? How does the story of the liturgy – text or performance – connect to the stories of individual suffering?

The analysis of the liturgical text prompts the discussion of what sin is and what suffering is, and how these two relate to each other (see also pp. 65–67). It may be helpful to turn *sin and suffering* into a polarity as well. Doing so secures a place for both, for, as we just saw, one polarity should not be isolated from the other. Moreover, by juxtaposing the different elements of the polarities they increase in meaning. Furthermore, the discussion becomes less polarized. That means that we do not have to choose between one meaning of the word 'sin' over the other. One meaning sheds light on the other instead.

The analysis of the interviews with participants shows yet another polarity: *text and context*. The participants point to many places of connection between the story of the liturgy and the story of their situation. These points of connection fall into two broad categories. On one hand, the participants mention specific liturgical elements, such as songs, confession, sermon, intercession, etc. On the other hand, they point to general factors, such as the atmosphere, orderliness, the fact that the liturgy is there every Sunday, daily prayer, etc. The two lists make clear that the liturgical text and even the liturgical performance are embedded in a larger liturgical context. Text and context correspond roughly to story and ritual. Anderson and Foley see an intricate relationship between the two. Storytelling is a ritual and rituals tell stories. Telling the liturgical story is a ritual and the liturgical ritual tells a story. This also relates to the polarity of moment and process. Each liturgical celebration is a moment in the longer process of subsequent celebrations, including daily prayer. Every liturgical celebration adds color to the bigger picture. But also all elements of a particular liturgy take place in a certain atmosphere. For example, adding to the atmosphere of the church service is the length and way in which the intercessions are done, or whether the participants stand in a semi-circle around the altar or kneel to receive Communion. Placing text and context on a polarity helps to draw attention to the mutual influence they have on each other.

Finally, we might wonder whether turning *Word and Table* into two poles helps to deepen the paradox of living faithfully. The ecumenical and liturgical movement of the twentieth century have encouraged balancing the two poles of Word and the Eucharistic sacrament, whereas, generally speaking, before this time the Word was emphasized in Protestant churches and the Eucharist in Roman Catholic churches. In Eucharistic services in *Common Worship* both have their place. The participants in worship confirm the importance of both for connecting the liturgy to their situation. Eighteen participants mention the Eucharist and 12 mention the sermon and/or Scripture reading. The observation of worship services, however, still shows that churches in the Anglo-Catholic tradition place less emphasis on the service of the Word and more on the Eucharist; churches in the Evangelical tradition emphasize the Word over the Eucharist. Seeing Word and Table as parts of a polarity helps to see the importance of both.

These parts of the liturgy are different in character and possibly in atmosphere. The readings and sermon give more direct opportunity to connect to the life stories of people than the Eucharist. Anderson and Foley write: "Music can touch deep into our emotions; architecture can invoke the wonder of the divine; and ritual can provide revelations and comfort beyond our words. It is, however, the preaching event, with all its narrative possibilities, that is perhaps the most potent vehicle for interweaving the human and the divine."[24] The present research project confirms that music is an important vehicle for connecting the divine story as told in the liturgy with the human stories of suffering (music is mentioned by half of the participants). The power of ritual is obvious in the story of Abigail (see above, 'Private, Public and Official,' pp. 50–51). However, our research does not confirm that the preaching event – i.e. readings and sermon, is "the most potent vehicle for interweaving the human and the divine." It is very important, as 12 out of 21 participants refer to it, but the most important point of connecting the divine story with the human stories is the Eucharistic celebration. We need to be careful of drawing conclusions, as both Anderson and Foley's research and ours do not draw on statistical data, and the sample does not aim at representative numbers. What the research does point to, though, is that the power of the Eucharistic ritual is not to be underestimated and is more important than one might think. This is not to diminish the importance of the preaching event. The statement by Anderson and Foley and our research together show the usefulness of regarding these two parts of the liturgy, Word and Table, as a polarity, gaining in meaning and importance by their juxtaposition, deepening the paradox of living faithfully.

Conclusion

The discussion of the polarities above has indicated how closely related the polarities themselves are. For example, in the polarity of moment and process, the official, public and private meanings also came to the fore, which in turn begs the question of ritual honesty, which has a lot to do with whether stories are concealing or revealing. Furthermore, the question of ritual honesty easily feeds into the polarity of myth and parable, as people are inclined to search for and live in myth rather than with parable. The new polarities that were proposed above also reveal the close relationship between several polarities. They are all part of a way of perceiving reality – in our case, the reality of liturgy in relation to suffering. Distinguishing the polarities helps to see the many layers of liturgy and allows for a deeper analysis of each.

Notes

1 John Dominic Crossan, *The Dark Interval: Towards a Theology of Story* (Sonoma, CA: Polebridge Press, 1994). See also Charles Gerkin's use of Crossan's theory in *The Living Human Document*, 161ff.
2 Robert W. Funk in Crossan, *The Dark Interval*, xi, cf. 32, 40. Note that 'myth' and 'parable' are used here as narrative, rather than biblical–theological, concepts.
3 Anderson and Foley, *Mighty Stories*, xii.
4 Ibid., 14.

5 Ibid., 12–16.
6 Ibid., 19.
7 Ibid., 46.
8 Ibid., 48–49.
9 Ibid., 7.
10 Ibid., 29–30; cf. Elaine Ramshaw for the concept of ritual honesty. *Ritual and Pastoral Care* (Philadelphia, PA: Fortress, 1987).
11 Anderson and Foley, *Mighty Stories*, 29; Margaret Mary Kelleher, "Liturgical Theology: A Task and a Method," *Worship* 62(1) (1 January 1988): 2–25.
12 Anderson and Foley, *Mighty Stories*, 7.
13 Ibid., 83–85.
14 Ibid., xii.
15 Abigail, 078.
16 Abigail, 078.
17 It is nonetheless interesting to see that the act of getting up and walking to the front gets filled with meaning by quite some participants – for example, as a sign of community or unity in diversity.
18 Day, *Reading the Liturgy*, 75.
19 Bridget Nichols, "Scripture, Time and Narrative in the Proper Prefaces of the Church of England's 'Common Worship'," *Studia Liturgica* 39(1) (1 January 2009): 127.
20 See for the relationship between liturgy and pastoral care Ramshaw, *Ritual and Pastoral Care*; William H. Willimon, *Worship as Pastoral Care* (Nashville, TN: Abingdon Press, 1979).
21 A.L. van Ommen, "Anglican Liturgy and Community: The Influence of the Experience of Community on the Experience of Liturgy as a Challenge for Liturgical Renewal and Formation," *Studia Liturgica*, 45(2) (2015): 221–234.
22 Anderson and Foley, *Mighty Stories*, 52.
23 Day, *Reading the Liturgy*, 63.
24 Anderson and Foley, *Mighty Stories*, 164.

4 Themes in addressing suffering through liturgy

In the previous chapters the text of *Common Worship*, the interviews with participants and liturgists and the observations of worship services were analysed and interpreted from a narrative and ritual point of view. These analyses and interpretations yielded a number of themes to be looked at. The present chapter brings together and discusses these themes.

Community

The theme of community stands out as most important in the stories of the participants and the interviews with chaplains; it is observed in the worship services and underlined by the use of the plural in the liturgical text. Community is key. In the previous chapter we observed a correlation between the participant's experience of community and their experience of liturgy. When community is experienced positively, the liturgy is as well. When community is experienced negatively, so is the experience of the liturgy.[1]

Caring for people happens not only in liturgy, but also in community. Hence the importance of the coffee fellowship afterwards, because, according to one chaplain, "that's where a lot of brokenness is mended even if not expressed."[2] The liturgists are aware of the role of the community in addressing suffering – six out of seven liturgists refer explicitly to the community. It is remarkable that both participants and liturgists mention the role of the time of fellowship after the liturgical worship service is done. One liturgist calls it a liturgical fellowship and there is much to commend such a designation of this part between the liturgy and daily life. It bears the character of an 'after-liturgy,' not unlike an after-party.

The liturgists make another important observation about community. All persons have to deal with brokenness in their life, which somehow places everyone at the same level in the community and in the liturgy. Furthermore, in the liturgy everyone is in the process of grafting their own story on to the story of Jesus, whether the mother who has lost her child or the student with insecurities about his future (that is not to say that the suffering is at the same level, but the dynamic or process of grafting is the similar). The interviews with participants do not speak about community in this way, but it is clear from the interviews that indeed a lot of suffering is going on in any community, and thus the interviews confirm the liturgists' statement that suffering is part of life. The observations of worship services affirm this as well – for example, in the prayers of intercession in which suffering is mentioned in various ways.

When analysing the liturgy through a narrative–ritual lens, it was mentioned that Anderson and Foley are concerned that the liturgy emphasizes the communal over the individual (see pp. 51–52). The question was raised whether the individuals do feel neglected because of the emphasis on the communal, and whether the liturgy is able to pick up the many stories the participants bring to the liturgical gathering. The interviews with participants make clear that usually participants do not feel neglected and they are able to connect their stories to the liturgy. The interviews with liturgists, furthermore, show that the liturgists are aware of the many stories present in the assembly, and they try to relate to those in the liturgy. The observation of worship services does not shed much light on this issue, although several instances of connecting to individual stories can be referred to, such as the rite of Thanksgiving for the Gift of a Child in St Stephan's.

Holy Communion

The liturgical element mentioned most often by the participants in worship and also mentioned by six out of seven liturgists, is Holy Communion. The importance of the Eucharistic rite is underlined by the liturgical text and performance in that it takes a good part of the whole liturgical celebration. Moreover, even if Word and Table are both important (see pp. 51–52), the readings and sermon are much more flexible in terms of wording and length than the Eucharistic rite with its extensive prayers. The Eucharist also stands out in that the rite should be led by an ordained minister – again, more flexibility in this regard is allowed for the liturgy of the Word – and that one of eight authorized prayers must be used. Proper prefaces can alter the storylines slightly and at various points the minister can choose one of several options, but overall the prayers are fixed. In narrative terms, here the original author and the authorizing body (the Liturgical Commission and the Archbishop's Council) exercise most authority over the liturgy, leaving little narrative space for the narrators. In light of this, it is even more striking that the Eucharist stands out as that place where the connection between liturgy and daily life is made for most participants.

The analysis of the interviews with participants shows that the Eucharist relates to their situation in different ways. For some, it has a direct relation to their suffering. For others, it is the communal aspect and the sense of bonding that relates to their situation. For yet others, the Eucharist has pastoral significance, not least in that there they feel accepted. To some, the mysterious and holy aspect of Communion speaks, and to others the ritual aspect of it. Apart from the different aspects of the Eucharist that people can relate to, the different elements of the rite speak differently to people. So, for some, it is the act of going forward and standing or kneeling at the altar rail which has deep meaning to them; for others, it is receiving together with those with whom they are in conflict; for yet other people, it is the mystery of the elements of bread and wine becoming Christ to them.

The liturgists also mention the ritual aspect of the Eucharist as important. The rite involves people physically; it draws them into the performance and thereby into the community. At the Table everyone is accepted and therefore the rite has huge pastoral significance. In terms of content, the Eucharist addresses suffering, transforms it and in a sense even overcomes it.

The observation of worship services confirms several aspects that were mentioned by the participants and liturgists. Indeed, going up to the altar involves people physically. Moreover, the observation of liturgical performances shows that the liturgical action is primarily done by the liturgists up-front. In the Eucharistic rite the distance between the liturgists and the people is overcome, and there the participation of the people becomes most obvious. This is clear in receiving bread and wine, but also in the exchange of peace at the beginning of the rite. At the same time, this moving around creates a sense of community. In one church this was symbolized by holding hands while singing a song, after bread and wine were distributed.

Interpreting the Eucharistic narratively and theologically, based upon the observation of the worship services, it is important to note that in the Eucharist God is most clearly seen as an actor in the liturgical performance, because of Christ sharing his body and blood. The Eucharist is a place where God gives of himself. In Anderson and Foley's terms, the Eucharist is a place where the divine story and the human story are interwoven most visibly. No wonder this part of the liturgy stands out as most important and that here people feel addressed in their situation of suffering.

In sum, the Eucharistic rite is of utmost importance in connecting to and addressing suffering. All data sources affirm the sense of community, of participation in the ritual by everyone, and that here suffering can even be transformed. Holy Communion speaks to people in many different ways because it contains so many aspects. From an empirical perspective one might suggest that the Eucharist speaks to so many people probably because it draws everyone in. From a theological perspective, one might suggest that it connects to so many people because here God gives of himself in a most obvious and powerful way.

Liturgy as a safe place

"If there wasn't church, I would have gone mad."[3] These words from Betty sum up the feeling of many participants who regard the church as their safe haven in stormy weather. Like Holy Communion, the theme of safety has many aspects to it. It is mentioned by 14 out of 21 participants and by three out of seven chaplains. Most participants who talk about safety feel safe in the liturgy for one of two reasons or both: the structure of the liturgy and the givenness of the liturgy.

The structure is the same every week, and that gives stability and even a sense of objectivity in the chaos of daily life. The givenness of the liturgy means that the liturgy and church are always there. One can be sure that next Sunday there will be a worship service again. This gives a sense of continuity when life is disruptive. Hannah: "It's there, it just goes on, you are part of it. And you don't have to be worrying all the time about what you feel. It's, it's there."[4] The paradox is that it is because of the contrast between the experience of liturgy and the experience of suffering that a connection between the two is established. The participants mention a couple of other things as well: the community in which the liturgical celebration takes place makes it a safe place for some. For others, it is being accepted in the community and at the Table which makes it a safe place.

For the three chaplains who mention safety it is an important issue. It is remarkable, though, that they relate this first and foremost to the community whereas the participants relate it primarily to the liturgy itself. The chaplains are concerned that the community needs to be a safe place for people. In the liturgy this starts with the anonymity every individual has, in the sense that all are drawn in into the same story. Yet the community can also be the place where individuals share their stories with each other. The level of safety experienced in the community has influence on the liturgical celebration and the chaplains mention especially the prayers of intercession and the matter of extempore intercession by anyone who wants. This requires a level of safety, which in one church is experienced but not in the other. The observation of worship services confirms that in one church people pray out loud and in the other church they do not. In terms of content of the liturgy one chaplain says that because suffering is a theme in the liturgy, it is safe for people to ask their questions and express their doubts and pain in the liturgy. However, according to another chaplain, the content of the liturgy may be unsafe in that it presents people with who they are and who they ideally would be.

The liturgists stress the importance of safety in relation to community. Some participants mention this, but most relate the theme of safety to the structure and givenness of the liturgy. These aspects are hardly mentioned by the liturgists, although it is arguable that the idea of anonymity in liturgy – because everyone is drawn into the same process of grafting one's story on to that of Jesus – comes close to the structure and givenness of the liturgy.

The observation of liturgical action does not reveal a lot about the theme of safety. One thing is worth mentioning, though. In St Stephan's the liturgy included the rite of Thanksgiving for the Gift of a Child. The word 'safety' is not mentioned in the rite, but the semantic field which surround safety is very much present, in words like 'love' and 'care' and in the image of babies, etc. The rite creates an atmosphere of warmth and comfort, and therefore of safety.

Clergy and pastoral awareness

From all data sources it is clear that the clergy play a significant part in the liturgy and in addressing suffering. Most of the participants assign an important role to the clergy in their stories, for better or worse. The role comes usually in two ways: the clergy are pastorally sensitive or not, and they support people or not – the latter role figures primarily in ordination stories. The experiences are very mixed, but the significance the clergy have is clear.

The clergy, in turn, show great pastoral awareness in their interviews. They know their congregations well and try to be sensitive to issues of suffering and brokenness. However, as the stories of participants demonstrate, the clergy sometimes do, and sometimes do not succeed in dealing with people as the people would have wanted. The clergy also show that pastoral awareness goes hand in hand with liturgical awareness. To craft a good liturgy that relates to the people one needs to be acquainted with the liturgical resources, but also with the stories of the people.

The observation of the liturgies make clear that the clergy and lay ministers are important in the liturgical celebration because they are the main actors in the liturgical performance, at least at face value. The observations also reveal a difference in styles between ministers. Some are more personal than others and some make it easier to identify with than others.[5]

The liturgical text, finally, shows the importance of the ministers in that they are mentioned in the rubrics time and again, in most instances as 'president.' The question can be raised whether they act as representatives of God – e.g. in declaring the absolution – or as one with the people – e.g. in saying the same prayers. The interviews with chaplains and participants do not indicate that they see themselves as representatives of God or that the people see them as such. However, as discussed in the present section, they play an important part in the stories of people, and in connecting the human and divine stories, whether in pastoral conversations or by presiding in the liturgy. Moreover, they have a crucial function in the liturgy in enabling people to make the connection between their situation and the story of the liturgy for themselves. The observation of the liturgies stresses their importance in the liturgical action. Together these observations do not answer the question who the clergy represent: God or people. Nevertheless, they do make clear that the clergy have a specific role in the life of the church and in the liturgy, a role that is not to be underestimated and that should be performed with great sensitivity and responsibility.

Experience of God

Eleven out of the 21 participants comment on their experience and view of God.[6] Ten of the 11 participants have a positive view of God. Six of them even never questioned God. The others had a negative view of God for some time, but later it changed to a more positive view. One person is not clear on his view of God. He longs for a relationship with God but seldom has the feeling he is in a relationship with God.

The two views of God in times of suffering that are both used by six participants and which are related, are the view that God is in control and that God is always there. In total, seven participants mentioned either of these views or both. Often these views overlap, but not always. For example, Olivia refers to a verse from Hosea which says "I took my beloved into the wilderness, that I might be close to her."[7] She comments: "That's difficult, cause that has the implication that God did it deliberately, so as to get me, which I don't think is right. But certainly God came into the wilderness with me."[8] Here is an example of someone who believes God was with her, but not necessarily that God is in control. Olivia believes that God was with her in her pain and in how she dealt with it. A strong image of control comes from Rebecca. She compares times of suffering to being at sea. God is there at sea as well, even in such a way that "If I go under, it is because he is taking me under, and I am with him."[9] The participants hold a variety of perspectives with regard to the question of theodicy. All arrive finally at the point of having a positive view of God.

It is hard to see how the roles of God attributed by the participants in their stories relate to the roles of God in the liturgy, but a couple of clues can help to see the relationship. One similarity is that in both the liturgical text and the stories of participants God is seen as the greater party. Also, the positive view of God is fostered by the liturgical script in the sense that God is benevolent towards his people. Furthermore, the view and experience of God being with the people in their situation resonates with many parts of the liturgy. Interestingly, the resonance starts at the beginning of the liturgy with the greeting and is there at the end as well in the blessing. Many other places can be mentioned here. The climax of God's presence with his people might said to be in the Eucharist, in the epiclesis and in the consummation of the elements of bread and wine.

Contrast between churches

The contrast between churches is a theme for the participants, but not really in any of the other data sources. Only one liturgist mentions the fact that in the Church of England the Eucharist is open to everyone, in contrast with some other churches. In the Benelux setting, which is traditionally partly Protestant, party Roman Catholic, the openness of Holy Communion is of pastoral significance. That Communion is open to everyone is a factor in some stories of the participants as well. Thus, the pastoral significance and the contrast between churches with regard to pastoral and dogmatic differences is underlined. The other contrasting factors mentioned by the participants are their experience of community, clergy and liturgy, which we deal with in other sections of this chapter.

Expatriate setting

The Anglican communities in the Benelux find themselves in an expatriate setting. The observation of worship services makes this obvious. A huge variety of cultures and languages is found in all churches. In many stories of participants the expatriate setting surfaces, but the influence of this setting seems to be low in most stories. Often the church is one of the few communities that expatriates relate to. Positively this gives them a 'home away from home,' as can be heard regularly in international settings. Negatively, it means that even when a person has negative experiences with this church, there is nowhere else to go.

The liturgists mention the presence of people from many different nationalities and denominations, as implied in the expatriate scene. One liturgist mentions that therefore it is not possible to work with standard rites and formulas when it comes to baptisms and weddings. The liturgist needs to work with the different cultures and denominational backgrounds. The liturgists differ in the consequences the expatriate scene has for the relations of people in the community. One chaplain holds that sometimes people feel they have a professional image to sustain, whereas another chaplain thinks that an expatriate setting is heterogeneous and therefore people are inclined to take their masks off sooner than in more monochrome settings. The interviews with participants show that both chaplains may be right: some participants do and some do not feel the level of safety that allows people to be open and vulnerable.

Healing

Suffering and healing are two sides of the same coin. In this book we focus on only one side of the coin – suffering. However, it does not come as a surprise that throughout the data sources, from time to time, healing comes to the fore. So the liturgical text makes clear that suffering is an important theme in the liturgy (although depending on the definition, see pp. 65–67), but it is not *the* theme. Rather, the storyline of wholeness includes a process from suffering to healing. In the interviews with participants and chaplains the topic of healing was never introduced by the interviewer, yet several people commented upon it. The stories of the participants demonstrate that healing can happen in a liturgical context and because of that context. Sometimes Holy Communion plays an important part in the healing process, although not always. Healing can also happen in liturgical rites other than the regular Sunday morning worship. Furthermore, the participants make clear that healing is a process, and the (cultural) understanding of healing as a quick fix is not appropriate. This opens up the question as to what healing is at all.[10] The liturgists state that the whole of the liturgy can foster healing. How this works itself out in practice is different for each congregation, as the observation of the four churches in this project shows. In one church healing was very much present in the worship services we observed. Yet the way it was addressed and dealt with was specific for this audience; in another church it could not have been done in exactly the same way.

In sum, when talking about suffering, the topic of healing is just around the corner. It is hardly possible to address one without the other. The data sources confirm this. In every data source the topic of healing was mentioned somehow. For the purposes of this book we will not elaborate further on the topic of healing, although we do come back to the issue later (pp. 123–128).

Putting on a brave face

The theme of putting on a brave face has to do with several issues. Whether someone chooses to tell her story or remain silent about it sometimes has to do with personality ('make it till you fake it'[11]), sometimes whether someone thinks the community will respond negatively about it, or still other reasons may have an influence. It is interesting that for some participants who choose not to tell their story in the community, or only in a later phase, this has a (negative) influence on or is related to their experience of the liturgy. For example, after her best friend dies when only a teenager, Katrina goes through a time of 'fake it till you make it.' During this time Katrina is not interested in church at all, and only goes to the worship services because her family goes. When she starts to recognize her need for healing, she starts wanting to get something out of the worship services again. However, the participants' experiences are too diverse to draw further conclusions from them.

The liturgists relate the theme to the level of authenticity and safety that is experienced in the community. Some recognize the role the minister has in modelling authenticity. But whether or not participants of worship share their experiences of suffering with each other, all are in the process of sharing it with Jesus in the liturgy. One may experience the community as not safe enough, but the liturgy itself is safe, according to one liturgist. Our suffering is placed within the context of Christ's suffering.

The first important thing to note here is that the theme of community comes back again. The second important issue is the level of safety that the liturgy provides, irrespective of community.

Experiences other than liturgy

It is clear that the experience of suffering in relation to the experience of God is not confined within the limits of the liturgy. So from time to time participants mention other experiences as well, such as attending a homegroup, personal prayer, etc. The liturgical text shows this already by including all of life in the prayers of confession and also in the storyline of living. The liturgy sends the people out in order to live for God's glory, in newness of life. The liturgists speak mainly about pastoral work when they speak of other moments at which suffering is addressed. They recognize that liturgy and pastoral work feed into each other, as also the polarity of moment/process (see pp. 52–53) expresses.

This theme highlights once more that the liturgy takes place in the context of broader church life, and that suffering is addressed on other occasions as well and not only in liturgy. The polarity of moment/process is especially helpful to frame these observations.

Liturgy causing suffering

A few participants had negative experiences with liturgy (in previous churches). Not surprisingly, the theme did not come up in the other data sources, and therefore we can hardly call it a theme here. Yet it is worthwhile to include this issue here as a reminder that something good and powerful can become something bad and powerful. Just as Psalm 88 is one of the few psalms in Scripture that ends in darkness, so this theme acts as a 'necessary irritant' for an overly optimistic view on liturgy.

Sin and suffering

In this chapter we discuss themes that have come up from the various data sources. It is remarkable that many themes are hardly related to the liturgical text. That is telling in itself when considering the question whether the liturgical text addresses suffering. However, the answer to this question depends on one's definition of suffering. In this section we show how suffering is, or is not, a theme in the liturgical text. Because of the complexity of this question, it deserves a more lengthy treatment than the other themes.

First, the liturgical text addresses the suffering of God. That suffering comes to the fore in Jesus' death and resurrection, which plays a role throughout the liturgy, starting from Easter to Pentecost with the acclamation that Christ is risen. Furthermore, the death and resurrection is referred to in the rite of confession, in the Gloria, the creed, and it forms the heart of the liturgy of the sacrament. The suffering of God has a big role in the theme of wholeness or salvation.[12] It makes salvation possible.

Second, in this book the working definition of suffering which steers our focus is: 'a major negative life event.' This understanding of suffering is hard to find in the liturgical text. Suffering in this sense is mentioned explicitly in the intercessions. Even here it does not need to be, but at least here is the explicit possibility for it to be mentioned, and the other data sources confirm that here suffering is mentioned indeed. Other parts might be the words of welcome, hymns or the sermon. Again, the participants of worship and the observation of worship services confirm the importance of at least the hymns and the sermon (and Scripture readings) for addressing suffering. The fact that the places where suffering may be addressed are all found in the rubrics rather than in the given text, reminds one once more of the responsibility of the presider to enhance the narrative competence of the participants, by employing the creativity and variety which the rubrics allow when he thinks appropriate. In other words, the liturgical presider plays a huge role in enabling the participants to connect their stories of suffering with the story of God as told by the liturgy.

Third, when the sinful state of humankind is interpreted as suffering, then it is present throughout the liturgy. Sinfulness as suffering is in that case present in the liturgy whenever the suffering of God is referred to. The death and resurrection of Christ are the means by which the sins of the people can be forgiven.

In this line of reasoning, suffering in the context of sin is the suffering of God in Christ. But is it also possible to think of suffering on the part of human beings as included in the theme of sin? Here we touch upon the issue of what sin is and what kind of sin is meant by the liturgical text, and also what suffering is. Two dominant interpretations of sin are sin as personal wrongdoing and sin as a general state of brokenness of the world. The question which interpretation is present in the liturgical text is relevant because it makes a huge difference to how people are addressed – as wrongdoers or as people who are afflicted by brokenness and suffering.

Presumably, most people interpret sin as the trespassing of certain commandments. One may or may not suffer as a result of this. Theologically, one must say that such sin does cause suffering indeed, and the classic reference is to the 'fall' of Adam and Eve in paradise. The liturgical text affirms this interpretation. This is clear in the rite of confession, where the Ten Commandments or a summary of the law, to which the people respond "Amen. Lord have mercy." The response indicates that the people know they have trespassed the law. The prayer of confession states unambiguously that "we have sinned against you and against our neighbour in thought and word and deed, through negligence, through weakness, through our own deliberate fault." Personal trespassing is a major feature when the liturgy mentions sin.

Another interpretation of sin is more holistic. In that interpretation sin refers to the broken state of creation, to the transient nature of human beings and to all the brokenness in the world. Such an interpretation includes natural disasters and suffering that is not because of personal wrongdoing but which happens to people anyway. Does the liturgical text allow for this interpretation of sin as well? If yes, suffering might be addressed when sin is mentioned. A couple of clues might be found in the text, yet analysing the text with the question in mind what is meant by sin in the liturgical text, it becomes clear that the dominant interpretation is that of personal wrongdoing. Because of people's trespassing they are not worthy and they need forgiveness.

Ganzevoort discusses the way liturgy addresses people when he writes about guilt and violence.[13] In a context of violence at least two parties play a part: the victim and the perpetrator.[14] The problem with liturgy which focuses on sin as personal wrongdoing for which forgiveness is needed is twofold. On one hand, victims tend to feel guilty without being guilty – the focus on guilt in the liturgy tends to make them feel even guiltier. They might even think that no forgiveness exists for their 'sin.' On the other hand, the perpetrator might feel forgiven way too easily by the general absolution of sin, and this person's problem (and sin) is not dealt with properly. Moreover, the victim hearing the forgiveness for the perpetrator might feel even worse.

Another point for discussion to include here is the dominant metaphor of God as Father and Christ as Son. It is outside the scope of the current research project to include a critique from feminism on the prominence of male metaphors in liturgy. This has been done already by many others, yet it is appropriate to flag the issue here in the context of suffering and how suffering people feel or do not feel addressed and can or cannot relate to the liturgy.[15]

This discussion shows that when the liturgy refers to sin, people who suffer and feel guilty about it without being guilty, might be put down by the liturgy. This problem will not be solved in this book. Yet it is important here to repeat that the liturgy of the Church of England is characterized by a pre-given structure and allows for the use of a great variety of resources (see pp. 7–11). That means that it should be possible to create liturgies that interpret sin in a more holistic way and declare absolution in a different way, if the minister felt this was needed. With this discussion the issue of narrative space and competence comes up again, and also the question of which roles the various characters have and which role the participants can take.

In summary, suffering as a major negative life event is hardly a theme in the liturgy. This contrasts the findings of the analysis of the liturgical text with the findings from the other data sources. At several points the liturgical text might be possible to address suffering as a negative life event, but the liturgy does not necessarily do so. These places are: the intercessions, the words of welcome, the sermon and the hymns. More indirectly it might be done through the storyline of wholeness which includes sin and forgiveness, but also the more holistic word 'salvation.'

Conclusion

In this chapter the various data sources are brought together and compared with regard to the themes that have come to the fore. Community and Holy Communion stand out as most important for addressing suffering and connecting with people who suffer. The comparison stresses the importance of the clergy in their roles as pastors and liturgists, especially since the liturgical text does not explicitly address suffering as major negative life events. The comparison makes clear that healing is never far off when talking about suffering. The question arises about the possibility of liturgy addressing suffering when the community (and sometimes the liturgy) are not experienced as safe places. The topic of community shows that liturgy takes place in the broader context of church life, and the experiences other than liturgy underline this fact.

By bringing together the data sources on these themes, a richer picture emerges than dealing with the themes in the individual data sources. The various data sources often highlight different aspects of a theme. The sum is more than its parts. For example, whereas the participants show the importance of community in relation to liturgy, the liturgists highlight the fact that everyone in the community suffers from brokenness. Another example concerns the importance of the liturgists. While the rubrics in the liturgical text make clear that the ministers have a specific role, the observations of liturgies highlight the distance that is created, whereas the participants further color the picture by saying how they (at least most of them) appreciate the ministers in their role as liturgical presiders and pastors.

Notes

1 van Ommen, "Anglican Liturgy and Community."
2 Ron, I, 207.
3 Betty, 203.
4 Hannah, 109.
5 For the dynamics of identification with leaders in the church, see Jack Barentsen, *Emerging Leadership in the Pauline Mission: A Social Identity Perspective on Local Leadership Development in Corinth and Ephesus* (Eugene, OR: Wipf and Stock Publishers, 2011).
6 The reason the other participants did not mention their views of God is because this particular topic was not part of the interview questions. Also the liturgists did hardly speak about this theme.
7 Cf. Hosea 2:14.
8 Olivia, 087.
9 Rebecca, 097.
10 For an in-depth discussion of healing, see Bruce T. Morrill, *Divine Worship and Human Healing: Liturgical Theology at the Margins of Life and Death* (Collegeville, MN: Liturgical Press, 2009), Chaps 2 and 3, esp. pp.71–80.
11 This is how Katrina describes her own approach, although she admits that in the end this approach does not work.
12 In classic theology it is denied that God can suffer. However, in more recent theological debates this position is debated. For example, Terrence Fretheim demonstrates convincingly from the Old Testament that God does suffer, not the least because of the sin of humankind, but also with humankind and for humankind. See *The Suffering of God: An Old Testament Perspective*, Overtures to Biblical Theology (Philadelphia, PA: Fortress Press, 1984).
13 R. Ruard Ganzevoort, "God Voor Schuldigen?," in *Vergeef Me ... Verzoening Tussen Mensen En God*, ed. W. Smouter and C. Blom (Zoetermeer: Boekencentrum, 2001), 84–96; R. Ruard Ganzevoort, "Familiaal Geweld Tegen Kinderen: Theologisch-Pastorale Reflecties," in *Wanneer "Liefde" Toeslaat: Over Geweld En Onrecht in Gezinnen*, ed. A. Dillen *et al.* (Leuven: Davidsfonds, 2006), 120–132.
14 Ganzevoort also mentions bystanders, but that is less relevant for our discussion.
15 See, for example, Denise Dijk and Joke Bruinsma-de Beer, "Sprekende Vrouwen: Narrativiteit in de Liturgie Vanuit Feministisch Perspectief," in *De Praxis Als Verhaal: Narrativiteit En Praktische Theologie*, ed. Reinder Ruard Ganzevoort, Kampen Studies (Kampen: Kok, 1998); Procter-Smith, *Praying with Our Eyes Open: Engendering Feminist Liturgical Prayer*; Procter-Smith, *In Her Own Rite*.

5 Suffering in worship
Empirical perspectives

This chapter serves as a summary and conclusion to the previous chapters, in which the empirical data sources were analysed and interpreted. Furthermore, this chapter serves as a bridge to the next part of this book, in which we approach the topic of suffering in worship from a liturgical–theological perspective. Because the main question is approached from different data sources, this makes for a multilayered answer. The first part of this chapter will answer the research questions of this project from an empirical perspective. The second part concludes the empirical part of this project.

Empirical perspectives

The central question for this book is: "How does or can Anglican liturgy in the archdeaconry of North West Europe in the Church of England's Diocese in Europe address and connect to people with regard to their narratives of serious negative life events?" For the ease of reference, Table 5.1 below shows the research questions and to which data source these questions relate specifically. This section reviews the research questions in the order of the table, thereby moving from the questions specifically for one data source to the questions that relate to more than one data source. The analysis of the interviews with participants and liturgists yielded also lists of points of connection in the liturgy between liturgy and suffering. These lists will be discussed under question 5.

The experience of liturgy in times of suffering

This book grounds the question and answers to that question in the first place in the experience of the participants. So the first subquestion of the main question how Anglican liturgy addresses and connects to people who suffer from a major negative life event asks for the participant's experience of liturgy. Most participants in worship experience the liturgy as positive. When they were negative about worship in their church at the time of suffering, they often moved on to another church. Most important in their experience are the experiences they have with the church community, with the Eucharist and with clergy. Many participants experience the liturgy as a safe place.

70 *Analysis of liturgy and stories of suffering*

Table 5.1 Research questions and data sources

1	How do people who suffer experience worship services during the period of suffering?	Participants
2	How do liturgists think they address suffering and suffering people?	Liturgists
3	Is suffering a category liturgists think of anyway?	Liturgists
4	Is suffering a theme in *Common Worship*?	Liturgical text (LT)
5	What opportunities does the liturgy in general and the liturgical text in particular provide for addressing and connecting to suffering people?	Participants, liturgists, LT
6	What happens when liturgy and suffering meet?	Participants, liturgists, observation
7	Does liturgy contribute to solidarity with those who suffer?	Participants, liturgists, LT, observation
8	Do worship services confirm the ideas expressed by chaplains and suffering people?	Observation

Liturgists addressing suffering?

The next questions are how liturgists think they address suffering and whether it is a theme they think of anyway. To start with the latter, the liturgists show great awareness of suffering that is going on in their congregations. And yes, the liturgy addresses suffering in many ways. As much as it is part of life it is also part of the liturgy. Suffering is not something most people think of immediately when talking about liturgy, but one only has to scratch the surface to find that, as a matter of fact, suffering is at the heart of the liturgy. One liturgist says that the liturgical image for suffering is baptism, which the confession and Eucharist reflect. The liturgists are also clear that liturgy is not the only place to address suffering. A lot happens in personal conversations, with the chaplains or with others. At this point the liturgists underline the importance of the fellowship time after the worship service.

Is suffering a theme in **Common Worship***?*

Listening to the experiences and reflections of the participants and liturgical presiders is one thing. Other input comes from the liturgical text. Is suffering a theme in *Common Worship, Order One*? The answer to that question is not straightforward and opens up the discussion of what we mean by suffering, whose suffering we mean and also whether the theme of sin includes suffering (see pp. 65–67). A working definition of suffering in this book is: suffering is a major negative life issue or event. As such, it is hardly a theme in the liturgical text. Interestingly, the points in the liturgy where this can be addressed are mostly stated as rubrics and not as prewritten texts. When one understands sin as not only personal wrongdoing, but more holistically as a state of brokenness in the world, then suffering is a theme throughout the liturgy. When the suffering of God in Christ is taken into account, suffering is a theme in the liturgy.

The liturgical potential to address suffering

The question that follows from the previous one is what opportunities the liturgy in general, and the liturgical text in particular, give to address suffering. The rubrics within *Order One* do give opportunities, especially the words of welcome, the sermon, intercessions and the hymns. Except for the words of welcome they are all mentioned by the participants as particularly powerful indeed. The words of welcome, or introduction to the theme of the service, are in some instances prewritten – e.g. in the liturgy for Palm Sunday. Furthermore, the discussion of sin, together with the observation that *Order One* provides a structure which allows for flexibility for drawing upon various liturgical resources, as much as a text, make clear that the storylines of wholeness might be tailored to the theme of suffering. The liturgists state that virtually all elements in the liturgy can be used to connect to suffering people in their situation.

At this point it is worthwhile to include a table with points of connection between liturgy and suffering as listed by the participants and liturgists (see Table 5.2). The table lists only those points that are in the liturgy or relate to the liturgy explicitly. The thematic analysis has shown that other elements are also very important, such as the experience of community and liturgy as being a safe place. The table shows that when it comes to the liturgy itself, for the participants the Eucharist stands out as singly the most important, to be followed by the singing of hymns, and the readings and sermon. The liturgists also refer to the sermon and readings, to the prayers of intercession and the liturgical year.

Here we need to repeat the warning that this is a qualitative and not a quantitative research project. That means that numbers are treated as an indication of the more important content behind the numbers. So when only four out of seven liturgists explicitly refer to the Eucharist as a point of connection with suffering, that does not mean that the other three think it is not. From the

Table 5.2 Points of connection according to participants and liturgists

	Participants (out of 21)	Liturgists (out of 7)
Greeting		1
Songs	10	4
Confession and absolution	4	2
Collect		1
Readings including psalms	8	6
Sermon	9	6
Prayers (of intercession)	7	5
Peace		2
Eucharist	18	4
Coffee afterwards	3	3
Liturgical year (esp. Advent, Lent, Good Friday)		5
Daily prayer	6	
Other rituals		2

various interviews, it is clear that for all of them the whole of the liturgy is important, including the Eucharist.

A number of participants mention elements which have to do with the context of the liturgy. They are not included in the list since they are often mentioned by only a couple of participants. These elements include things like careful performance, the beauty of the language, orderliness, time for reflection, the mere fact that the liturgy is there, and others. This shows that the answer to the question of how liturgy connects to suffering people must include more than only a list of liturgical elements as in the table above. The thematic analysis demonstrates that liturgy itself as well as the context in which liturgy takes place are both important in making the connection with suffering people.

Furthermore, the liturgists make clear that the various elements of the liturgy do not stand alone. According to Ross, together they make for a symphony that can be as beautiful as Bach. Suffering is inherent in the liturgy and invites people to bring their suffering to the liturgy, in the words of Al, to graft their own stories upon the story of Jesus. While the liturgy and its script give many opportunities to address suffering, the liturgy needs to be used with creativity. The liturgical text itself invites to be imaginative. To address suffering in the liturgy and connect to people is nothing less than a craft, for which both pastoral and liturgical awareness are indispensable skills.

When liturgy and suffering meet

The question of what happens when liturgy and suffering meet states the main question in another way. It is admittedly a question for which it is hard to pin down the answer, and therefore it cannot serve as the guiding main question. Yet it is important to keep asking this question, for it acknowledges that the liturgy is about more than saying texts and singing songs. From an empirical point of view, it is clear that all kinds of social and psychological processes are going on in the liturgical gathering. From a theological point of view, the liturgy is about a meeting between God and people. The present research is not in the field of the sociology or psychology of religion, but within the limits of the narrative and theological framework of this project it is necessary to ask the question what is going on beyond turning up on a Sunday and going through the motions.[1]

All data sources indicate that more is going on than that. The liturgical text makes clear the theological point that the liturgy is not just a social gathering, but is an expression of the relation between God and people, in which much storytelling and relational positioning is going on. From the text itself it is not possible to say what is happening in the experiences of the people, but the text does invite people to graft their stories on to God's story, including their stories of suffering, as one chaplain helpfully said.

From the interviews with the participants it is clear that no blueprint can be given as to what happens when liturgy and suffering meet. Different people have different experiences. Nevertheless, it is clear that for almost all participants the liturgy is important during times of suffering, and a number of them have powerful experiences. The stories of the participants also show that the potential power of the liturgy needs to be used well, for a wrong use of it can put people off.

The liturgists start by pointing out that whatever happens in the liturgy, it happens within community (the liturgical text underlines this fact by consistently using the plural). The community both helps to realize that no one is alone in their suffering since all have experiences of suffering, and it has a supportive role, whether that is implicitly or explicitly. The level of safety in the community that the suffering person experiences is an important factor with regard to what extent this person dares to open up. Furthermore, for something to happen in the liturgy, a connection between liturgy and life needs to be made. Theoretically, all the liturgy is about all of life, but this is not necessarily experienced, and there is a need for an inductive liturgy which engages with the stories of the people.[2] If all of this is in place, then nothing less than transformation is possible through the liturgy. Some powerful experiences by the participants confirm this statement.

As with the liturgical text, from the observation of worship services it is hard to say what happens for those who deal with difficult situations. Nevertheless, the observations do confirm that the liturgy gives opportunities, and that the liturgists deal creatively with them. At least the potential for something to happen in the connection between liturgy and suffering is there.

In conclusion, although the question of what happens when liturgy and suffering meet is not easy to answer, the review of the answers from various data sources make clear that a lot does happen.

Solidarity with those who suffer

As was said in Chapter 1, this book has an emancipatory interest. The connection between liturgy and suffering is not the subject of much scholarly writing, and therefore the voices of suffering people are often absent from the liturgical discourse. The emancipatory research interest brings with it the question whether the liturgy itself fosters solidarity with those who suffer. Our research does not reveal much about this, but a couple of clues can be given and can serve as a start to further research and reflection.

All data sources make clear that the key to solidarity lies in the community and communal nature of the liturgy. The correlation between the experience of community and the experience of liturgy we observed is a primary example of this key. The liturgical text is written in the plural, and that runs parallel with the statement of the liturgists: no one is alone in the liturgy. Whether that means a huge sense of solidarity because of friendships in the community or in the anonymity of the group, but solidarity in that everyone is in the same process of grafting their story on to Jesus' story is another matter. The other side of community and solidarity becomes also evident from the stories of the participants. When they decide not to open up and to conceal their story, they exclude the possibility of solidarity themselves.

Another clue to solidarity in the liturgy is the prayer of intercession. This is one of the places in which suffering can be addressed most explicitly and where solidarity can be expressed with those who are suffering within and outside the community. Other chances for or examples of solidarity mentioned are: special rituals, the collection, Communion by extension, the fact that the liturgy is the same throughout many times and places, and that the Eucharist is open to everyone (including divorced people). From the analysis of the liturgical text comes the observation that in the liturgy God expresses solidarity with the people, especially in the Eucharist. Furthermore, in one worship service we observed there was a rite for the Thanksgiving for the Gift of a Child, in which the community expressed its solidarity with the parents of the child.

In short, solidarity with those who suffer is not the first issue that comes to mind when talking about liturgy and suffering. Yet the data sources give a few clues about how the liturgy fosters solidarity with those who suffer. It needs the creativity of the liturgical presider to make the theme explicit and foster further solidarity.

What is said and what is done

Having discussed the views of liturgists and participants with regard to the research questions, the last question needs to be whether the observation of worship services confirms the ideas as expressed by the liturgists and participants. As a matter of fact, this question is already answered on several occasions in answering the previous questions. It is not possible to comment on all issues from the observation of the liturgical action. As far as it is possible, the observation confirms what was found in the analysis of the interviews with liturgists and chaplains and gives more colour to the picture. It also confirmed the storylines of the liturgical text. Sometimes these storylines did not change at all, sometimes they were coloured in and at other times they were set within the particular framework of a certain theme, often according to the liturgical year.

In conclusion, the multilayered analysis of the main research question, with the help of the eight research questions just discussed, and from the perspective of liturgists, participants, the liturgical text and the observation of worship services, makes for a varied but consistent picture.

Identity and meaning-making

The narrative framework and the analysis of all data raised a number of questions that have not been addressed explicitly yet. In this section we pick up these questions and formulate answers from a narrative perspective in line with the narrative approach of this research project. The leading concepts stem from narrative theory: identity and meaning-making.

The starting point of narrative theory is that stories shape our identity. Human beings try to make sense of what happens by telling stories and by fitting the events that happen into their larger story of their lives. In this way they give meaning to circumstances and events from their own life story and thus their life stories are expanded. Human beings are indeed shaped by the stories they fashion because of the just mentioned dynamic. Stephen Crites, an important voice in narrative theory, states that human beings do not make up sacred stories, but awaken to them.[3] In the stories of the participants we found this to be true. The participants list many points of connection between the story of the liturgy and the story of their life. We argued already that the participants make the connection themselves. However, at the same time the points at which this may take place can come unexpectedly: a hymn that touches them, a verse from Scripture that all of a sudden takes on a whole new meaning in the context of their situation, the theme of life and death that resounds in the Eucharistic prayer seemingly more than before. In all these cases they do not "think themselves up a sacred story. They awaken to a sacred story ... "[4] Because all these experiences and the moments of connection add influence to the life stories as much as the life stories influence the interpretation of the divine story of the liturgy, all of this forms the identity of the people.

A powerful image that one chaplain used in the interview and which we referred to already is that in the liturgy the people graft their own story on to the story of Jesus Christ. The image helps to address several questions. The first observation in the image is that the story of Jesus Christ is dominant, for the other stories are grafted on to his story. Juliette Day affirms this order of stories. "Participation in the liturgy permits me to embed my narrative in the narrative of salvation."[5] However, this notion is not without problems. In narrative theory a distinction is sometimes made between canonical narrative theology and constructive narrative theology.[6] The images of grafting and embedding fit well with the canonical strand, in which Scripture is dominant and normative. Constructive narrative theology, on the other hand, challenges the primacy of Scripture by voices of alternative experiences. We do not need to choose between approaches to see what the critical point is in the discussion: what is the place for deviant stories, for deviant views of God, for alternative experiences? The image of grafting is helpful in seeing the dynamic of what is going on in the liturgy. The polarity myth/parable makes clear that the story of Jesus was a deviant story in his own time, and Scripture makes clear that "God's ways are not our ways" (cf. Isa. 55:8–9). It seems that even a canonical narrative approach leaves enough room for alternative experiences, if the dominant liturgical authors are honest enough to allow Scripture to speak for itself.[7]

The image of grafting helps in another way to see what is going on in the liturgy from a narrative perspective, which we might call 'filling the gaps.' This happens in the process of understanding the liturgy and also in connecting the story of the liturgy to the story of one's life. The first is elaborated on by Day in a chapter on intertextuality. Intertexts are texts that are inserted into other texts, such as quotations or references to other texts. For example, the liturgy is the text, and the greeting at the beginning of the liturgy "Grace, mercy and peace from God our Father and the Lord Jesus Christ" is a common way for St. Paul to start his letters. Day says that when several references to other texts come together and the connection between the texts is not made by the text, then "the meaning-making task of the reader is to fill in the gaps between them, to create connections where there may be none in and between the source texts … "[8] A similar process is going on in the liturgy on the scale of connecting one's own story to the story of the liturgy. Alastair Daniel comments that this is a common strategy in storytelling. In several ways the narrator can deliberately leave gaps, which heightens the participation of the audience because they need to fill in these gaps.[9] In the liturgy many stories come together and it is up to the participants to make the connection with their story themselves. In others words, they fill in the gaps between the divine and the human stories and thus weave those stories together. The result is a process of meaning-making and identity-formation.

Conclusion

Finally, we are in the position to answer the main research question from the empirical perspective taken in this book so far. The question is: 'How does or can Anglican liturgy in the archdeaconry of North-West Europe in the Church of England's Diocese in Europe address and connect to people with regard to their narratives of serious negative life events?' The answer follows the order of the previous chapters: authors and audiences, narrative elements, polarities and themes. The section on research questions already gave answers to the main question by being derived from the main question. That section was already directly related to the main question and the answers there will not be repeated here. Furthermore, the aim of the present paragraph is not to repeat all the above discussions, but to point out how each section provides part of the answer to the main question.

Authors and audiences

The discussion of who the authors of the liturgy are shows that the phrase 'Anglican liturgy' in the research question is a layered phrase. Liturgy is a combination of several authors and narrators who perform a script. To connect to 'narratives of serious negative life events' is a matter of a combination of all these elements. Several authors are narrating, and which story is told in the end is the result of a negotiation between different authors, primarily the script and the liturgical professional. Therefore, it has been necessary to look at these different authors as different data sources, because they all give their own input for answering the research question.

The question is directed towards people whose stories involve major negative life events. The formulation of the research question makes these people the recipients of the liturgy. However, these people are also authors of the liturgy, or at least narrators. They are not passive recipients of something that happens to them, nor are they only audience, but they are characters in the play themselves, and thereby shape the liturgical performance and the liturgy itself for that matter. How the liturgical performance connects to them, therefore, depends partly on themselves. This observation is in line with one important finding in this research: the connection between liturgy and suffering can be fostered by the liturgical text, by the liturgical presider and other characters, but eventually the connection is made by the participants themselves.

Still, the responsibility for connecting the story of the liturgy and the stories of suffering cannot rest with the participants alone. The narrative space for the participants to tell their own story is very limited. The script is prewritten to a large extent, and most of the choices that the script allows for are made by the liturgists. Since the narrative space for the participants in worship is so limited, it requires a high level of narrative competence to make the connection with the story of the liturgy. Most participants have this level of competence, as evidenced by the many points of connection between the liturgy and their story which they can think of.

Yet the issue of narrative space and competence needs to be taken seriously. Two examples illustrate this. The first example is Betty, one of the participants. At a certain point in her story, she says, she could even not sing or pray or listen to the sermon. The only thing she could do was just be there. This may have been fine for that moment, but it is clear that this is not an ideal situation. However, she was not able to participate in the liturgy to the extent of connecting the stories. The second example comes from an article by Heather Walton. She sees the value of narrative in pastoral counselling, but she warns that some suffering is beyond words. Sometimes people cannot express their suffering. Sometimes another language is called for: "not narrative but poesies: images, symbols and metaphors that carry the pain of trauma without committing the blasphemy of trying to represent, comprehend or reconcile the horror in story form."[10] The question arises whether the liturgy is such a place. Because of its ritual character it might be, to a certain extent. Suffering is most explicit in the act or symbol of breaking the body of Christ and pouring out his blood in the Eucharist. Walton's quote expresses the need not to explain everything that happens in the Eucharist, but to leave the mystery. In line with her statement, we are warned not to try to reconcile the suffering of people with devout reflections on Christ's broken body. The Eucharist is a great opportunity to confess that the offering of a Son is horrendous and we do not understand, just as we often do not understand our own suffering. These two examples show that not everyone has the high level of narrative competence at all times, which the liturgy requires. This leaves all authors of the liturgy with the question what other languages can be devised.

Narrative elements

We now turn to the narrative elements of Ganzevoort's method. The narrative approach has deepened the analysis and understanding of the various data sources.

It is not necessary to repeat everything that the narrative analysis has brought to the fore. The focus is now on how the narrative elements contribute to answering the main question.

In terms of *structure*, of the three storylines 'wholeness,' 'glory' and 'living,' the first one is most directly related to suffering. The theme of suffering, as far as present in the liturgical text (see pp. 65–67), comes to the fore primarily in that storyline. But the discussion of this storyline 'wholeness' with regard to the question of whether suffering is a theme in the liturgical text revealed that this storyline includes more than suffering. In this storyline suffering is transformed and sometimes healed. From the element *perspective* the issue of power comes to the fore. As said above, the phrase 'Anglican liturgy' is a layered phrase because of different authors and narrators and audiences. Thus, in the liturgy a negotiation of perspectives is going on. The narrative space for the participants is limited, so the power to author the story rests with the Liturgical Commission and with the liturgical presiders. Our research shows that this does not have to lead to conflict, as the worshipers choose to come to the worship service themselves, and more importantly, the liturgists show great pastoral awareness and try to tailor the liturgy to the stories of the participants as much as possible. Nevertheless, the element of *experience* shows that the connection depends primarily on where persons are in their faith journey or journey of suffering rather than on particular genres. The discussion in that section also pointed out that the frailty of human life is hardly explicitly addressed in the texts that *Common Worship, Order One* offers, but rather in 'flexible' elements of liturgy. The element of *role assignment* shows that the protagonists in the liturgical story are God and people. God is the greater party who takes the initiative to connect with people. The liturgical ministers play a vital part in enabling this connection to happen.

The last two narrative elements focus on how the story is told. The *relational positioning* that happens by telling the story shows again God as greater party and the people seeking reconciliation with God. Their script is to ask forgiveness for personal wrongdoing. The question remains how suffering that one experiences not because of one's own fault has a place in the story. The narrative space is limited, and an inductive liturgy, which thoroughly engages with the stories of the participants, is called for. It is important to note that the roles attributed to God by the text are not necessarily the same as attributed by the participants, although in both cases God is seen as benevolent. But there is a discrepancy between the view of God in the text and that of the participants. This is a disconnection between the story of the liturgy and the stories of people, although nowhere has this been seen as problematic in the Anglican context.[11] The element of *audience*, finally, stresses the need for narrative competence of the liturgists. It has been noted a couple of times that the narrative space of the participants is limited. That of the Liturgical Commission, as official author of the liturgical text, is huge, but once it is written on paper they no longer exercise influence over it. That leaves the liturgical minister with most narrative space. She has most power to shape the liturgy and its script. Her narrative competence means that she needs to think both pastorally, knowing the stories of the people, and liturgically, knowing the story of God. It is a delicate and sensitive work to craft the liturgy. The interviews show that the liturgists and most participants are positive about the narrative competence of the liturgists.

Polarities

We now turn to the various polarities that were used to analyse and interpret the data sources. Myth/parable has to do with the genre in which stories are told. Both the liturgical text and most stories of participants are in the genre of novel or comedy which are both related to the myth: the belief in the possibility of reconciliation, of a world in which all is well that ends well.[12] However, the liturgical story does not arrive at that mythic endpoint easily. Central in the liturgical story are the mighty acts of God in Jesus Christ, who is the "ultimate parable."[13] Furthermore, most, if not all, stories of the participants contain elements of the parabolic as well. Thus, the polarity of myth/parable demonstrates a huge possibility to connect the story of the liturgy with the stories of participants.

When a story is revealing rather than concealing, narrative space is created for authors to tell their stories. In the liturgy this translates as points of connection, where the participants recognize their own story as relating to that place in the liturgy or to liturgy in general. According to the participants and liturgists, the liturgy does create such spaces, and therefore the liturgy can be said to be revealing and as inviting people to tell stories that are revealing. Yet it was also remarked that this is only possible for the narratively competent participant, and that also the narrative competence of all other authors is needed.

The polarity private/public meaning, expanded to include 'official meaning,' asks whether these meanings are the same, in which case it is likely that the ritual is 'honest.' When a ritual is honest and meanings conflate, it is more likely that the liturgy does address and connect to people's narratives of major negative life issues and experiences. Indeed, in most stories it is the case that the meanings conflate. So, in most stories the private meaning that people attach to the liturgy is similar to or the same as the public and/or official meaning.

The polarity moment/process makes clear that several processes are at work. In the liturgy itself the process of reconciliation and being made whole again takes place. Each liturgical celebration, in turn, is part of a chain of liturgies, which together tell an even more complete picture of God's story. Moreover, the liturgy is celebrated in the wider context of church life, and the interaction between liturgy and pastoral work is mutually influential. It is important to note that this interaction partly answers the need for narrative competence. In pastoral conversations meanings of the liturgy can be explored and connected to the situation of the suffering person, which then bear on further interpretations and experiences of and in liturgy.

The polarities discussed so far are all put forward by Anderson and Foley. Throughout the analysis and interpretation of the various data sources some more polarities came to the fore. The first one is liturgy/community, stressing the fact that liturgy takes place in community. The experience of liturgy correlates with the experience of community. The answer to the question how Anglican liturgy can or does connect to suffering people, therefore, must take into account the importance of community. So far this section in which we answer the main question has highlighted the roles of the liturgical minister and of the participants in making the connection. The polarity liturgy/community shows that the community has a huge role in whether or not suffering is addressed, and that has a direct relation to whether or not suffering persons can relate to the liturgy and therefore connect to the story of the liturgy. The role of the community comes back below, especially when discussing community and the liturgy as a safe place. The polarity individual/liturgical story questions the narrative space of each author and narrator once more, and it is not necessary to repeat the discussion here. We proposed to put the different meanings of the word 'sin' on a polarity in order to keep the value of different interpretations. This relates to answering the main question by asking what sin and suffering is. When suffering is included in the word 'sin', then it is easy to show many references to suffering in the liturgical script. However, when 'sin' means personal wrongdoing, it is much less easy to find references to suffering in the liturgical text itself. Note that the liturgists and participants do not have much difficulty pointing out points of connection between the liturgy and their situation, as one might suppose from the analysis of the liturgical text in itself. The next polarity, text/context, demonstrates that the answer to the main question needs be looked for not only in the liturgical elements, such as confession, readings, sermon or Eucharist, but also in the context of the liturgy. For example, for a number of participants the mere fact of the liturgy being there is comforting. Finally, turning Table and Word into a polarity helps to see the importance of both. Indeed, almost all participants mention the Eucharist as being important to them in times of suffering, but more than half of them also mention the readings and sermons.

Themes

Community is key. It is the most important theme that comes up in the data sources. Liturgy is embedded in the wider context of church life, which is communal in nature, as is the liturgical celebration itself. Suffering people find support in the community. Moreover, everyone in the community has to deal with suffering from time to time. The polarity liturgy/community above already picked up the correlation between the experience of liturgy and the experience of community. Any liturgy that aims at addressing and connecting to suffering people needs to foster a community in which this is possible. Such a community is marked by a level of safety in which it is not necessary to conceal stories or to put on a brave face when going through a bad patch.

The second most important theme in relation to suffering is the celebration of the Eucharist. Even though in terms of text the liturgy seems not to open much narrative space for the participants, it is here that nearly all participants make a connection between the story of the liturgy and their own stories. It was suggested above that, empirically speaking, the Eucharist connects to so many people because it draws them in physically, more obviously than other parts of the liturgy. Theologically speaking, it might connect to so many people because here God shares of himself in a most obvious and powerful way.

The third theme that stands out is that for many participants the liturgy is a safe place in times of hardship. Two factors for making it a safe place are mentioned most often: the structure of the liturgy and the mere givenness that the liturgy is there. The paradox is that the point of connection with the stories of suffering people is exactly that which contrasts most: a structure and a givenness, both certainties in times that are often characterized by uncertainty and chaos. The liturgists relate the theme of safety primarily to the level of safety that can be experienced in the community. The participants confirm the importance of community, as we just saw, but do not relate it necessarily to safety, although it is arguably part of it.

The fourth theme is clergy and pastoral awareness. The importance of the role of the clergy is clear from the stories of the participants. Their pastoral sensitivity, or lack thereof, has often huge influence on the stories. The liturgists themselves are aware of the pastoral issues in the congregation and try to deal pastorally and liturgically with them in a sensitive way. In terms of liturgical celebration, they have an important role, both in narrating the story as in selecting beforehand what will be narrated. The liturgists have a huge responsibility in enabling the connection between liturgy and suffering to happen, as they have most narrative space.

The theme of healing shows that the main question of this project might be taken one step further. The question deliberately formulates the question with regard to addressing suffering and connecting to people's narratives of suffering. However, the research shows that the liturgy might do more than only address suffering, but it actually transforms suffering, connects it with Christ's suffering, and therefore with the hope of resurrection and healing or wholeness.

Other themes have come up throughout the analyses, but it seems that the five themes reviewed here give most direct input to answer the main question. The other themes still add to the bigger picture and some are de facto included in other themes – e.g. 'putting on a brave face' is included in 'community' and 'safety.'

In conclusion, the empirical research shows that the question is multilayered and the narrative framework of this book accounts for many layers. Several themes keep coming back through the several layers. It is worth pointing out the themes that keep coming back. These are:

- the narrative competence of all authors and narrators, their roles and relational positioning;
- the question what sin and suffering is and how that is included in the liturgy;

- the several polarities are interrelated but most important seem to be myth/parable and individual/communal and with the latter the importance of community;
- Holy Communion;
- liturgy as a safe place;
- healing;
- and liturgy happens within the broader context of church life.

Furthermore, a powerful metaphor that helps understand the dynamic of connecting the story of the liturgy with the stories of suffering people is that of grafting. In the liturgy the participants are grafting their own stories on to the story of Jesus. All these themes include other themes and polarities and narrative elements. In the bigger picture, these themes present themselves as main colours, although other colours in the background are still important for the picture.

Notes

1 The present and previous chapters focus on the empirical point of view. The theological framework comes stronger into view in the next chapters.
2 For more on inductive liturgy, see Lukken, *Rituals in Abundance*, 333ff.; and Anderson and Foley, *Mighty Stories*, Chap. 8. The next chapters in the present book will also deal with importance of listening to the human stories and with inductive liturgy – see esp. pp. 122–123.
3 Stephen D. Crites, "The Narrative Quality of Experience," *Journal of the American Academy of Religion* 39(3) (September 1, 1971): 291–311.
4 Ibid., 296.
5 Day, *Reading the Liturgy*, 63.
6 Elaine Graham, Heather Walton, and Frances Ward, *Theological Reflection: Methods* (London: SCM Press, 2005), Chaps 2 and 3.
7 In this regard it is interesting to note that lectionaries tend to be selective. Lester Meyer points out that while more than one third of the Psalms are psalms of lament, the lectionaries include a small minority of these psalms compared to – e.g. psalms of praise. This might raise the question whether the lectionaries are influenced by a culture which does not know anymore how to deal with lament. Lester Meyer, "A Lack of Laments in the Church's Use of the Psalter," *Lutheran Quarterly*, 1993, 67–78; cf. Brown and Miller, *Lament*; Billman and Migliore, *Rachel's Cry*.
8 Day, *Reading the Liturgy*, 86.
9 Daniel, *Storytelling*, 46–49.
10 Heather Walton, "Speaking in Signs: Narrative and Trauma in Pastoral Theology," *Scottish Journal of Healthcare Chaplaincy* 5(2) (2002): 4.
11 One or two participants did struggle with this in the context of other churches which were not Anglican.
12 See Chapter 3 for the meaning of these terms in this specific context.
13 Crossan, *The Dark Interval*, 101–105; Anderson and Foley, *Mighty Stories*, xii.

Part II

Liturgical theology
Human tears and divine tears

Part II of this book moves from the empirical findings to liturgical–theological reflection upon the question how Anglican liturgy can address and connect to narratives of major negative life experiences. The connection between Part I and Part II is made in three ways.

First, the connection is made by means of the narrative framework underlying the whole project. In laying out the approach the present study has taken, we argued that liturgy is narrative in itself, both in the specific narrative elements it contains and in its overall structure. The latter is true in two ways: each individual worship service has a narrative structure, and so has the liturgical year. In the next chapters several significant liturgical narrative features will be elaborated on – e.g. the concepts of remembrance, identity and meaning-making. A further argument for approaching our study from a narrative point of view is that such an approach is relatively new in liturgical scholarship. In this part, therefore, we will make connections with the wider academic liturgical community. It is expected that this will lead to a mutually fruitful dialogue.

Second, following the practical–theological method of Osmer, we now move on to the third and theologically normative task. For this task we discuss the question how Anglican liturgy can address suffering from a liturgical–theological point of view. By doing so we move quite naturally to the fourth step, which is the pragmatic or strategic step: how can we move on from here? The aim is not to lay out a detailed strategy, though. It is expected that the discussion in the next chapters will offer enough for the reader to take away and apply in his or her own context.

Third, the most salient findings of Part I will be related to and viewed from a theoretical stance. For an elaborate overview of these findings, see pp. 76–82 in Chapter 5. All these themes will come back in the discussions of the present chapter, although some more prominently than others.

The question of this project is about the connection between the human stories of suffering and God's story as it is told in the liturgy. Because the connection between the human and the divine is ultimately the question of Anderson and Foley, whose 'polarities' have served as interpretive lenses in Part I, it is appropriate for Part II to start with them. They conclude in their last chapter that underlying all these polarities is a spirituality of reconciliation.

In Part II we will develop such a spirituality with regard to the place of suffering in the liturgical community. The connection between the story of God and the story of human beings is further deepened by suffering itself, according to Nicholas Wolterstorff. Chapter 6 discusses the proposals of Anderson and Foley and of Wolterstorff. It will become clear that a key concept in narrative and suffering is 'remembrance.' This is also liturgically and biblically a key concept. A spirituality of reconciliation must be grounded in remembrance. Chapter 7 explores the narrative, biblical and liturgical dimensions of remembrance. The framework of a spirituality of reconciliation in which divine and human stories intersect will provide substantial ground on which to explore the liturgical narrative space for God and people (Chapter 8). In Chapter 9 we will discuss what happens when narrative space is found and stories told. In Chapter 10 we return to Anderson and Foley's proposal of a spirituality of reconciliation. On the basis of the discussions and explorations in this chapter, we will show how this spirituality might look like for a liturgical community that seeks to give narrative space for suffering.

6 Connections

Human tears and divine tears

The question to which we seek to find an answer in this project is one that asks for connections – i.e. the connection between the story of the liturgy and the stories of suffering people. Anderson and Foley call these the divine and the human stories. Their book *Mighty Stories, Dangerous Rituals* is aimed at finding connections between these stories, or, in their words, their book is aimed at 'weaving' them together. The first section of this chapter explores how a spirituality of reconciliation might help to address the question of suffering and liturgy. While such a spirituality is foundational to the life of the (liturgical) community, it does not fully answer the question of how the divine and human stories connect or intersect. Nicholas Wolterstorff finds an answer to this question in suffering itself, but not only our suffering but also the suffering of God. The final section elaborates on this link between the human and divine.

Weaving together human and divine stories

Anderson and Foley draw heavily on the dynamic of several polarities in order to establish connections between divine and human stories. We have used these as an analytical and interpretative framework in our methodology. The polarities are an expression of "the paradox of faithful living." In the last chapter of their book the authors argue that underlying these polarities and this paradox of faithful living is a spirituality of reconciliation.[1] In their own words: "In order to honour both human and divine narratives in the stories we tell and the rituals we enact, we need to foster a spirituality of reconciliation."[2]

Reconciliation is called for whenever stories and rituals are not authentic, and often they are not. A birthday party might reveal the tension between family members. Or people may have a perspective on their life that is concealing rather than revealing, so at the rite of confession they think there is nothing to say sorry for, or others may be so much caught up in their guilt that the words of absolution cannot sink in. While stories and rituals are potentially powerful agents of reconciliation, they may be in need of reconciliation themselves as well.[3] Moreover, reconciliation is called for in a world that is divided by wars on terror, by conflicts between religious groups, by polarizing political parties. Anderson and Foley point out that diversity is part of creation, but more than ever before the diversity is visible in the neighbourhoods we live in. Reconciling both ends of the polarities has become a matter of urgency. Reconciliation is no longer only "a way of healing broken relationships and restoring people and communities .... It is necessary that we practice reconciliation as a way of living in order to foster understanding as well as restore brokenness."[4] This leads to nothing less than a "particular disposition" – indeed, a spirituality "for respectful living in the midst of ambiguity. It presumes a way of being in the world that not only admits of the possibility of ambiguity and paradox but embraces their reality."[5]

The reality of suffering in the world, and suffering in the lives of individuals and communities, together with the innate hope for healing and wholeness, brings out clearly the tension of "living in the midst of ambiguity." Suffering is part of life, the participants and liturgists in our research recognized. The parabolic is all around. The mythic hope for and the belief in the possibility of reconciliation are constantly undermined.[6] Yet human beings are inclined to the mythic. Moreover, the Christian faith looks toward a mythic end in which God "will wipe every tear from their eyes," where "there will be no more death or mourning or crying or pain."[7] At the same time the story of Jesus shows that this mythic end will not come about without suffering. Therefore, the parabolic is as much at the heart of the Christian story as the myth. To live with this tension requires a spirituality of reconciliation in which both myth and parable have their necessary place. The question for this chapter is how such a spirituality may take shape liturgically and in the liturgical community.

Before discussing the characteristics of a spirituality of reconciliation, Anderson and Foley remind their readers of what reconciliation is not. Reconciliation is not forgetting, it is not bargaining and it is not revenge. Building on the work of Robert J. Schreiter, Anderson and Foley state that when we forget we create the "narrative of the lie."[8] Such a narrative conceals the truth, and "ignores or glosses over the injustice."[9] The opposite of the narrative of the lie is what Schreiter calls a "redeeming narrative." Such narratives create space for truth-telling, for an honest account of the injustice, violence or any other form of suffering. They are authentic and have liberating power. Key to such narratives is honest remembering of what happened. Remembering is the opposite of concealing and forgetting.[10] A spirituality of reconciliation reframes stories and rituals. The aim is not to forget, but to remember in a different way – in God's way.[11] When it is not possible to give voice to one's suffering, for whatever reason, the truth is concealed. In most of the stories in our research the participants felt enough room to tell their story. However, in some stories they felt it was difficult to tell their story or they felt a strong disconnect between the liturgy and their own situation. Testimonies of people who feel excluded abound in the literature on liturgy and suffering. Such exclusion adds to the suffering those people experience already.[12] The antidote to exclusion of suffering, and therefore to the exclusion of suffering people, is remembering.

Reconciliation is not forgetting, neither is it bargaining. Elsewhere in their book Anderson and Foley bring to attention the fact that many dying people bargain with God in order to live longer.[13] However, not only dying people make such bargains, as a matter of fact everyone does it all the time. However, while the practice of bargaining with God happens a lot, it is odd, according to Anderson and Foley. Bargaining presumes that both parties have something to offer. The problem is that this does not lead to true reconciliation. It is a balancing act in which both parties may have something to offer, but both are required to give up something. Therefore, not all the story ought to be told. "Stories are held in check; certain episodes are not mentioned; ordinary meetings that might precipitate conflict are avoided; and sacrifice is seldom perceived by both sides to be equal."[14] Thus, bargaining does not lead to wholeness and healing, whereas true reconciliation does. When stories are not told authentically, healing cannot occur. As Melissa Johnston-Barrett states: "In a real sense, telling stories regains the world for the sufferer."[15] Healing can only occur if the suffering is addressed.[16]

Finally, reconciliation is not revenge. Anderson and Foley point to the fact that revenge is a popular theme, especially in movies. Everyone likes to see the underdog taking revenge on his oppressor, and we feel that justice is done. However, revenge 'evens the score,' "but it does not eliminate the pain or alter the story of suffering."[17] While the other may now also feel the pain, it does not lead to true empathy. Anderson and Foley describe empathy as "your pain in my heart."[18] Empathy is the act of listening carefully to the other and entering the other person's world. When both victim and victimiser do so, reconciliation becomes possible. In several stories in our project people felt hurt by others. Sometimes in these stories it is desirable that this wounded person and people from within the liturgical community or this community as a whole are reconciled with each other – for example, in the story of Olivia who felt more or less betrayed by her church council and vicar who turned her down for ordination, or in the stories of Peter and Judith, neither of whom found room to tell their story and were put off by their communities.[19] How can the liturgical community become a community of reconciliation, which is able to hold together pain and joy, suffering and healing, the happily married and the broken divorced or desperate singles, or people with different sexual orientations? The question is most relevant because the experience of community runs parallel with the experience of the extent to which suffering persons feel connected with the liturgy (see pp. 57–58).

A community of reconciliation bears the marks of true reconciliation: it embraces contradiction, it honours the other, it is hospitable to the stranger and it has the courage to be surprised by grace.[20] Embracing contradictions, such as pain and joy, suffering and healing, heterosexuals and homosexuals, married and divorced, is not only necessary to live in today's Western societies, but for Christians it is essentially following in the pattern of Christ. He was both God and human, he died and rose again. The ultimate Christian paradox is that to live is to die. In the words of Luke 17:33: "Whoever tries to keep their life will lose it, and whoever loses their life will preserve it." And St Paul asserts: "For to me, to live is Christ and to die is gain."[21] The Christian life is one of paradox and it embraces contradictions in a spirit of reconciliation.

A community of reconciliation honours the other as a logical consequence of embracing contradictions. It means seeing "the world of the other as a gift instead of a threat." Anderson and Foley recognize that this is not an easy way of looking at the other. "When we are able, however, our world is enlarged through our engagement with the world of the other."[22] For our enquiry, this raises the question of to what extent the liturgical community hears the voices of suffering and how these voices enrich the community, and indeed the liturgy itself.

The other can also be a stranger. Anderson and Foley argue that we need the other, including the anxiety and fear we have for the other, because these experiences remind us of the distance between us and God who is *der Ganz Andere*. They continue by pointing out that every person is a stranger, including ourselves. In unfamiliar settings or groups we do not belong to, we discover that we are the stranger ourselves. In the Gospels, the most powerful story about hospitality to a stranger is the story in which Jesus is the stranger, walking with two disciples on the road to Emmaus. They only recognize who Jesus is in the ritual of breaking the bread. "This early Eucharistic story underscores in a particularly pointed way that Eucharist is not possible without the stranger, without the other, without the different."[23] Relating these considerations to suffering and liturgy, the question is who the stranger is. Is it the person who suffers and is 'odd'? She might be, because Western societies tend to ignore pain and suffering.[24] Judith encountered this societal weakness when she found that even in church, people would not know what to do with her story of having lost her daughter. Yet from the perspective of the suffering person, the community might be the stranger. Who is the stranger when the community advises to have an abortion while you hold strongly to the unborn life (the story of Hannah)? And in the relationship between people and God, which the liturgy renegotiates, who is the stranger: God or people? The holy or the not-so-holy? A community of reconciliation wrestles with these questions and takes the risky step of welcoming the stranger.[25]

Finally, a community of reconciliation has the courage to be surprised by grace. Reconciliation leads us to unexplored places, because once reconciled, the situation is different than it has ever been before. Therefore, "in order to embody a spirituality of reconciliation, we need the courage to be surprised."[26] The courage to be surprised includes the courage "to love the questions and live the contradictions of the stories and rituals that bring them to life. To do so in a spirit of reconciliation does not demand resolution but allows transformation as we never imagined it and grace where we least expect it."[27] In previous chapters it has become clear that we cannot speak only of suffering, but that the horizon of suffering is healing and wholeness – indeed, transformation. A spirituality of reconciliation underlies and warrants such a horizon. Moreover, wholeness can be at the horizon because the liturgy seeks to connect the divine story with the human stories.

In sum, reconciliation is not forgetting, it is not bargaining and it is not taking revenge. To formulate it positively, a spirituality of reconciliation is marked by remembrance, storytelling that is revealing and empathy. Furthermore, such a spirituality embraces contradictions and therefore honours and is open to the other who might even be a stranger. If a community has the courage to face otherness and contradiction, it will be surprised by grace. Suffering is such a parabolic contradiction to the mythic expectations of life. It is to the suffering in both divine and human stories that we now turn.

Human tears and divine tears

In his article "Liturgy, Justice, and Tears," Nicholas Wolterstorff argues that liturgy and the struggle for justice are closely related.[28] The article is most relevant to our discussion for several reasons. First, Wolterstorff makes clear that, while the discussion in the article starts from the angle of injustice, nevertheless suffering in general is in view and his arguments are applicable to the discussion of liturgy and suffering in this book. Second, Wolterstorff arrives at the conclusion that the link between liturgy and the struggle for justice – Anderson and Foley would say the link between the divine and the human stories – is in suffering itself. Third, Wolterstorff distinguishes between sin and suffering, which bears upon our discussion of these terms (see pp. 65–67). Finally, the article fits well with the spirituality of reconciliation as discussed in the previous section. A number of connections between Wolterstorff's arguments and such a spirituality present themselves. Therefore, it is appropriate in our quest for the connection between the story of the liturgy and the stories of suffering people to take Wolterstorff's article as a starting point.

A key to Wolterstorff's case is the recognition that when people gather for the liturgical celebration, they come with all of their experiences of life. That includes joy but also pain, blessing but also the experience of the absence of God, especially in times of suffering. The experience of suffering is not only ours, but one of all who have gone before us. The liturgy remembers how they responded by using many of their responses, in the songs we sing and the psalms we recite. Yet we do not just remember the responses of our forebears and of ancient Israel; we make their language our own by appropriating these words for ourselves. "Not only do we hold in memory the psalms of ancient Israel and the hymns and acclamations of the church; we say and sing them so that they become *our* psalms and *our* canticles and *our* acclamations."[29] The tension that Wolterstorff points out is that even if we use our forebears' responses to suffering – i.e. the language of lament, the question is whether we really appropriate this language to ourselves. Before exploring this tension in more detail, it is necessary to see that remembrance is a key concept in liturgy as such.

According to Wolterstorff, the liturgy is a response to divine action, and within the liturgy the "reciprocal process of divine action and human response" is going on as well.[30] In the liturgy the divine actions are remembered: "exodus, return from exile, incarnation, crucifixion, resurrection, Pentecost."[31] The experience of God in the present and the experience of God by prior generations are related and even intertwined. Wolterstorff contends that when "either the present experiencing, or the remembering of the prior experiencing, is diminished, then Christian existence is distorted."[32] He continues with pointing out that not only past and present are related, the concept of remembrance includes something of the future as well. "Since part of what is remembered is the promises of God, we can even say that full-orbed Christian existence is a complex interplay of remembering and experiencing, and *expecting* the workings of God. Correspondingly, then, the Eucharistic response of the Christian not only catches up what God does do, but what he *did* and *will* do."[33] In sum, remembrance is integral to the experience of God in Christian life in general, and in a particular way in the liturgy, especially in the Eucharistic celebration. Furthermore, remembering the responses of our forebears to God's actions in the world necessarily holds in balance praise, penitence and lament.

Now we come back to the question of the usage of lament. Wolterstorff follows Claus Westermann in saying that God is encountered in three ways in Scripture: as the one who blesses, as the one who judges and as the one who saves. God saves in many ways, but they all come down to two categories: salvation from sin and salvation from suffering.[34] The human response to blessing is to give God glory. The response to sin is penitence. For both these responses the liturgy gives language, as our analysis of the liturgical text confirmed. The human response to suffering is lament. However, that language is much harder to find in the liturgy. Westermann does not find this language in the liturgy at all, but Wolterstorff is a bit more nuanced. He points to the phrase *kyrie eleison*, which is nowadays often attached to the prayers of confession, but it is part of the prayers of intercession as well. Furthermore, the Eucharistic prayer gives voice to the suffering of Jesus on the cross. And finally, the language of lament is encountered when the lectionary is observed. Nevertheless, Wolterstorff admits that Westermann's claim that the language of lament is absent from worship is correct in substance. Wolterstorff puts it very well when he says:

> Though the lament is not entirely missing from the Christian liturgy, its sound is muffled. Praise and confession one cannot miss; for the lament, one has to look. The person with thankful heart and the person with penitent heart will find much in the liturgy which expresses her feeling. The person with bleeding heart will only now and then find something. Such a person may find consolation in the liturgy, may find her participation in the liturgy to be a healing experience. Only now and then, however, will she be presented with words that express her suffering. We do not like tears in church.[35]

These words by Wolterstorff ring true to the findings of our research, even if it is more than 25 years since his article was published. Our research confirms that quite a number of people do find healing in liturgy. The participants can point to many elements in the liturgy that connect to their story of suffering. Yet suffering is not the first subject that comes to mind when asking what liturgy is about.

These observations work into two directions. On one hand, it is true that our research did not reveal that the language of lament is employed. If it was employed regularly it had certainly surfaced in our analysis of the various data sources, but it did not. Wolterstorff, Westermann and other scholars make clear that lament is the language *par excellence* to give voice to suffering. Lament is one way in which liturgy *can* address narratives of suffering people, as our research question asks. Because the academic discourse about liturgy and suffering suggests that lament is part of the answer to our question, we will elaborate on this in Chapter 8. On the other hand, the fact that most participants do find their suffering addressed in the liturgy needs to make one cautious about overstating the case that suffering can hardly be expressed in worship. Wolterstorff makes the same point when he nuances Westermann's claim that lament is entirely absent from worship. Our research revealed that suffering is expressed, or at least connected to in many other ways, most importantly in the experience of community and the Eucharist. So when the literature claims that suffering is not expressed because the language of lament is virtually absent, the literature may be right about the absence of lament but not about their claim that therefore suffering cannot be expressed.

Wolterstorff states that including lament in liturgy "touches fundamental theological points."[36] In his article he does not elaborate on these in-depth, but he gives a starting point to explore these points. He finds the starting point in Jesus' words "Blessed are those who mourn." According to Wolterstorff, in this beatitude we are all invited to become mourners. It is worthwhile to quote him at length here:

> [Jesus] invites all of us to become mourners – mourners not just for the sins of the world but mourners for the manifold ways in which that mode of human flourishing which the Bible calls *shalom* is lacking in our midst. We, who realize that in God's realm of *shalom* there is no one hungry, are to mourn whenever we see someone starving. We, who realize that in God's realm of *shalom* there is no one falsely accused, are to mourn whenever we see someone imprisoned unjustly. We, who realize that in God's realm of *shalom* there is no one who fails to see God, are to mourn whenever we see someone unbelieving. We, who realize that in God's realm of *shalom* there is no one who suffers oppression, are to mourn whenever we see someone beat down – and yes, to confess if we have helped in the beating down. We are invited by God himself to be mourners; accordingly our theological understanding of God must be shaped in consistency with that invitation. And our liturgies, if they are to express what is fundamental in our existence, must give voice to our mourning.[37]

From this quote is it clear that all suffering is to be lamented, since all suffering is an impediment to the realm of *shalom*. These words from Wolterstorff also point to the communal nature of such mourning. Note that Wolterstorff does not talk about mourning over our own inflictions (although that is certainly part of it), but he says that the community is invited to mourn over the suffering of others. To the marks of a community of reconciliation we can add that such a community stands in solidarity with those who mourn by becoming a community of mourning itself. Wolterstorff sharply warns against a liturgical community that does not mourn with those who mourn. "Insofar as our liturgies do not find adequate place for this lament, our experience of injustice and our cry for deliverance will not find their full and proper voice in the liturgy. Insofar as the liturgy does not make place for the lament, those who cry out from the pain of injustice and those who mourn that pain will find the liturgy alien to some of their deepest experience."[38] This warning shows that there is a pressing need to deal with stories of suffering in a way that honours these stories and make room for authentic, revealing instead of concealing, storytelling.

The importance of lament notwithstanding, there is yet a deeper connection between the human and divine stories, Wolterstorff says. Not only do human beings suffer, the Scriptures also speak about the suffering of God. The passages of the Suffering Servant in the prophet Isaiah are a case in point, as well as the language of love and compassion that pervade Scripture and therefore the language of God's broken heart, but also anger over the apostasy of his people (cf. Jer. 3:19–20; 12:7–8).[39] Ultimately, the cry of lament in the psalm becomes the cry of lament on the lips of the Suffering Servant himself: "My God, my God, why have you forsaken me?" Because of God's suffering Wolterstorff suggests "that it is not only *our* tears which constitute a link between justice and liturgy – or rather, between *injustice* and liturgy. It is also the tears of the *divine* which constitute such a link."[40] Referring to John Calvin, Wolterstorff claims that the demands of justice lie in God. Human beings are icons of God. "To commit injustice is to inflict suffering on God."[41] What Wolterstorff says about injustice holds true for suffering in general, as suffering also spoils the image of God.

> And now we can spy a very deep connection indeed between justice and liturgy. For it is that same vulnerable love of God which constitutes the organizing centre of the Christian liturgy. Or better, it is the *wounded* love of God which constitutes the organizing centre. Or perhaps better yet, it is the *actions* of God to which he was moved *by* his wounded love for us, his wayward suffering icons, that constitutes the organizing center.[42]

Liturgy remembers the suffering of God and the suffering of people in that it remembers Jesus Christ at its center. The core ritual in regular worship that remembers Jesus Christ is the Eucharist. Wolterstorff argues that this ritual is not only *eucharistia*, but also a lament, although in his observation traditional liturgies conceal this aspect. So he proposes that the anaphora prayer of Holy Communion should not only be *eucharistia*, but also lament.

By now it will be clear that the way in which Wolterstorff sees the connection between suffering and liturgy relates well to a spirituality of reconciliation as sketched by Anderson and Foley. The latter authors are keen that stories and rituals are authentic and therefore remember instead of forget. Wolterstorff uses the same language of remembrance and connects the remembrance of suffering of both God and people to liturgical remembrance. Wolterstorff colours liturgically the spirituality of reconciliation. Chapter 7 furthers the case to see remembrance as a key concept for connecting the human and divine stories and also demonstrates that it fits well within a narrative framework.

Notes

1 Anderson and Foley, *Mighty Stories*, Chap. 9. For the expression 'paradox of faithful living,' see p. 52.
2 Ibid., 167.
3 Ibid.
4 Ibid., 168. We may add that in the 15 years since Anderson and Foley wrote their book diversity and its concomitant tensions have only increased. As we focused the empirical work for this book on Anglican liturgy, it is relevant to note that reconciliation is at the heart of the Anglican Communion and is one of the top priorities of the Archbishop of Canterbury. Reconciliation projects are facilitated by the Continuing Indaba program. For more on this, see Phil Groves and Angharad Parry Jones, *Living Reconciliation* (Cincinnati, OH: Forward Movement, 2014) and http://living-reconciliation.org/ (accessed on 3 December 2015).
5 Anderson and Foley, *Mighty Stories*, 168.
6 For an explanation of 'myth' and 'parable' as they function in Anderson and Foley's book, based on John Dominic Crossan's *The Dark Interval*, see Chap. 3.
7 Revelation 21:4. All quotations from Scripture are taken from the New International Version, unless otherwise stated.
8 We will deal with the work of Schreiter himself in Chapter 10. Here we will stay close to Anderson and Foley's work since the purpose of the present paragraph is to make the transition from our methodological framework, which drew partly upon Anderson and Foley, to the liturgical–theological reflections in this part.
9 Anderson and Foley, *Mighty Stories*, 171. The term 'narrative of the lie' comes from Schreiter; see his *Reconciliation: Mission and Ministry in a Changing Social Order* (Maryknoll, NY; Cambridge, MA: Orbis Books, 1992). Schreiter develops this concept in the context of violence, but it is broadly applicable. The book by Anderson and Foley is a case in point. Another example is the application of the concept in a study on disability and liturgy by Helen Betenbaugh and Marjorie Procter-Smith; see "Disabling the Lie: Prayers of Truth and Transformation," in *Human Disability and the Service of God: Reassessing Religious Practice*, ed. Nancy L. Eiesland and Don E. Saliers (Nashville, TN: Abingdon Press, 1998), 281–303.
10 Cf. Betenbaugh and Procter-Smith, "Disabling the Lie," 292 and elsewhere.
11 Anderson and Foley, *Mighty Stories*, 172–173.
12 To name just a few groups: women, LGBT, disabled people, victims of domestic violence. For literature, see for example Procter-Smith, *In Her Own Rite*; Eiesland and Saliers, *Human Disability and the Service of God*; Vereene Parnell, "Risking Redemption: A Case Study in HIV/AIDS and the Healing of Christian Liturgy," in *Human Disability and the Service of God*, 249–266; Ganzevoort, "Familiaal Geweld."
13 Anderson and Foley, *Mighty Stories*, Chap. 6, esp. p. 104.
14 Ibid., 174.

15 Melissa Johnston-Barrett, "Making Space: Silence, Voice, and Suffering," *Word & World* 25(3) (1 June 2005): 333.
16 David A. Hogue, *Remembering the Future, Imagining the Past: Story, Ritual, and the Human Brain* (Eugene, OR: Wipf and Stock Publishers, 2003), 90.
17 Anderson and Foley, *Mighty Stories*, 178.
18 Ibid., 177.
19 Peter's story is about his struggle with his sexual identity and the concomitant struggle with the church. Judith's story is about losing her daughter and the response of the church to her grief.
20 Anderson and Foley, *Mighty Stories*, 178–183.
21 Phil. 1:21.
22 Anderson and Foley, *Mighty Stories*, 181.
23 Ibid., 182.
24 Christian Beker contends that the usual responses to questions surrounding suffering are either "we repress hope and become cynics or we repress suffering and become credulous ideologues, happily swallowing the images of false hope produced by apocalyptic prophets of doom and by ecclesial and secular technocrats. And when we seek the middle way between cynicism and credulity, we often strive to create private, danger-free zones and egocentric projects of survival." Quoted in Marva J. Dawn, *Reaching Out without Dumbing Down: A Theology of Worship for the Turn-of-the-Century Culture* (Grand Rapids, MI: William B. Eerdmans, 1995), 39. Cf. Bruce T. Morrill, *Anamnesis as Dangerous Memory: Political and Liturgical Theology in Dialogue* (Collegeville, MN: Pueblo Books, 2000), 179. See also Morrill's extensive discussion of postmodern society's views on illness and pain in *Divine Worship and Human Healing*, Chap. 2 and elsewhere.
25 Cf. Swinton, *Raging with Compassion*, 224ff.
26 Anderson and Foley, *Mighty Stories*, 182.
27 Ibid., 183.
28 Nicholas Wolterstorff, "Liturgy, Justice, and Tears," *Worship* 62(5) (September 1, 1988): 386–403.
29 Ibid., 390.
30 Ibid., 389.
31 Ibid., 390.
32 Ibid.
33 Ibid.
34 Ibid., 392–393.
35 Ibid., 396.
36 Ibid., 397.
37 Ibid.
38 Ibid., 397–398.
39 For more examples of God's passion in the book of Jeremiah, see Terence E. Fretheim, *God and World in the Old Testament: A Relational Theology of Creation* (Nashville, TN: Abingdon Press, 2005), 173–174.
40 Wolterstorff, "Liturgy, Justice, and Tears," 398.
41 Ibid., 401.
42 Ibid.

7 Remembering

At the heart of a spirituality of reconciliation is remembrance, as an antidote to forgetting and as a way of authentic storytelling. Remembrance is also a key concept to understanding liturgy, as Wolterstorff explains. This chapter demonstrates the rich potential of the concept for our question how the story of the liturgy can connect to the narratives of suffering people. In the first section, remembrance as a concept is grounded in narrative, so it fits well with the present research. Second, it is also a thoroughly biblical concept. The third section demonstrates how intertwined remembrance is with the Eucharist. Finally, we will comment on the importance of remembrance for the whole of the liturgy and in relation with the rest of life.

Remembering as a narrative concept

Catherine Kohler Riessman, an authoritative voice in narrative research, argues that storytelling can have several functions, but "remembering the past is the most familiar."[1] However, the issue of time is a complicated one in narrative. Even when a person tells a story of the past, it is told in the present. At the same time as remembering the past experiences, the storyteller tries to make meaning of the past by telling the story in the present, thereby constructing her identity.[2] Moreover, she probably wants to achieve something for the future. Byron Anderson connects memory to the act of remembering, and he points out that past, present and future are all in view in this act. Memory is not a passive object and it is not data retrieval. On the contrary, "the performance of memory enables a person to re-member, to construct a self."[3] Remembering does not only look to the past, but it remembers with a view toward the future and in function of this imagined and hoped for future. Anderson writes: "What I am suggesting here is that the present of the person holds within itself the relationship between the past and future in such a way that the past as constructed within the self 'shadows forth' the future, a future which always remains unknown yet which can be perceived by way of imagination, hope, and anticipation."[4] In remembering, the storyteller includes the future and wants to achieve something for the future in terms of identity and relationships. The model of Ganzevoort with which we have been working in this book makes this clear. The last two features of his narrative theory have to do with the act of storytelling rather than with the story itself. In storytelling relationships are negotiated, while the storyteller tries to satisfy his audience. Here we are reminded of the goal of storytelling: to begin, maintain, shape and end relationships. Thus, the concept of remembrance immediately brings out several aspects that are inherent in narrative: time, meaning-making, identity and relationships.

Remembrance opens up these inherently narrative concepts; at the same time these concepts point to narrative in turn. In the previous chapter we saw that the antidote for forgetting is remembrance and that authentic storytelling that is revealing rather than concealing includes remembrance. An insightful discussion of remembering suffering comes from Elizabeth O'Donnell Gandolfo. Taking the remembrance of the massacre at El Mozote in El Salvador as a case study, she argues how remembrance of suffering in and of itself gives hope.[5] Referring to Johann Baptist Metz she states that totalizing and oppressive regimes try to erase memories, and thereby in effect diminish identities. According to Metz "dangerous memories" that challenge are needed in order not to forget.[6] O'Donnell Gandolfo continues to say that "remembered suffering thus has subversive power to *interrupt* received narratives about 'the way things are,' subvert official versions of the past, and uncover reality for what it truly is."[7]

Although O'Donnell Gandolfo speaks in the context of grave injustice of a communal character, the underlying dynamic of forgetting – whether or not because of totalizing and oppressive forces and narratives – versus remembering remains in the context of suffering of major negative life experiences of individuals, as in the stories in this book. The participants in our research affirm that they do find points of connection between the story of the liturgy and their stories of suffering. Yet we also observed that suffering is not on the surface in the liturgy. Above, we saw how Wolterstorff hits the nail on its head when he says that one is hard-pressed to find suffering and lament in liturgy, and thus remembrance of these experiences and the language to give voice to suffering. Back to O'Donnell Gandolfo, the question is what the dominant narratives are that we live by, both in society and in church. In spite of suffering, people finding consolation in the liturgy, the dominant narratives are those of praise and sin as personal wrongdoing. The dominant narrative seems to be not one of remembering suffering. This (empirical) observation stands in contrast with the liturgical–theological claim that remembrance is at the heart of the Eucharist. Apparently, there is a disconnect between liturgical theology and maybe even the liturgical act itself on one hand, and how the liturgy communicates and is experienced on the other hand. The fact that suffering people can point out to many places in the liturgy at which they find themselves addressed in their suffering on one hand shows the power and potential of the liturgy to address suffering; on the other hand, it might point to the lack of a clear focal point at which suffering is expressed – in other words, to the lack of clear occasions of and for remembrance.

Remembering as a biblical concept

The concept of remembrance is central in the covenantal theology of Scripture.[8] The words in the Old Testament used for remembrance of remembering derive from the root *zkr*. In the New Testament the words belong to the *mne-* group. These roots and most of their derivatives are used in common language and in both Testaments are used this way. However, in both Testaments they gain theological significance. Brevard Childs suggests that "a new and highly theological usage of *zkr* emerged from Israel's attempt to reinterpret the significance of her tradition."[9] This suggestion affirms what narrative scholars claim – i.e. remembrance always involves interpretation and this interpretation is done with a view to the future and helps to construct identity, as we just learned.

Both God and people remember. Leslie Allen identifies several meanings and connotations of *zkr* for people's remembrance. The bottom line Allen states as follows: "On the human level, the words embrace reflection, especially on what is in the past. Such reflection may lead to regret or relief, or more actively appreciation and commitment."[10] What becomes clear is that remembering precedes action. When reflection leads to regret, often the subsequent action is to lament. Remembering God's covenant leads to praise (e.g. 1 Chron. 16:12). Remembering God can even transform the community. "Recalling God's past saving work becomes a bridge from a grim present to a blessed future," Allen contends. The Exodus event is paradigmatic. Allen gives several examples and then concludes: "Many of these examples focus on the Exodus not simply as an event in history but as a window through which to glimpse God's redemptive will for his people and individual believers in every generation."[11] Thus, remembering is not just a mental act but it is tantamount to participation in God's salvific history.

God also remembers. Allen sums up: "God's remembering has to do with his attention and intervention, whether in grace or in judgment."[12] In lamenting, people plead with God to remember his covenant, his faithfulness, his sympathy with those who suffer. In narratives, God responds to crises, such as reversing a woman's barrenness. But when God remembers, he can also remember the sins of the people, which results in divine judgement.

According to Childs, the meaning of the noun form *zikkārôn* falls into two broad categories. One is passive and denotes things worthy of remembrance in themselves. The second category is active and refers to "a memorial which calls something else to remembrance."[13] It is mostly used of cultic objects, and therefore in the setting of worship. The overtly theological meaning of the word remembrance in this context becomes clear in the following passage:

> The concern of the Priestly theology is not to relate present Israel to a past event. There is no tension between past and present because the past mediated an eternal order. Rather, the concern is to maintain the sacred order and relate Israel to it. The memorials as cultic objects serve to insure Israel's

relation to God's order by reminding both God and Israel. Yahweh is reminded of his purpose with Israel and his memory is equivalent to his action. Israel is reminded of the eternal order and she again relates herself to it by cultic participation in the events which mediated the order. The Priestly terminology conceives of history as the unfolding of the divine purpose through the interaction of divine and human memory.[14]

This quote from Childs underlines the fact that remembering is much more than an abstract thought about a past event. Remembering sets both God and people in motion. The believers call upon God to be faithful to his covenant. God calls upon people to do exactly the same.

Childs goes on to discuss the meaning of another noun form of *zkr* – *zēkher*. He states that the word is used parallel to the Hebrew word for name, *šēm*. Childs discusses the importance of a name in the Hebrew culture. A name expresses a person's identity. Therefore, "the destroying of one's name is synonymous with annihilation (cf. Jer. 11.19; Job 18.17). A similar situation is true of the *zēkher*. If a name cannot be uttered, it is soon forgotten. A large number of passages deal with the destruction of the enemy by means of cutting off all mention of the name."[15] Scholars like Metz point exactly to this quality of remembrance. History tends to forget and even suppress the memories of those who suffer.[16] In doing so, those in power alter the identity of the weak. In biblical terms, they try to annihilate their names. The biblical witness, on the contrary, asks for exactly the opposite – namely, that the name of the enemy (i.e. the powerful) be erased.

Finally, in the New Testament, in 72 per cent of the passages which contain some form of the word remembering, the meaning corresponds to normal Greek usage, according to Bartels.[17] In these cases remembering often leads to a particular consequence in one's behaviour. When the word is used in a specific biblical way, it means to intercede, to proclaim, to believe or to confess.[18]

One specific way in which the word *anamnesis* is used is in the accounts of the Last Supper: "Do this in remembrance of me" (Luke 22:19; 1 Cor. 11:24–25). This is probably the most well-known use of the word, resounding every time the Eucharist is celebrated. The next section zooms in on this use of remembrance, before zooming out to the whole of the liturgy in the section after that.

Remembering in the Eucharist: *anamnesis*

"Humanity needs a whole new way to speak of itself in the memory of suffering, even at a time when it often hides the suffering, the dying, and the dead from view."[19] David Power argues that such a way of speaking is found in the liturgy – more specifically, in the mystery of the Eucharist. Remembrance, or *anamnesis*, that happens in the Eucharist, opens up a new way of speaking.

The word *anamnesis* has taken on a significant liturgical meaning because it is a key word in the celebration of Holy Communion. "Remembrance or memorial is at the heart of the eucharistic action."[20] It is outside the scope of the present chapter to even begin to summarize the many discussions that the phrase "Do this in remembrance of me" has aroused, especially in the second half of the twentieth century.[21] The purpose of this section is to point to the importance of the phrase for liturgy and to show its relevance for our discussion.

Discussion has aroused over the meaning of the phrase. Bartels states: "Traditionally, these words have been generally understood to mean that the Lord's Supper was Jesus' appointed means of being present in the hearts and minds of the community of the church."[22] The presence of Christ in the Eucharist has been a deeply dividing issue at the time of the European Reformations. Only in the last decades have churches been able to overcome the issue to a certain extent – for example, in the Lima statement *Baptism, Eucharist and Ministry*.[23] It is not necessary for us to rehearse the discussion and take a stance. For now it is important to point out that the New Testament *anamnesis* in the accounts of the Last Supper is very similar to the Hebrew *zikkārôn*. As we saw above, this is active and refers to "a memorial which calls something else to remembrance."[24] The past is actualized in the present. Morrill summarizes: "A 'real event' occurs in the commemorative celebration, in its present contextual import, whereby a redemptive event of the past enables a 'genuine encounter' in the present."[25] The genuine encounter which happens in the Eucharist is with Jesus Christ. The Eucharist reminds not only of Jesus' death, but also of his resurrection. The remembrance is a remembrance "of me," so the participant in the Eucharist is drawn into the whole life of Jesus Christ, and by extension into all the saving deeds of God, indeed unto God self.[26]

Remembering in liturgy and beyond

We have seen that both God and people remember and we have explored several meanings of remembering. According to Allen, "religious worship is the context where human and divine usage come together, in the fellowship of praise and blessing."[27] Remembering does not only happen in the Eucharistic rite, but in the whole of the liturgy. This fact is widely acclaimed by liturgical scholars, although many keep a focus on *anamnesis* in the Eucharistic rite.[28] According to Morrill, it is important to keep in mind the interrelatedness of the Eucharist and other Christian practices of remembrance, "for it demonstrates that the celebration of the Lord's Supper does not function in isolation from the rest of the Church's practices of proclamation, commemoration, and decisions for action in the world."[29] Remembering God and God remembering his people happens throughout the liturgy – for example, in confession and absolution, in saying the creed, in a profound sense in exchanging the peace, etc.

Moreover, liturgy is interrelated with the rest of life. Remembrance leads to action, as the discussion of remembrance above has made clear. In our empirical research we found that the liturgy is embedded in the rest of (church) life.[30] Behind Metz's concept of dangerous memory, discussed above, lies this relationship between contemplation and action. In his radical call for a theology that "must be able to define and call upon a praxis in which Christians can break through the complex social, historical and psychological conditions governing history and society," nothing less than "a praxis of faith in mystical and political imitation" is needed.[31] Morrill points to the fact that the phrase 'dangerous memory' has been seminal, but that most theologians have focused on the political pole, and that the mystical pole in Metz's work has been largely ignored.[32] Yet Morrill demonstrates in his book the importance of both the mystical and the political. On the basis of Metz's theology, Morrill states:

> The biblical God is the one to whom afflicted people, people without a future, prayed and from whom they received deliverance from their oppressors. The "mysticism" of their prayer and the "politics" of their deliverance together constituted the pattern of their lives "in the presence of God." This pattern realizes its fulfilment and its universality in the mission, death, and resurrection of Jesus.[33]

This statement contains a lot to be unpacked, which Morrill does in his book. It is outside the limits of this book to review this. For now, it is important to bring this statement back to the argument of the present chapter.

It is immediately clear that Metz writes with suffering persons in view, just as we do. In our research, the suffering people are not always without future, although the suffering does impact their future a great deal, and in some cases makes one wonder about the future (for example, when one struggles with being single, with conceiving, or with a failed process to ordination). 'Mysticism' points to remembering God in prayer, but also to call upon God to remember the suffering person. Yet remembrance leads to action. On God's behalf, when he 'delivers from evil,' on behalf of the people when they engage in (political) acts towards healing and freedom. We are reminded here of what Rebecca Chopp calls 'narrative agency.' When people find power to (re)write their own story, they can find power to act for their own interests and freedom. This process involves imagination, which "includes the conditions of possibility for subjects to place themselves in new roles, stories, and patterns .... Imagination is the ability to think differently about the past, the present, and the future."[34] When liturgy (mysticism) gives narrative space to those who suffer, this is the beginning of agency in their situation.[35] Such remembrance brings one into the presence of the living God and his redemptive time. It finds its fulfilment in Jesus Christ, whom we remember in the liturgy and more specifically in the Eucharist.

Conclusion

The concept of remembrance plays a vital role in a spirituality of reconciliation and in connecting the divine and human stories. This chapter has demonstrated how remembrance is a fundamental concept in narrative theory where it is related to time (past, present and future), meaning-making and identity. It is also a fundamental concept in the worship of Israel, and from the beginning also in the worship of the Christian communities. The Eucharist is most clearly an occasion of remembrance, but remembering happens throughout the liturgy and eventually leads to action. This chapter has not only shown the importance of the concept of remembrance for understanding liturgy, and in particular a narrative understanding of liturgy, but it has also laid a foundation for the question of the narrative space of both God and suffering people. It is to this question that we now turn.

Notes

1 Catherine Kohler Riessman, *Narrative Methods for the Human Sciences* (Los Angeles, London, New Delhi, Singapore: SAGE Publications, 2008), 8.
2 See Miroslav Volf, *The End of Memory: Remembering Rightly in a Violent World* (Grand Rapids, MI and Cambridge: William B. Eerdmans, 2006); and Miroslav Volf, *Exclusion and Embrace: A Theological Exploration of Identity, Otherness, and Reconciliation* (Nashville, TN: Abingdon Press, 1996).
3 E. Byron Anderson, "Memory, Tradition, and the Re-Membering of Suffering," *Religious Education* 105(2) (1 March 2010): 126.
4 Ibid., 128.
5 Elizabeth O'Donnell Gandolfo, "Remembering the Massacre at El Mozote: A Case for the Dangerous Memory of Suffering as Christian Formation in Hope," *International Journal of Practical Theology* 17(1) (1 January 2013): 62–87.
6 The original German reads "gefährliche Erinnerung." Johann Baptist Metz, *Glaube in Geschichte Und Gesellschaft. Studien Zu Einer Praktischen Fundamentaltheologie*, 5. Auflage, (Mainz: Matthias Grünewald Verlag, 1992), 79. For the sake of readability, hereafter we will refer to the English translation: Johann Baptist Metz, *Faith in History and Society: Toward a Practical Fundamental Theology* (New York: The Crossroad Publishing Company, 2007).
7 Gandolfo, "Remembering the Massacre," 71.
8 Our discussion of remembrance in Scripture draws primarily on Leslie C. Allen for the use of the word in the Old Testament and on K.H. Bartels and C. Brown for the New Testament discussion. Leslie C. Allen, "Zkr I," *New International Dictionary of Old Testament Theology and Exegesis* (Carlisle: Paternoster Press, 1997); K.H. Bartels and C. Brown, "Remember, Remembrance," *New International Dictionary of New Testament Theology* (Carlisle: Paternoster Press, 1992). For both articles Brevard C. Childs' study is foundational, see Brevard S. Childs, *Memory and Tradition in Israel* (Chatham: W. & J. MacKay, 1962).
9 Childs, *Memory*, 50.
10 Allen, "Zkr," 1101.
11 Ibid., 1102–1103.
12 Ibid., 1101.
13 Childs, *Memory*, 66.
14 Ibid., 68.
15 Ibid., 71.
16 Metz, *Faith in History and Society*, 66.
17 Bartels and Brown, "Remember, Remembrance," 240.
18 See for further discussion of the use in the New Testament Bartels and Brown, "Remember, Remembrance"; Nils Alstrup Dahl, *Jesus in the Memory of the Early Church: Essays* (Minneapolis, MN: Augsburg Pub. House, 1976); see also Morrill, *Anamnesis as Dangerous Memory*, 155–162. Morrill bases his discussion primarily on Dahl's essays.
19 Power, *The Eucharistic Mystery*, viii.

102 *Liturgical theology*

20 Paul Bradshaw, Gordon Giles, and Simon Kershaw, "Holy Communion," in *Companion to Common Worship*, ed. Paul Bradshaw, Vol. 1, Alcuin Club Collections 78 (London: SPCK, 2001), 125.
21 For such a discussion, see Paul Bradshaw, "Anamnesis in Modern Eucharistic Debate," in *Memory and History in Christianity and Judaism* (Notre Dame, IN: University of Notre Dame Press, 2001), 73–84. A discussion of contemporary Anglican views on *anamnesis* can be found in Julie Gittoes, *Anamnesis and the Eucharist: Contemporary Anglican Approaches* (Aldershot: Ashgate, 2008).
22 Bartels and Brown, "Remember, Remembrance," 243–244.
23 World Council of Churches, *Baptism, Eucharist and Ministry*, Faith and Order Paper 111 (Geneva: World Council of Churches, 1982).
24 Childs, *Memory*, 66. Note that Lawrence Hoffman argues that the word 'remember' is better rendered as 'to point to.' God's memory is drawn to his grace by various 'pointers.' For example, 'This' in 'Do this in remembrance of me' points "to Jesus, who himself is the primary pointer, the second lamb like the first, who points God's way toward merciful redemption." Lawrence A. Hoffman, "Does God Remember? A Liturigcal Theology of Memory," in *Memory and History in Christianity and Judaism* (Notre Dame, IN: University of Notre Dame Press, 2001), 66.
25 Morrill, *Anamnesis as Dangerous Memory*, 177.
26 Ibid., 178ff. Most contemporary liturgical scholars agree with the statement that the *anamnesis* refers to the whole of Jesus' life, although this position is contested by some. For a balanced discussion, see Bradshaw, "Anamnesis."
27 Allen, "Zkr," 1101.
28 To give just a few examples which substantiate this claim: The concept of remembrance pervades Don Salier's description of liturgy in the first chapter of his *Worship as Theology*. Dirk Lange writes: "liturgy is about remembering and, particularly, remembering God's acts in history." Julie Gittoes contends: "The church is a community that gathers for *anamnesis*, and is in a profound sense formed and shaped by it. The sacraments form a focal point for this ongoing process …. This is perhaps most evident in the Eucharist, and most fully developed in the sense of remembrance and anticipation at its heart." Morrill, in his overview of Alexander Schmemann's thought writes that the whole liturgy is a remembrance of God's salvific acts; indeed, "the remembrance, the *anamnesis* of the Kingdom is the source of everything else in the Church." Lange, *Trauma Recalled*, 6; Gittoes, *Anamnesis and the Eucharist*, 1; Morrill, *Anamnesis as Dangerous Memory*, 114ff., quote on p. 116.
29 Morrill, *Anamnesis as Dangerous Memory*, 166.
30 For a profound treatment of the relation between liturgy and life, see Zimmerman, *Liturgy as Living Faith: A Liturgical Spirituality*. For a recent discussion of the relation between liturgy and mission, see Ruth A. Meyers, "Mission," in *The Study of Liturgy and Worship*, ed. Juliette Day and Benjamin Gordon-Taylor, An Alcuin Guide (London: SPCK, 2013), 202–211. In her article intercession has an important role. In terms of our discussion, intercession may be seen as the place where people remember in prayer the world they live in, and at the same time call upon God to remember this world.
31 Metz, *Faith in History and Society*, 77.
32 Morrill, *Anamnesis as Dangerous Memory*, xiii–xiv.
33 Ibid., 36.
34 Rebecca S. Chopp, *Saving Work: Feminist Practices of Theological Education* (Louisville, KY: Westminster John Knox Press, 1995), 43.
35 Ibid., 34ff.

8 Remembering suffering

In Part I, we argued that the people and God are the main characters in the story of the liturgy. Both are addressed by the other and both tell their stories. However, our empirical observations made clear that as a matter of fact the liturgical presider has much more narrative space than the main characters. In the present chapter we will search by way of theological reflection what the consequences are of the limits to the narrative space of God and people, and how this space might be enlarged. In line with the research question for this project, the focus is on the narrative space for suffering.

Remembering the suffering of God: narrative space for God

The question of how liturgy can address and connect to stories of suffering implies the question in which ways suffering is a theme in the liturgy. The analysis of the liturgical text made clear that the liturgical script as such, as far as it addresses suffering, focuses on the suffering of God in Jesus Christ. Death and resurrection are referred to in the acclamation from Easter Day to Pentecost as part of the greeting at the beginning of the liturgy, in the rite of confession, in the Gloria, in the creed and in the rite of the Eucharist. In terms of suffering especially the death of Christ is in view.

Classical theology has long claimed the impassibility of God. However, more recent (biblical) scholarship has demonstrated that the Scriptures witness quite a lot to the suffering of God. We have already discussed Wolterstorff's thesis that it is the suffering of both God and human beings that makes for the connection between the divine and human stories, and thus between liturgy and stories of suffering people. Therefore, we need to look closer at the suffering of God as witnessed in the Scriptures. A major contribution to this aspect of the Bible comes from Terence Fretheim. His distinction between God's suffering *because of, with* and *for* his people is particularly relevant for our discussion.[1]

Fretheim places his discussion of the suffering of God in the context of the relationship between God and people. This relationship is not distant but rather full of passion. Even images of marriage and parenting are used to describe the

104   *Liturgical theology*

relationship. When Israel breaks the relationship, God is deeply hurt by it, and he suffers *because of* this breach. For example, Jer. 3:19b–20 reads:

> I myself said,
> How gladly would I treat you like my children
>   and give you a pleasant land,
>   the most beautiful inheritance of any nation.
> I thought you would call me 'Father'
>   and not turn away from following me.
> But like a woman unfaithful to her husband,
>   so you, Israel, have been unfaithful to me.

Note that Fretheim relates this aspect of God's suffering to God's memory. God remembers how it used to be and therefore Israel's unfaithfulness is so painful. Fretheim emphasizes that God's sorrow comes before his judgement. The opening words of Isaiah are a case in point:

> I reared my children and brought them up,
>   but they have rebelled against me.
> The ox knows its master,
>   the donkey its owner's manger,
> but Israel does not know,
>   my people do not understand.[2]

These words express sorrow rather than anger. Pointing out the very similar beginning of Jeremiah (2:2), Fretheim comments:

> All the subsequent accusations and announcements of judgment can only be understood properly if seen as spoken out of the deeply pained heart of God. God's memory-filled grief informs all that follows, making it clear that these developments are the last thing in the world God wanted.[3]

Israel's unfaithfulness will finally lead to judgement. However, the passion God has for his people shows that God is never a distant judge. As a matter of fact, God goes to great lengths to bear the sin of the people. "A relationship is at stake, not an agreement or a contract or a set of rules. The judgement that does fall may in fact entail an 'eye for an eye' correspondence, but that comes only on the far side of a slowness to anger revealing a fundamental 'lack of fairness' on God's part, if God's actions are measured in terms of a strict standard of justice."[4] God knows that judgement means the end of the life of Israel. So the call to repentance is to turn and live (e.g. Ez. 18:32; 33:11). Because of his love for his people God chooses to let himself be afflicted by the sins of the people, although the divine patience is not unlimited. God suffers *for* the people.

However, when judgement comes, God laments and mourns *with* the people over the destruction of the land and the people. Fretheim shows that the order is not always judgement and then lament. For example, in the book of Amos at one point the lament comes before the judgement (5:1–2). This is not a rhetorical device in order to call the people to repentance; the judgement seems inescapable. But the lament, which Amos sees as descriptive of God's Word which follows from verse 3, shows God's genuine mourning over Israel. "Thus, we are presented with the kind of response to be expected from God upon the death of Israel: God will undertake lamentation .... God will join the people in taking up a lament over what has happened; God mourns as they do."[5] God suffers with the people.

In the final chapter of his book, Fretheim convincingly argues that the prophet not only speaks but also embodies God's Word. When the people hear and see the prophet, they hear and see God. One way in which this becomes apparent is in a number of oracles in the book of Jeremiah. "The suffering of prophet and God are so interconnected that it is difficult to sort out who is speaking in many texts. Nor should one try to make too sharp a distinction. As if with one voice, prophet and God express their anguish over the suffering of the people."[6] Through the prophet God enters into the situation of his people. As God suffers because of, with and for the people, so does the prophet, and indeed God through the prophet. But something good comes out of this. When God suffers, this is never the end. "For God to mourn with those who mourn is to enter into their situation; and where God is at work, mourning is not the end .... This experience means entering into a death-filled situation with the people, not only so that God can experience it, but so that God can work creatively from within it and raise them up to be a part of a new world."[7] In the Old Testament the identification between God and prophet finds its climax in the songs of the Suffering Servant. Traditionally, the Suffering Servant is interpreted as Jesus Christ, who stands in this prophetic tradition, and in whom the suffering of God and the suffering of human beings are both taken up and become one. It is clear from the Gospel stories how Jesus suffers because of, with and for people. By entering into the experience and pain of humanity in the person of Jesus Christ, God ultimately works a new world from within.

The liturgy is centred around the possibility of new life in Christ, through the Holy Spirit, to the glory of the Father. As we saw above, Wolterstorff claims that the organizing centre of the liturgy is "the *actions* of God to which he was moved *by* his wounded love for us."[8] Having explored the suffering of God in Scripture, the question of remembrance needs to be asked again in relation to the question of this project. What does the liturgical *anamnesis* refer to? In the liturgical text the death of Christ is in view, and his death serves as atonement for the sins of the people. Sin seems to mean primarily personal wrongdoing. This theology is also in view in Fretheim's discussion of the suffering of God. Jesus' death is because of the broken relationship between God and people. The suffering of God because of his people could not be taken further. Judgement falls. As Fretheim said, this is the end of life. But the radical twist in the suffering of Christ is that judgement falls on him instead of on the people.

The suffering because becomes suffering for. Remembering God in the liturgy, and more specifically remembering the suffering of God in Christ, expresses this storyline.

Yet the question remains to what extent the liturgy expresses the storyline of God's suffering *with* his people, and it is not necessary to restrict the question to God's mourning over the destruction of the land and the people as result of their own sinfulness, as in Amos. One needs only to look at the psalms of lament to see that we can legitimately expand the question to God's suffering with people who are faithful and yet broken. In the liturgy, is God also remembered as the one who suffers *with* people? Does liturgical *anamnesis* only refer to the death of Christ, or can it refer to more than that? Morrill discusses this question and wonders why some scholars are adamant to keep the focus solely on the death of Christ. He does not see what the theological and pastoral issues are at stake in that view and why a 'diffusion of the focus' should be a problem. Might the problem be that "modern, bourgeois religiosity exhibits the faulty tendency of wanting to ignore the memory of suffering and death?"[9] With reference to Xavier Léon-Dufour, Morrill reminds his readers that Jesus at the Last Supper says: "Do this in remembrance *of me*," and not "*of my death*."[10] Léon-Dufour draws parallels between the Passover meal of Israel to remember the exodus and the Eucharistic meal. There are many resemblances, but there is one important difference: the Eucharistic meal is identified with a person. So in the Eucharist, remembering is about the person of Jesus Christ. This person suffers because of and for the people. But remembering the person of Jesus Christ brings much more to mind than only his atoning death on the cross. It brings to mind the Incarnation – God's entering into "a death-filled situation with the people," in Fretheim's words. It brings to mind Jesus' identification with the powerless, whom he restored to society and whom he gave entrance to the worship cult again. It brings to mind Jesus' mourning and his invitation to become mourners ourselves (see Wolterstorff, p. 91). It brings to mind the embodiment of the spirituality of reconciliation Anderson and Foley propose (pp. 85–89). In sum, liturgical *anamnesis* potentially brings to mind much more than Jesus' atoning death for sinners – it brings to mind his suffering *with* those who suffer.

Back to our question of how liturgy does or can address and connect to narratives of those who suffer. In the conclusion to the empirical chapters we stated that the question remains how suffering that happens not because of one's fault has a place in the liturgical story. This is a very important question given that the suffering in the stories of the participants is not because of their own fault. They are victims, not perpetrators. We have seen that they do find connections in the liturgy, but not necessarily in the *anamnesis*. Liturgical theology takes much interest in the concept of *anamnesis*, but if it is narrowly defined as remembering the atoning death of Christ, then the connection with those who suffer from major negative life experiences is perhaps minimal. However, the discussion in this section has shown that the God of the Bible, who is confessed in the liturgy, is a compassionate God who enters human reality and suffers with those who suffer. Liturgical remembering should include the aspect of God's suffering *with*. This is one way in which the liturgy *can* address and connect to those who suffer. Note that although we have focused on the remembrance in the Eucharistic rite, and more specifically on *anamnesis* as in the Institutional Words, there is no reason to limit these reflections to this part of the liturgy. On the contrary, other parts of the liturgy have huge potential to stress God's suffering (and healing) presence in situations of suffering. This might be done in words of welcome, in carefully chosen confessions and absolutions, in the sermon, in the prayers of intercession and of course in other parts of the Eucharistic rite (as Wolterstorff said, the anaphora might be lament as well as *eucharistia*). As the empirical chapters have shown, it might happen anywhere in the liturgy.

How does this discussion fit with the proposed spirituality of reconciliation? One point of connection lies in the word 'empathy.' Above, we saw that Anderson and Foley describe empathy as "your pain in my heart."[11] Empathy is to enter into each other's world. The discussion of the suffering of God showed that this is exactly what God does: he enters the world of frail humanity. Saliers catches this in the concepts of divine ethos and human pathos. Divine ethos is God's self-giving, most clearly seen in the liturgy. Human pathos refers to all human life and especially to suffering. In Saliers' view, liturgy is in its essence about the divine ethos in relation to the pathos of humanity.[12] Richard Osmer speaks about the *pathos* of God. God's *pathos* is in essence the suffering of God as described by Fretheim. The sympathy of human beings for each other needs to be grounded in the God's *pathos*, according to Osmer. "*Sympathy* is human participation in God's pathos, God's suffering over the life of the covenant people and creation as a whole. We cannot understand what is meant by sympathy without first grasping the concept of divine pathos."[13] Divine and human feelings and stories do connect and interrelate when they empathize with each other. This forms the spiritual basis for sympathy for each other. Such sympathy is an antidote against revenge, as Anderson and Foley argue. Again, this sits well with Fretheim's discussion of God's suffering. When judgement finally must come, God does not celebrate but mourns. In God's judgement is no thought of satisfaction that justice has been done.[14] Rather, sympathy means to mourn with those who mourn. It is entering the world of each other. To do so is a key element of a spirituality of reconciliation.

Remembering the suffering of people and communities: narrative space for people

The narrative space for God seems to be focusing on his story of suffering because and for. In the previous paragraph we argued that it is crucial to enlarge God's narrative space by including God's storyline of suffering with people. Now we turn to the narrative space for people. We find this primarily in the language of lament. After having discussed silence and lament in the next section, we will comment on the issue of identity and meaning-making as inherent to remembrance and narrative.

Silence and lament

In Chapter 7 we noted a disconnection between the experience of liturgy and liturgical theology. The dominant narrative of society that also creeps into our liturgical celebrations is one that has a hard time acknowledging suffering. Wolterstorff rightly says that the language of praise and confession is obviously present in the liturgy; for language to express pain one has to look hard. This stands in contrast with liturgical theology that sees suffering at the heart of the Eucharist and therefore at the heart of the liturgy. We concluded that the liturgy has huge potential to address suffering, given the many points of connection participants refer to, but that it might lack a clear focal point to express suffering. In other words, we have seen that the participants make the connection with their situation themselves and that the points of connection are often implicit rather than explicit. When it is recognized that the narrative space of the participants is limited, the question arises how liturgy can express suffering more explicitly. Or, to phrase it in terms of Fretheim's reflections on God's suffering, the liturgy makes clear that God suffers *because of* his wayward people and that he suffers *for* them. But does liturgy also make clear that God suffers *with* those who suffer?[15]

Wolterstorff finds the connection between the liturgy and situations of suffering in the biblical genre of lament. But he and a number of other writers bemoan the apparent lack of lament in the liturgies of the Western churches. The personal testimony by Samuel Balentine is telling:

> The church taught me how to pray and, more subtly, how not to pray. One was to praise God, but not protest; to petition God, but not interrogate; and in all things to accept and submit to the sometimes incomprehensible will of God, never challenge or rebel. Yet when life's circumstances would not permit either such passivity or such piety, this advocacy of a rather monotonic relation to God seemed destined to silence if not exclude me and, I suspected, other struggling questioners from the ranks of the truly committed, the genuinely faithful. 'You must not question God.' If one cannot question God, then to whom does one direct the questions?[16]

In the discussion of remembrance we saw the importance of remembrance as an antidote to silencing and excluding those who suffer. Balentine suggests that the way that liturgical communities pray and not pray makes them complicit in silencing and excluding.[17] His testimony begs the question whether suffering has a place before God. No doubt most people immediately say 'yes' to that question. However, as Balentine and others witness, most churches have a difficult time to use the language *par excellence* to express suffering – i.e. the language of lament.

Kathleen Billman and Daniel Migliore have written one of the few monographs on the subject of lament. At the end of their book they once more state the need for lament:

> As long as the purposes of God are not yet completely realized, as long as there is an abyss between the fullness of life promised in the gospel and the lived experience of women and men, there is a need for the prayer of lament. The ministry and prayer of the church cannot be whole and wholesome unless it makes room for this prayer in its pastoral care, worship, work for justice, and theological study.[18]

This quote brings the need for lament close to home: suffering is the opposite of fullness of life. In all the stories of suffering that we have encountered in our research project, lament is an appropriate means to express the brokenness. If lament is the language *par excellence* to express suffering, we need to look closer at the possibilities it gives in connecting the divine and human stories in liturgy at times of suffering. But before lament, there is silence.

Billman and Migliore state that suffering often defies language. This might mean that someone does not feel safe anywhere to tell her story. Or it might mean that the suffering is beyond words. In an insightful article about silence, voice and suffering, Melissa Johnston-Barrett writes that even "those who *are* able to speak (and speak coherently) about their suffering find their words constantly frustrated, because what is felt – bodily, emotionally, mentally, and spiritually – cannot be captured in language."[19] Suffering silences.

However, those who are able to listen do not need words. Suffering expresses itself first and foremost in the body.[20] Scripture regularly pictures suffering in the body – for example, the pain of Job. Therefore, those who care need to learn the skills to listen not only to words, but also to that which is not said verbally but non-verbally. "The cry of lament begins in the body," as Billman and Migliore put it. "Before words, there are emotions and memories, carried and felt in the body."[21] So the language of lament might start without words and it needs sensitivity of the community to listen to these silent cries.[22] John Swinton remarks of Job's friends that their solidarity in silence was healing, but it went wrong when they began to speak.[23] Latin-American theologian Elsa Tamez says about the the silence of the friends of Job that this form of silence "was the highest wisdom." Their silent solidarity gathered their tears into one.[24] Swinton discusses the silence of suffering at some length, and relates this to the silence of Christ on the cross. Usually, theologians and others focus on the words Jesus speaks on the cross, Swinton says, but these few words can only be understood by the six hours of silence. In being silent, God shows his solidarity with those who are equally silenced by suffering.

Still, as we have noted, healing can only begin to occur when suffering finds a language. At first, this language is perhaps incoherent and broken. The road to telling the story of suffering may be travelled by taking only small steps. Yet it "is only at the threshold of speech that the sufferer can begin to regain a sense of agency and identification with oneself and others. These small steps begin to reconnect the sufferer to others."[25] The term 'agency' is important. If liturgy gives little narrative space to people who suffer, then their narrative agency is diminished rather than enhanced.[26] For liturgy to be healing, it needs to find opportunities to give a voice and a language to those who suffer.

Lament is such a language. In the lament the suffering person cries out to God for deliverance. She calls upon the God who appears to be absent in the situation. The hidden God is called back on to the scene.[27] However, lament is not therapeutic catharsis (although it might have similar effects) and it is not (only) an outburst of anger and despair. Lament in Scripture is first and foremost prayer. Lament has an address: "My God, my God, why have you forsaken me?!"[28] Even in the difficult language of accusing God the psalms of lament express a 'my-God-theology.' Swinton:

> Lament has a purpose and an endpoint beyond the simple expression of pain: reconciliation with and a deeper love of God. As a form of prayer, lament is both transformative and subversive. It is a profound statement against the world and the assumptions that drive the world.[29]

Swinton mentions several functions of the prayer of lament in this quote: expression of pain, reconciliation, love, transformation, and lament is subversive. The transformative and subversive functions of the prayer of lament help to put things into perspective. In other words, they bear upon the meaning-making framework.

When a major negative event intrudes on life, the meaning-making framework is shaken.[30] The crisis that suffering causes is not necessarily a crisis of faith, but a crisis of understanding.[31] In such a context the lament is uttered. The suffering person experiences God differently from whom he thought God was. Instead of God's benevolence, he experiences God's absence. Rather than resigning his faith, he calls upon God to act on behalf of the righteous, to make right the situation, and to be true to the covenantal relationship he has with his people. Brueggemann notes that this is bold speech because it dares to name the suffering. Moreover, it dares to name the suffering before God and claims it as a proper subject for conversation with God. "Everything properly belongs in this conversation of the heart. To withhold parts of life from that conversation is in fact to withhold part of life from the sovereignty of God. Thus, these psalms make the important connection: everything must be brought to speech, and everything brought to speech must be addressed to God, who is the final reference for all of life."[32] In the words of Westermann:

> The theological significance of the personal lament lies first of all in the fact that it gives voice to suffering. The lament is the language of suffering; in it suffering is given the dignity of language: It will not stay silent![33]

Thus, the person who laments engages in bold truth-telling and seeks to frame her understanding of the world, her meaning-making framework, in relation to God.[34]

Lament sets free from the bondage to revenge and hatred. Meaning-making now happens within the context of trusting God, even if God appears to be absent. In the prayer of lament the suffering person expresses his anger over the injustice of the suffering and often aims his anger at the enemies. Yet he does not ask for personal power to take revenge, but he rather lets the revenge be God's. As such, the prayer of lament does not fuel anger but instead brings it to God and asks God to deal with the enemy.[35] Thus, lament is a very appropriate language within a spirituality of reconciliation, which is emphatically opposed to revenge.

Free from revenge and hatred, the road to reconciliation begins to open up. It is difficult to enter that road. Swinton remarks that it is much easier to hold on to memories of suffering and feelings of anger, revenge and hate than it is to think about the possibility of forgiving the perpetrator of evil and maybe even reconciling with her.[36] Yet ultimately Christians take their anger in lament to the cross, where, out of the suffering silence, the first words are: "Father, forgive them, for they do not know what they are doing." The cross is the paradox of the Christian faith, where evil is overcome by suffering evil to its deadly consequences and where the circle of anger, hatred, revenge and violence is broken. Christ shows the difficult road to forgiveness and reconciliation. Lament still has its place. Jesus himself takes on his lips the agonizing question why God has forsaken him. By doing so, he legitimizes this central part of Israel's prayer.

Lament transforms. It transforms anger from being destructive to something that can become constructive. Especially when the community is able to lament with those who suffer, or even on their behalf when the suffering person is not able to do so any more, the community constructively brings the lament before God. Doing so keeps the suffering person in the community and in a real sense it keeps God in the community.[37] Thus, lament resists the silencing and isolating power of suffering.[38] From the perspective of pastoral work, Eugene Peterson argues along the same lines. He mentions several functions of joining private grief with communal lament. First, by doing so suffering "develops significance .... The community votes with its tears that there is suffering that is worth weeping over." Second, suffering dehumanizes. By bringing suffering into the community, it is set within a human environment. Third, "when the community joins in the lament, sanction is given for the expression of loss – the outpouring of emotion is legitimized ..."[39] Peterson concludes by highlighting the need for pastoral counselling to be part of the ministry of the liturgical community. He states eloquently: "Pastoral work among the suffering wears a path between home and sanctuary."[40] We will return to this theme in Chapter 10.

The lament petitions God to act, but it also moves the community to action. This is yet another function of lament and a further capacity for transformation. As Billman and Migliore say, it is not possible for a community to bewail the death of teenagers on a train crossing and not at the same time demand safety equipment.[41] We are reminded of Metz's concept of dangerous memory, which is grounded in 'mysticism' (which includes prayer) and stands up against injustice. Lament remembers and this remembering does not remain without consequences.[42] Lament is an act of solidarity and leads to solidarity in action.

The prayer of lament does not take away suffering, but it does reframe it. Swinton says that the "reframe is a spiritual one that opens up new possibilities that were not previously available."[43] The lament gives hope that God listens and as an appeal to God it trusts that he will do something about the situation. David Power writes about the 'liberating power of memory,' that "the memory of all who suffered is taken into the memory of Christ .... In faith and anticipative memory, Christian peoples can always give testimony to an alternative world, in which love and justice prevail."[44] Therefore, the lament can move towards or include praise.[45] From a faith perspective, it ultimately gives hope because of the cross and resurrection of Jesus Christ.

Neil Pembroke argues for including lament in liturgy on the basis of his pastoral and liturgical experience, but also from a psychological point of view. Apart from his psychological underpinning of the argument to include lament in worship, two insights are important for our discussion. First, he relates the expression of anger (lament) to psychological research on assertiveness. It seems that assertiveness "puts a strain on the relationship."[46] Therefore, psychologists advise their clients often to take an empathic rather than a direct approach. This is socially more acceptable. Pembroke argues that often a 'soft' form of lament suffices for most people and will also be more easily accepted in the community. A soft form might be to ask 'Why?' and 'How long?' – typical language of lament psalms. Still, there is a place for the 'hard' form, which is met in the psalms of lament as well. His second insight that adds to our discussion is that psychological research shows that only ventilating emotions is not constructive; it becomes constructive when it is combined with reframing one's view on the situation. Liturgically, such a reframing happens ultimately through the parabolic dynamic of cross and resurrection.

While Pembroke's insights are valuable contributions to the topic of lament in liturgy, two points need to be added to his theory. First, in his examples of liturgical introductions to lament prayers, he is pastorally sensitive to those who suffer and those who do not. Pembroke asks the latter people to think back to a time when they did suffer. However, it speaks of solidarity of the community with those who suffer if they could perhaps pray on behalf of and for those who suffer. Second, the question arises whether Pembroke makes the transition to praise too quickly. Sometimes it is not possible for the suffering person to make this transition at that point. Having said this, it should be emphasized that Pembroke's insights are most helpful to the discourse on lament.

In sum, lament is first an expression of suffering. Such an expression is not often found in Western churches, but biblical and other evidence make clear that it is a powerful and legitimate language. The prayers of lament are an important resource to address suffering in the liturgy. It gives narrative space to those who suffer. It fits a spirituality of reconciliation because it binds the community and the suffering person together and, after appropriate silence and listening, gives them a language to share the pain and bring it before God in prayer. Lament does even more. It moves towards solidarity and action. As such, remembering the suffering in the prayer of lament becomes "dangerous remembering." Praying with the language of lament has transformative power for those who suffer and the community around them.

Identity and meaning-making

Lament brings suffering before God and reframes it. When the meaning-making framework is shattered, people engage in coping strategies to make sense of the world anew. Moreover, they try to find a new place for themselves in that new understanding of the world. The search for identity is grounded in memory. In relation to the liturgical narrative space that people have and the narrative agency they can or are allowed to execute, the question is how liturgy helps in the search for identity and meaning when people's lives are shattered. In a sense, this entire book revolves around this question. The aim of the present section is to see how identity and meaning-making work out in the question for narrative space for people and remembering their suffering.

Byron Anderson argues that identity is bound up with time.[47] If someone conceives of herself as being only in the present, then it is impossible to answer the question 'Where am I?' and 'Who am I?' The present is always fleeting. For someone to answer these questions she needs a sense of her history and her future. When people say who they are, they start telling a version of their life story. So memory plays an important part. Memory is not a passive object, but is only possible in the act of remembering. Also, "memory is not data retrieval. The performance of memory enables a person to re-member, to construct a self."[48] Anderson refers to David Hogue who says: "Because memories constitute the self, each time we remember an event from our own lives, the self is transformed. The act of re-membering is an act of self-reconstruction. Each time we re-member the events that have shaped our lives, we are re-membering who we are."[49] A similar process is at work with regard to the future. Identity is formed not only by memories of the past, but also by how a person imagines his future.[50] Past, present and future are all part of anyone's life story and meaning-making framework.

The story of the liturgy works with the same time dimensions, as the analysis of the liturgical text has shown (see Chapter 2). As the story of the liturgy reveals the memory of God in his mighty deeds, so the liturgical community finds its identity in this story of God. The memory of God's past dealings with people and the imagination of God's future with people shape the identity of the liturgical community in the present. The mighty deeds of God are remembered in the liturgy, especially the climax of cross and resurrection. Even the suffering of God is remembered in liturgy – although it is questionable to what extent God is remembered as the one who suffers *with* people, as we have discussed above.

The question arises whether the memories of the people find a place in the liturgy as well, especially memories of suffering. The evidence suggests that at least the most obvious language for the remembrance of suffering, the language of lament, is usually absent in the liturgy. Our research has made clear that suffering is addressed (and therefore remembered) at several occasions in the liturgy, or at least that the liturgy provides this opportunity. However, often this is implicit and the suffering person is left on his own to make the connection with his own life. Seeing identity and meaning-making in the context of remembering raises the question whether such implicit addressing of suffering is enough. Maybe it is, for the individual person. But when the remembrance of suffering remains at an abstract and implicit level, it will be harder for the community to join the sufferer on his "mourning bench."[51] It will be harder for the memory to become a 'dangerous memory.' And so it will be harder for the community to express its solidarity and put solidarity into action. The identity of the suffering person might be shaped by implicit remembering, but the identity of the community will not. Moreover, if a person's identity is found in community, then even the sufferer's own identity will not be formed as fully as possible.[52] Also, when a person is allowed and able to tell her story, it will help to overcome isolation and put the person back in the community.[53]

Notes

1 Note that the suffering of God is distinct from the suffering of people in that it does not incapacitate God. See Fretheim, *The Suffering of God*, 124.
2 Isa. 1:2–3.
3 Fretheim, *The Suffering of God*, 115.
4 Ibid., 125.
5 Ibid., 131.
6 Ibid., 160.
7 Ibid., 136, 166.
8 Wolterstorff, "Liturgy, Justice, and Tears," 401.
9 Morrill, *Anamnesis as Dangerous Memory*, 179.
10 Ibid., 180.
11 Anderson and Foley, *Mighty Stories*, 177.
12 Saliers, *Worship as Theology*, 1994. Saliers develops these concepts in Chapter 1 of his book. They form a basso continuo in his work, not least in his chapters on lament and intercession.
13 Osmer, *Practical Theology*, 136. Note that in this research we use this book by Osmer primarily because of the practical–theological methodology which we follow in broad lines. However, to engage with his description of 'sympathy' is appropriate here because he sees sympathy (or empathy) as foundation to a spirituality of prophetic discernment, which in turn is underlying the third and normative step in his methodology, the step we are taking in this chapter. Furthermore, the connection Osmer makes between the prophetic office and sympathy fits well with the discussion above.
14 Fretheim, *The Suffering of God*, 136.
15 An additional argument for including narrative space for people and suffering in liturgy comes from the field of trauma theory. Storm Swain claims that when suffering is part of people's larger worldview, they are better able to cope with suffering than when their worldview excludes suffering. Arguably liturgy plays a part in the formation of worldviews. Storm Swain, *Trauma and Transformation at Ground Zero: A Pastoral Theology* (Minneapolis, MN: Fortress Press, 2011), 7. In her book, Swain integrates a Trinitarian pastoral model with D.W. Winnicot's trauma theory. Important concepts in Winnicot's theory are holding, suffering and transforming.

These Swain relates to God as Earth-Maker, Pain-Bearer and Life-Giver (after the paraphrase of the Lord's Prayer by Jim Cotter in *A New Zealand Prayer Book – He Karakia Mihinare O Aotearoa*). Thus, she arrives at a pastoral model in which pastoral counsellors, and by extension, the community, hold out with people (earth-making), suffer with them (pain-bearing) and seek transformation through suffering (life-giving). In this book we focus on liturgical–theological literature. However, at several points Swain's work is helpful so when relevant we will refer to her pastoral model. These references also show that our discussion is not a strictly internal liturgical discussion, but has relevance outside the liturgical field.

16 Samuel E. Balentine, *Prayer in the Hebrew Bible: The Drama of Divine-Human Dialogue* (Minneapolis, MN: Fortress Press, 1993), quoted in Billman and Migliore, *Rachel's Cry*, 7.
17 Cf. John Swinton who argues that thoughtlessness makes societies and churches complicit when evil develops. Thoughtfulness, therefore, is one means of resisting evil. Swinton, *Raging with Compassion*, Chap. 7.
18 Billman and Migliore, *Rachel's Cry*, 149.
19 Johnston-Barrett, "Making Space: Silence, Voice, and Suffering," 330.
20 Elaine Scarry, *The Body in Pain: The Making and Unmaking of the World* (New York: Oxford University Press, 1985).
21 Billman and Migliore, *Rachel's Cry*, 136, 137.
22 Storm Swain refers to Dorothee Sölle, who argues that unbearable pain silences, and therefore a first step in overcoming suffering is to find a language of lament. While this is important indeed, Swain's interviews with chaplains at Ground Zero show that even in silence empathic solidarity is possible which breaks through the isolation brought by suffering. Swain, *Trauma and Transformation at Ground Zero*, 96–97.
23 Swinton, *Raging with Compassion*, 102.
24 Elsa Tamez, "Job: Dat Is Onrechtvaardig, Roep Ik, Maar Niemand Gaat Erop In!," *Concilium* 5 (1997): 66.
25 Johnston-Barrett, "Making Space: Silence, Voice, and Suffering," 333.
26 Chopp, *Saving Work*, 34ff.
27 Fretheim discusses God's absence and presence, and puts this in terms of more or less intense presence. Fretheim, *The Suffering of God*, Chap. 5. Cf. Saliers: in liturgy, by praying Scripture, "we remind God to be God! What God has done, what God used to mean for us in the past, is a promise of who God will be for us in the future. We are so polite with God. Why be so polite with one who knows us so well?" Saliers, *Worship as Theology*, 1994, 35.
28 Psalm 22:1.
29 Swinton, *Raging with Compassion*, 111.
30 For an overview of theories and empirical research in the area of psychology of religion with regard to meaning-making, see Crystal L. Park, "Making Sense of the Meaning Literature: An Integrative Review of Meaning Making and Its Effects on Adjustment to Stressful Life Events," *Psychological Bulletin*, 2010, 257–301. A classic textbook which discusses the role of religion in coping is Kenneth I. Pargament, *The Psychology of Religion and Coping: Theory, Research, Practice*, 1st edn (New York: The Guilford Press, 1997).
31 Swinton, *Raging with Compassion*, 111.
32 Walter Brueggemann, *The Message of the Psalms* (Minneapolis, MN: Augsburg Press, 1984), 52.
33 Claus Westermann, "The Role of the Lament in the Theology of the Old Testament," *Interpretation* 28 (1974): 31.
34 For lament as truth-telling, including an example of a lament written from the perspective of disabled people, see Betenbaugh and Procter-Smith, "Disabling the Lie." See also Billman and Migliore, *Rachel's Cry*, 139–140.
35 Billman and Migliore, *Rachel's Cry*, 119–122.

116 *Liturgical theology*

36 Swinton, *Raging with Compassion*, 131.
37 Meyer, "A Lack of Laments in the Church's Use of the Psalter," 73. For the notion of keeping God in the community, see Samuel E. Balentine, "Enthroned on the Praises and Laments of Israel," in *The Lord's Prayer: Perspectives for Reclaiming Christian Prayer* (Grand Rapids, MI: William B. Eerdmans, 1993), 33.
38 That is not to say that suffering no longer isolates. In *Lament for a Son*, Wolterstorff writes: "I have been daily grateful for the friend who remarked that grief isolates. He did not mean only that I, grieving, am isolated from you, happy. He meant also that *shared* grief isolates the sharers from each other. Though united in that we are grieving, we grief differently." *Lament for a Son* (Grand Rapids, MI: William B. Eerdmans, 1987), 56.
39 Eugene H. Peterson, *Five Smooth Stones for Pastoral Work*, (Grand Rapids, MI: William B. Eerdmans, 1992), 143.
40 Ibid., 145.
41 Billman and Migliore, *Rachel's Cry*, 120.
42 It is significant that the "appeal to remember frequently features in lament petitions." Allen, "Zkr," 1103. Brown confirms: "The Psalms contain the largest number of instances of *zākar*, the overwhelming majority of which occur in the individual complaint Psalms." Bartels and Brown, "Remember, Remembrance," 236.
43 Swinton, *Raging with Compassion*, 109.
44 Power, *The Eucharistic Mystery*, 347. Interestingly, he calls this a 'dangerous memory,' although without referring to Moltmann. Power also argues for the need of including lament in Eucharistic prayer and gives an example of how this might be done. See pp. 335–339.
45 Most lament psalms move from lament to praise. Thus, the structure supports its function. See Walter Brueggemann, "Formfulness of Grief," *Interpretation* 31, No. 3 (1 July 1977): 263–275; Swinton, *Raging with Compassion*, 106–109.
46 Neil Pembroke, *Pastoral Care in Worship: Liturgy and Psychology in Dialogue* (London: T&T Clark, 2010), 60.
47 Anderson, "Memory, Tradition, and the Re-Membering of Suffering," 125ff.
48 Ibid., 126.
49 Ibid. The quote from David Hogue comes from *Remembering*, 75.
50 Anderson, "Memory, Tradition, and the Re-Membering of Suffering," 127ff.
51 The expression is Wolterstorff's: "What I need to hear from you is that you recognize how painful it is. I need to hear from you that you are with me in my desperation. To comfort me, you have to come close. Come sit beside me on my mourning bench." *Lament for a Son*, 34.
52 Cf. Gandolfo, "Remembering the Massacre," 77.
53 Johnston-Barrett, "Making Space: Silence, Voice, and Suffering," 333. Note that these questions are not an argument to share every situation of suffering publicly. It requires sensitivity to know when and how to voice suffering. Yet our discussion of remembrance and lament in the previous paragraphs warrant the question how much suffering does get expressed in liturgy. For suffering and isolation, see Elaine Scarry. She writes about the 'unsharability' of pain. Suffering isolates because someone else can never fully know your pain. Scarry, *The Body in Pain*, 4. Here we should also mention the work of Judith Herman on trauma and recovery, mentioned by Swain. She states that the first stage in recovery from trauma is to find safety; the second is remembering and mourning; the third to be reconnected to social life. It is remarkable how close these stages correspond to our discussions in the present chapter. Swain, *Trauma and Transformation at Ground Zero*, 99–101.

9 When stories meet

Liturgy as transformation and healing

When the narrative spaces for God and people are found, the divine and human stories can be told and can meet in the liturgy. We will now explore what happens when these story worlds meet; this meeting may even lead to transformation and healing in and through Christ. We have argued that at the horizon of suffering is healing. Suffering and healing are two sides of the same coin. The focus in this book is on suffering, but the treatment of the topic is not complete without – however briefly – including a discussion of healing. John Swinton aptly states: "Sin, evil, and suffering are undoubtedly realities in the world, but they are secondary realities, intruders into the goodness of the world."[1] Therefore, our study cannot close with a full stop after discussing how liturgy addresses suffering. The liturgy itself, insofar as it addresses suffering, does not stop there. Apart from this basic dialectic of suffering and healing, our research has pointed to at least three other reasons to address the topic of transformation and healing. First, healing is a significant topic for the participants in worship. Second, the literature on liturgy and suffering that we studied for the purpose of the previous chapters does virtually always mention the transformative nature of liturgy. Third, healing and the transformative nature of liturgy are grounded in imagination – the narrative counterpart of remembrance.

The meeting of story worlds

We will start our discussion with a brief note on the concept of imagination. Rebecca Chopp defines imagination as "the ability to think differently about the past, the present, and the future."[2] Imagination is an important feature in (re-)writing one's life, as people do when coping with suffering.[3] David Hogue mentions three ways in which narrative theory and theology can create conditions for gaining new perspectives on one's story.[4] First, storytelling itself may be healing (and we have seen already that being able to tell one's story is often seen as a prerequisite for healing). Second, healing might include rewriting one's story. Hogue stresses that this is not an act of delusion or denial. Any storytelling includes interpretation of events, and the selection of which events and which aspects will be included in or excluded from the story. Thus, the meaning of a story is shaped. Pastoral care has the task of helping to author one's story and might help to shed new perspectives on life events. Third, when someone rewrites her story radically, she might find herself eventually in a new story that redefines her life.[5] A clear example of such rewriting of one's life story is conversion. Life takes on new meaning in the light of the new-found faith. This process is very similar to the image of grafting put forward by liturgist Al, an image that we have commented on at various places in Part I for example. In the liturgy the participants are engaged in the process of grafting their own story on to that of Jesus Christ. The stories of life are rewritten, reimagined, in the light of the new story of Jesus.

When narrative space is found for both God and people, and they start telling their stories authentically, liturgy is transformative. The literature on narrative, liturgy and suffering captures this in several images. The first image we will explore is storytelling itself. The verbal and non-verbal language we use to rehearse the Christian story evokes a reality that we do not see if we do not have the eyes to see.[6] At the same time, the liturgy rehearses the human story. The level to which that happens is a matter of discussion as we have seen throughout this book and especially in the previous chapter. Yet this is what the liturgy hopes to do, and when the divine and human stories are brought together, it has transformative power. Anderson and Foley assert that when "my stories and the stories of a faith tradition" enter into a conversation, they "merge into a new narrative that is liberating and empowering."[7] They continue by pointing out the aims of pastoral counselling in the light of this assertion, aims that can well be ascribed to the liturgy too: "In the light of these influences, we understand that the primary aim of pastoral care is to assist people in weaving the stories of their lives and God's stories as mediated through the community into a transformative narrative that will confirm their sense of belonging, strengthen them to live responsibly as disciples in the world, and liberate them from confinement."[8] The point to note here is that bringing the stories together makes for a new and transformative narrative.

With the notion of conversation a second image has come to the fore, that of a dialogue. Marjorie Procter-Smith elaborates on liturgy as dialogue. Noteworthy for our discussion is that she comes to this discussion after first having attended to the concepts of remembrance and imagination in the chapter before. Important as these concepts may be, she says, they are not bringing change, even though they are necessary for change (we are reminded of the importance of remembrance for constructing identity and writing new personal and communal narratives – see the discussion of remembrance above). Yet change is at the heart of the liturgy, Procter-Smith holds, "or what in theological terms is called *metanoia*, conversion, transformation." She continues: "This process of transformation is central to the liturgy because the primary action of liturgy is dialogue. Liturgy is a dialogue with God, an encounter with the one who calls us into community with one another. And as an inevitable result of that encounter, we are changed."[9] When transformation does not happen, it is not because God is not present in the liturgy. "It is we who are sometimes absent, or reluctant, or resistant to opening ourselves to the transforming dialogue with God which lies at the heart of Christian liturgy. A dialogue always requires two participants."[10] A dialogue also requires some common ground between the dialogue partners. In the dialogue between humankind and God this is difficult to imagine, but the traditional ending of prayer gives a clue to find common ground: we pray 'in the name of Jesus,' or in the liturgy often 'to God through Christ in the Holy Spirit.' "Jesus Christ, as our 'common ground', makes dialogue with God possible."[11] To link the image of dialogue with the first image of storytelling, we can say that the dialogue partners both (or all) bring their life stories and select which aspects they want to tell to their dialogue partner. The extent to which it is possible for the dialogue to be transformative depends on the extent to which the storytelling of both dialogue partners is authentic (cf. the polarity of concealing/revealing).

The third image is that of bringing together two 'worlds.' This notion comes from Paul Ricoeur's work on hermeneutics and is applied to liturgy by several scholars. For the sake of brevity, we will engage only with the works of Joyce Ann Zimmerman and Crina Gschwandtner, which are most relevant to our present discussion. Zimmerman shows how the three methodological moments of reading texts, as proposed by Ricoeur, are applicable to the liturgical text and the performance thereof. The three moments are participation, distanciation and appropriation.[12] Participation includes pre-understanding. When we read a text, we come to it with pre-suppositions. The same is true for participation in the liturgy. This is not something to be avoided – it cannot even be avoided – but as a matter of fact pre-understanding is necessary in order to participate. The second moment, however, is to distance "self from self." Zimmerman writes: "While participation is the condition of possibility for the articulation of self-experience, distanciation allows for an analytical moment verifying the meaning of that experience .... Without distancing, the possibilities presented by the text are lost to the 'comfort' of a known interpretation."[13] The analytical moment also allows for explanation. The dialectic of participation and distanciation leads to the third moment, called 'appropriation.' Through the first two steps new possibilities for their situations are presented to the worshippers, which lead to new self-understanding. "Is not the purpose of a liturgical text in a worshipping community to present possibilities for self-understanding to the community? Further, is not the challenge to let go of the ego that is brought to the celebration (one side of the text) in order that, through the text's celebration, a new self might emerge (the other side of the text)?"[14] The willingness and capacity to engage with new worlds of understanding is the "grace of imagination."[15]

While this brief overview of the three moments stresses the importance of the human story in relation to the text and liturgy, the discussion of Ricoeur's notion of the world of the text by Gschwandtner emphasizes the divine story breaking into the human story. According to Gschwandtner, "the reader must allow this world [of the text] to unfold and represent its 'issue'."[16] It is a multidimensional world, and it "comes to rupture our world and to call us to decision in light of it."[17] Gschwandtner points out the usefulness of this concept for the analysis of the liturgy. Moreover, many scholars engage with the same concepts, even when not working with Ricoeur's terminology. This is particularly clear in the emphasis liturgical scholars place on the eschatological dimension of the Christian story and therefore of the liturgy.[18] Gschwandtner concludes: the task of opening a world is central to the liturgy. It speaks with hope of the future kingdom which becomes present and begins within the liturgy."[19] The notion of two worlds coming together sits comfortably alongside the first two images of story and dialogue. The story world of one dialogue partner meets with the story world of the other. Via participation, distanciation and appropriation the liturgical world is experienced ever anew, opening ever new possibilities for the participants to see their story world within the light of another, a transformative, story world.

The fourth image that is worth exploring here is again one of story worlds, but this time not in the sense of two stories coming together, but in the sense of being transported into another world. The image comes from narrative theory as explained by Alastair Daniel.[20] Theatre and ritual, he says, are liminal (in between or threshold) experiences. Therefore, these experiences set apart this time from everyday time. The opening of the story (the abstract; the most classic example is "Once upon a time ...") transports the listeners into the world of the story. The conclusion (the coda) takes them back to their own worlds.[21] The liturgy does the same thing. The abstract suggested by the liturgical text is:

> In the name of the Father,
> and of the Son,
> and of the Holy Spirit.

The people consent to being taken away and led in their thoughts and experiences by their common 'Amen.'[22] It might be argued that the abstract in the liturgical setting is more elaborate, as the people have left their houses and gathered for this particular occasion. The dynamic remains the same nonetheless. As we have seen, through the liturgy another world is met with, the world of the divine. Here the paschal mystery is celebrated and remembered. Here the suffering person can find solace, comfort, maybe healing. Here the body of Christ is broken and broken lives are mended. The coda functions to take the people back to their own story worlds, although the liturgical coda is not clearcut. The smallest definition might be the sending:

> Go in peace to love and serve the Lord.
> **In the name of Christ. Amen.**[23]

However, if the coda has the function of bringing the people back from the story world to their own worlds, it might be argued that the whole of the dismissal functions this way, and it is noteworthy that some churches include notices regarding the life of the church community here. It might even be argued that the sending starts already with the prayer after communion:

**Send us out
in the power of your Spirit
to live and work
to your praise and glory.
Amen.**[24]

However, as with the abstract, the dynamic of leaving the story world of the liturgy remains the same. To substantiate this narrative process theologically, it is worthwhile quoting David Hogue at some length. About the liminal experience of the liturgy he writes:

> Our most transformative religious practices are liminal experiences – boundaried periods of time in which routine is left behind, norms and rules are suspended, and we experience life as if it were some other way. Memory and imagination locate us in history by telling and hearing stories of past, present, and future. Paradoxically, rituals also lift us beyond time. They transform by transporting us to worlds that are yet to be and returning us to our everyday worlds as new creations. The more deeply we realize and enact the ritual nature of spiritual practice, the more we are open to the uniquely sacred. We experience life the way it could be, or should be, if the presence of God were more fully recognized and welcomed in the world.[25]

Hogue usefully connects liminality to the important narrative concepts of memory and imagination.

However, the concept of liminality is both helpful and unhelpful. It is helpful in appreciating the distinctive nature of the liturgical gathering, performance and sending. It takes people out of their daily routine and enables an encounter with the divine. But it is unhelpful if moving into and leaving another world, the world of the story, means to leave our own stories behind. We are reminded by Ricoeur's first moment of participation that this is even not entirely possible; we can only understand a text (or story world) because of our pre-understandings. Moreover, the argument of this section, and by extension of the previous and the present chapter, is that liturgy needs to weave together two stories: the new and divine story of the liturgy *and* the stories of our daily lives, including stories of brokenness. We have argued that to remember the stories of human suffering the liturgy needs to seek actively to voice these stories – the language of lament being a most obvious way to do so and inductive liturgy (see below) the most obvious shape for the liturgy. It is when the two stories intersect that new meaning and a new story can be forged. Liturgy calls us to remember God, and therefore we are transported into the divine story world. But liturgy also calls upon God to remember us in our daily circumstances. Dare we say that the liturgy transports God into our story world? When both parties re-member, stories are transformed.[26]

In the light of the analytical lens of the polarities that we have used in this book, we might ask the question whether the coming together of human and divine – whether captured in the image of stories, dialogue, or worlds – points to another polarity. The polarities express aspects of the paradox of living faithfully, Anderson and Foley hold. Living faithfully requires remembering the human stories of suffering but also remembering the story of God. Is it too much to say that the polarity human/divine represents just another aspect of the paradox? Like most other polarities, the two poles need each other. This is a bold theological claim, and one can argue that God is self-sufficient. Yet he chooses to be engaged with his creation, even when this causes suffering (cf. pp. 103–107). The other way around, that creation needs God, is an axiom of the Christian faith and does not need to be argued here. The question, then, is what the value is of putting forward human and divine as a polarity. The value lies in the need for each other. For the liturgy, this means the need for telling both the story of God and the story of human beings.

But here we need to pause for a moment. It might seem obvious that liturgy tells both stories. However, we have pointed to the limited narrative space of God and human beings. Scholars like Gerard Lukken, Morrill, and Anderson and Foley have argued that the liturgy often tells the divine story in beautiful ways, but at the expense of the human stories. Such liturgy results in "a disastrous liturgy of complete answers and half-truths," in the words of Morrill.[27] He claims that it *is* possible to overemphasize the divine. This happens when "it takes on the sense of 'the transcendent' or miraculous but not the sense of the *biblical God* of Jesus. The latter is about the humanity of God. It *is* hard to believe in that and easier to believe that God does not really get mixed up in human affairs ..."[28] Liturgy needs "an integral, narrative connection between the stories of their lives and the story of God's salvific work in history."[29] An important reason why the churches are empty is because liturgy often fails to make this connection.[30]

Lukken observes the same problem and calls for an inductive liturgy which is marked by attention to the small stories. Lukken argues that the Bible is not one story but instead contains thousands of stories. It does not present a finished book of complete doctrines, but rather starts with the here and now, with stories of particular people in a particular place and in particular circumstances. The same is true for the liturgy:

> Liturgy is the story of our repeatedly remembering, confessing, acknowledging, entreating, lamenting, praising, searching and singing in the past and present, looking to the future, as a people who are travelling with their God – a sometimes understandable, but just as often absent or difficult God, an elusive friend. 'What faithful people picture concerning the meaning of their existence, what meaning they will give to their life, what

they believe regarding their future, that is all represented in the liturgy in stories, songs and prayers.' Essentially, a culture that cultivates an interest in the here and now and for the small stories, is a favourable time for liturgy.[31]

This quotation makes clear the grounding of the concept of inductive liturgy in a narrative understanding of liturgy.[32] Inductive liturgy means starting with the small stories and is contrary to deductive liturgy. The latter makes the movement from the bigger picture to the human life but by doing so is not able to relate this bigger picture to *this* particular human life. The movement is one of 'trans-*de*-scendence.' Inductive liturgy moves from the particularities of the present situation to the bigger picture, thereby connecting human and divine. "It begins with *these* people, who are confronted with *this* death."[33] The movement is one of 'trans-*a*-scendence.'[34] Still, the worship service starts in the name of the Father, the Son and the Holy Spirit. Rather than this being an element of a deductive kind of liturgy, this opening sets the scene in which the stories are told. The people could tell their stories anywhere, in any context, but here they choose to tell their stories in the framework of the liturgy, which brings together the divine and the human.

Liturgy has transformative power and it is potentially healing, but it needs to bring together two stories, two worlds, two dialogue partners. An inductive liturgy has much better chances for doing so than a deductive liturgy.

Healing in Christ

When two worlds come together, change occurs, and possibly healing. In the light of our discussion, a couple of theological observations are in place. We begin with the definition of healing as put forward by Bruce Morrill, because he holds together the human and divine, and his definition resembles much of what we have been arguing for in this chapter. In two chapters he extensively discusses what healing is, and he summarizes:

> It is a communal process addressing the suffering of individual members due to physical, psychological, social, or spiritual causes (or a combination thereof) against the horizon of meaning that their crisis or chronic health conditions put in question. Healing is a matter of re-establishing a sense of wholeness within a worldview, a transformation of the experience of misfortune by arriving at renewed or deepened meaning. Christians do this in terms of the person of Christ and the paschal mystery, but these as they become evident in the concrete conditions of their lives.[35]

The theological clue is in the last sentence. For the Christian, meaning and wholeness, and thus healing, are found in the person of Jesus Christ and in the climax of his death and resurrection.[36] While Morrill emphasizes Jesus' healing ministry on earth and his death and resurrection, it is important to give due attention to the person of Jesus Christ as incarnated God. The Incarnation is the theological foundation for bringing the two story worlds together. In Jesus Christ the human and the divine are completely interwoven. Anderson and Foley assert: "For Christians, the dual impulse of desiring to become part of God's story and simultaneously hoping that God will be present to our own narrative finds convergence in Jesus Christ – the essential mediation of the human and divine narrative."[37] Thus, the Incarnation becomes the model for relating human stories of suffering to the story of God. From this foundation we can move on to the life of Jesus Christ on earth and to the paschal mystery.

Morrill makes clear that in the healing ministry of Jesus the physical cure was only one aspect of the healing. When persons were ill, often they suffered isolation from their social environment.[38] When Jesus healed people, he responded to a "broad range of illnesses and misfortunes that, far from being narrowly defined biomedical diseases, were complex personal somatic, spiritual and social (religious, economic, political, and so forth) constructions."[39] The question for the Church today is how it can continue Jesus' healing ministry. The liturgical rites that the Church can dispose of are very different from the miracles Jesus performed. "Still, the purpose in both cases remains the same: healing as a transformation of people's experiences of illness, misfortune, and death such that they find renewed meaning (faith, trust) for life and death in the presence of God and within their world."[40] Ultimately, healing has to do with salvation, because meaning and wholeness are found in God. Morrill puts it this way: "Since healing in any concrete instance of life is fundamentally a matter of renegotiated meaning, all Christian healing comes through a restoration of afflicted persons' sense of self and world in relation to Christ Jesus and the reign of God he has inaugurated: divine solidarity with human brokenness, God's glory in human wholeness."[41] Gerard Lukken points out that from the second and third centuries Christian liturgy has had healing in view, seeing Christ as physician. Via Augustine's use of terms like *salus*, healing and salvation became intertwined. So, Christian liturgy "is about salvific healing or a healing salvation, because Christian ritual touches the depths of a person's injured being, and returns this to integrity."[42] Looking at the life of Jesus Christ this makes perfect sense. However, we need to be cautious with defining the purpose of the liturgy to find healing. Marjory Procter-Smith rightly claims that "the liturgy is the worship of God; it is not therapy, education, or social work."[43] In the light of this claim David Tripp's statement that "Christian worship is prayer for healing" might be a bit too blunt.[44]

The question arises of what the place of healing in liturgy is. The key lies exactly in Morrill's definition of healing as finding renegotiated meaning and a renewed understanding of oneself. Inductive liturgy enables people to bring their stories to make the connection between the divine story told in the liturgy and their own story of suffering. Worshipping God, that which worship is all about, directs our attention from ourselves to God. It is in the story of God, as revealed through the Scriptures and in the Incarnation, life, suffering, death, resurrection and ascension of Jesus Christ, that new possibilities are found. Liturgy opens a new world. The participants in worship are invited to see their stories in the light of God's story and thereby find new meaning. Moreover, all of this happens in a community. Authentic participation in the liturgy can indeed bring about transformation and healing. Seeing the relationship between liturgy and healing this way, we might reformulate Tripp's statement: "Christian worship is prayer; therefore it is healing."

All of this is still reasoned from the perspective of the suffering person telling her story in the liturgy. Yet the liturgy also contains the story of God. Therefore, from a faith perspective it must be said that God is also at work in the liturgy. Terrence Fretheim states, as we saw before, that "for God to mourn with those who mourn is to enter into their situation; and where God is at work, mourning is not the end."[45] Although Fretheim does not write this in the context of liturgy, it applies well to the liturgy. God's activity in the liturgy is highlighted by Michael Perham when he writes that

> the fundamental point lies in the transformation of the gifts we bring. What we bring, God uses, God touches, and we receive back what we have brought, but it has been transformed. The concern and anxiety we bring in our heart, as much as the bread and wine that we symbolically set before God in the eucharist, is touched by the hand of God and given back transformed. That is the real point of connection between liturgy and life. It is, as often as not, an argument for time in worship for silence and reflection, as much as for urgent, fervent prayer, time for God to touch and thus to heal.[46]

This quote illustrates the potential for liturgy to transform and heal when the stories of people and God meet. The discussion above has shown that this only works when liturgy is celebrated authentically. God touches and heals, but can do so only to what people authentically bring to the liturgy.

Healing and hope ultimately are found in the suffering, death and resurrection of Jesus Christ – in the words of Morrill's definition, the paschal mystery. This mystery is the heart of the Christian story and the heart of Eucharistic liturgy.[47] It is also the difference between Jesus' healing ministry and the healing rites of the Church.[48] The reality of Jesus' suffering, death and resurrection points to the fact that this all happened in history. This is crucial for the understanding of liturgy and healing, because "the risen Christ's gift of the Spirit sets the lives of believers in the same pattern of encountering the unseen God in the concrete circumstances of their own time and place."[49] That means that people can come to God, through the liturgy or through other means, with their concrete reality of pain, sorrow and suffering. The language of mystery is a warning that while God is known in history, he is also incomprehensible. We cannot control healing and salvation. Yet the history of salvation gives new meaning to those who suffer. It gives hope that as God acted once on behalf of those at the margins, he will do so again in present situations of suffering.

The reality of the Jesus story in history also points to the necessity of authentic storytelling. Morrill refers to Louis-Marie Chauvet who "describes faith as 'the assent to a loss,' a continuous letting go of our projections of what we imagine God should be like."[50] But the Other is encountered most real when he or she resists our projected imaginations. God can only be the healing God he is when we let him be who he is. That means that for healing to take place in the most profound sense, it is not only necessary for people be authentic in the stories they tell, but also that the story of God is authentically told. Therefore a continuous study of liturgy and other ways in which God's story is told in the Christian community is important.[51]

The paschal mystery is liturgically expressed most essentially in the celebration of Holy Communion. If healing is found in the person of Jesus Christ, then Holy Communion is the place for healing *par excellence*. In the words of one of our respondents, here the divine enters the human for a few seconds. In eating the body of Christ and drinking his blood, Christ enters materially our material bodies.

The Eucharistic prayers are full of hope, mostly captured in the language of death and resurrection. So, after the words of institution in which God is asked that "these gifts of bread and wine may be to us the body and blood of our Lord Jesus Christ," one of the acclamations is: "Dying you destroyed our death, rising you restored our life: Lord Jesus, come in glory."[52] However, the language of healing itself is used only twice in *Order One*. It is used once in Eucharistic prayer F:

> Look with favour on your people
> and in your mercy hear the cry of our hearts.
> Bless the earth,
> heal the sick,
> let the oppressed go free
> and fill your Church with power from on high.[53]

The other instance is also in the Eucharistic rite, in one of the invitations to communion, where the people respond:

> Jesus is the Lamb of God
> who takes away the sin of the world.
> Blessed are those who are called to his supper.
> Lord, I am not worthy to receive you,
> but only say the word, and I shall be healed.[54]

In the supplementary texts for Holy Communion the literal language of healing is used once in penitential material and twice in forms of intercession. This brief analysis of the use of 'healing' in *Common Worship, Order One* affirms our analysis of the liturgical text earlier: if healing is the counterpart of suffering, then it becomes clear once more that suffering, in the sense of experiencing major negative life events, is not emphasized in the liturgical text. And even the use of healing in the response to the invitation to Communion does not necessarily denote healing from suffering.

The limited references to suffering and healing notwithstanding, the symbol of the Eucharist does invite one to bring one's suffering in prayer and to the table. John Swinton writes:

> Sharing the Eucharist, with its symbolism of brokenness and unity embodied in the bread and the wine, mingles naturally with the cries of lament, the need for reconciliation, and the demand for a hopeful future. Within the theological movement of the Eucharist, the shift from despair to hope is cemented through the passionate meaning of the bread and the wine.[55]

The Eucharistic sacrament most fully reveals the foundational paradox of the Christian faith: life comes through the cross. Furthermore, the analysis of the stories of the participants in worship has shown that the Eucharist is the most important ritual element of the liturgy for them, although for various reasons. Two aspects of Holy Communion need discussion here. The first is in the light of the discussion of remembrance above and the second in the light of our research question.

First, at the heart of the Eucharistic rite are the words of institution, in which Jesus says: "Do this in remembrance of me." Liturgical theologians have discussed the meaning of *anamnesis* extensively, and we have briefly commented on the concept and shown how it fits well with a narrative understanding of liturgy. The use of the word 're-membering' by some scholars, as 're-membering,' demonstrates the idea that remembering unites. Swinton comments: "To re-member something is to take that which is broken (dismembered) and make it whole again."[56] Remembering brings together past, present and future. It brings together the community when people are willing to accept authentic storytelling, including passages of injustice, suffering and otherness. However, the Eucharistic act of remembering is odd because it seems to do the opposite. When Jesus says "remember me," he breaks bread and shares it. The Eucharistic act of breaking bread is an act of remembering brokenness in the broken body of Christ. Yet in order to remember his broken body, it is broken again every time and dispersed among the community. The body of Christ as represented by the bread is not re-membered but dispersed among the community. It gets even stranger: by this act not that which is broken (the body) is re-membered, but in a real sense the community is re-membered. The members of the community are united. One person being broken unites many persons among whom he is shared. By sharing the body of Christ the participants share in the divine life. By the brokenness of Christ the people can be healed. By taking part of the body of Christ, the community becomes the body of Christ. Therefore, healing is found in the Eucharistic community.[57]

The second aspect of Holy Communion has to do with the suffering of Jesus Christ and the suffering of people. It is hard to think of an element in the Eucharistic liturgy which more clearly reveals Christ's suffering. In the rite it is made visible by the breaking of bread and the pouring of wine. It seems quite self-evident to look here for the connection between the story of the liturgy and the story of suffering people. (Note that, while for many respondents in our research the Eucharist is very important in relation to their story, hardly anyone relates this explicitly to the suffering of Christ.) People might relate their suffering to the suffering of Christ. However, one should be careful with drawing this parallel. There are similarities but also dissimilarities. Marie Fortune distinguishes helpfully between voluntarily and involuntarily suffering.[58] The similarity is that in both cases, when suffering is the consequence of injustice, it should never be justified. But the difference is that the former has a purpose, the latter not. The former chooses to bear the consequences of a certain commitment, even if the consequence is suffering (e.g. those standing for equal rights in the Civil Rights Movement in the 1960s in the United States). Jesus' suffering was voluntary. He chose to bear the suffering consequence of his passionate love for humankind. Fortune's distinction shows that it is problematic to take Jesus' suffering as a model when suffering is involuntary because in that case there is no purpose. The stories of the participants in our research are all examples of involuntary suffering. But this is not to say that the Eucharistic rite leaves the involuntary sufferer void of hope. Jesus' suffering had a purpose indeed: to overcome all suffering, maybe especially involuntary suffering. This runs parallel with the observation above. The dispersion of Christ's broken body as an act of remembering his suffering and death brings hope and healing and wholeness for those who partake. In remembering the voluntary suffering of Jesus Christ, the involuntary suffering of those who do suffer is re-membered.

In sum, liturgy is transformational if authentic storytelling on the side of the human and divine occurs. This may be captured in the image of worlds coming together, of being transported into another world, of a dialogue taking place, or in the image of storytelling itself. To include the human story in the liturgical story, an inductive liturgy gives best chances. When the stories come together, suffering persons are invited to find new meaning for their stories in the divine story, especially in the story of the incarnation, suffering, death and resurrection of Christ. The paschal mystery is the defining moment for Christian hope. The whole of the liturgy remembers this mystery, but it is most condensed in the celebration of Holy Communion.

Notes

1 Swinton, *Raging with Compassion*, 57.
2 Chopp, *Saving Work*, 43. Also within feminist theology Marjorie Procter-Smith argues for the place of imagination in liturgy as well as remembrance. *In Her Own Rite*, 43–47.
3 Chopp, *Saving Work*, 43.
4 Hogue, *Remembering*, 104–108.
5 Each of these three points is also argued for by Ernst Bohlmeijer, as he develops a narrative psychological method. *De Verhalen*, see esp. Chapter 1. See also Daphne Noonan, "The Ripple Effect: A Story of the Transformational Nature of Narrative Care," in *Storying Later Life: Issues, Investigations, and Interventions in Narrative Gerontology*, ed. Gary Kenyon, Ernst Bohlmeijer, and William L. Randall (New York: Oxford University Press, 2011), 354–365.

6 Cf. 1 Cor. 2:14: "The person without the Spirit does not accept the things that come from the Spirit of God but considers them foolishness, and cannot understand them because they are discerned only through the Spirit." The Bible is replete with this kind of imagery.
7 Anderson and Foley, *Mighty Stories*, 48.
8 Ibid. We realize that liturgy and pastoral care have specific aims of themselves, but the aims mentioned here are applicable to both.
9 Procter-Smith, *In Her Own Rite*, 48.
10 Ibid., 48–49.
11 Ibid., 49.
12 Joyce Ann Zimmerman, *Liturgy as Language of Faith: A Liturgical Methodology in the Mode of Paul Ricoeur's Textual Hermeneutics* (Lanham, MD: University Press of America, 1988), 87–91, 171–195.
13 Ibid., 89–90.
14 Ibid., 90.
15 Ibid., 187. The term is Ricoeur's; see Paul Ricoeur, "The Language of Faith," in *The Philosophy of Paul Ricoeur: An Anthology of His Work*, ed. Charles E. Reagan and David Stewart (Boston, MA: Beacon Press, 1978), 237.
16 Crina Gschwandtner, "Toward a Ricoeurian Hermeneutics of Liturgy," *Worship* 86(6) (2012): 488.
17 Ibid.
18 Gschwandtner refers in this regard to Alexander Schmemann and Kevin Irwin.
19 Gschwandtner, "Toward a Ricoeurian Hermeneutics of Liturgy," 490.
20 Daniel, *Storytelling*, 36–37. We referred to Daniel in Chapter 5, p. 76. The first part of his book deals with narrative theory which he applies to classroom storytelling. Because of his engagement with narrative theory in general his views are useful for our purposes.
21 "Through the abstract, the storyteller says 'now listen to me, I am going to lead our thinking, and take us somewhere else'; in the coda, they say 'now we are going to return to the world of the here and now, and I am handing your thoughts back to you.'" Ibid., 37.
22 *Common Worship: Services and Prayers for the Church of England* (London: Church House Publishing, 2000), 167.
23 Ibid., 183.
24 Ibid., 182.
25 Hogue, *Remembering*, 154–155.
26 Cf. Saliers: "Christian liturgy transforms and empowers when the vulnerability of human pathos is met by the ethos of God's vulnerability in word and sacrament." *Worship as Theology*, 22.
27 Morrill, *Divine Worship and Human Healing*, 102ff.
28 Ibid., 107.
29 Ibid., 108.
30 This point is also made by Anderson and Foley, who refer to this as the problem of inadequate storytelling. See *Mighty Stories*, Ch. 8.
31 Lukken, *Rituals in Abundance*, 337. Lukken quotes H.A.J. Wegman, *Riten en Mythen: Liturgie in de Geschiedenis van het Christendom* (Kampen: Kok, 1991), 9.
32 Lukken does not make this explicit except for referring to narrative in a footnote at the end of this quote.
33 Lukken, *Rituals in Abundance*, 338.
34 Ibid., 338–339. Lukken gives many examples of the difference between the two kinds of liturgy and of how an inductive liturgy might be shaped. Power develops a narrative biblical–theological underpinning for the same concept, although using different terminology. He argues that in the biblical prophetic tradition salvific events were not seen as once for all and forever clear, but they had to be reinterpreted

130 *Liturgical theology*

in the light of the contingencies of the present. The best way of remembering the salvific events, therefore, is not to start from those events themselves, but from the present situation which urges remembering the events. *The Eucharistic Mystery*, 308–309; see also 47–50.

35 Morrill, *Divine Worship and Human Healing*, 159. Note that Morrill does not refer to healing as a physical cure, although it may involve that, but rather in terms of meaning-making and wholeness of the total human being in its social context. See for an extensive discussion Chapters 2 and 3 of his book.

36 We have argued that wholeness is one of the three storylines of the liturgical text. It is remarkable that the word comes back here from the side of the liturgical–theological discourse on suffering and healing. Also, the Anglican report *A Time to Heal* uses exactly this word for the concept of healing. It supports the appropriateness of the name of this storyline. "More than before in the last hundred years, many in our society realize there is a spiritual as well as a physical and a mental dimension to healthy living. 'Wholeness' is the in-word: it is what everyone longs for." The report also attests that "scholars tell us that in biblical theology there is a close connection between 'healing', 'salvation' and 'wholeness.'" *A Time to Heal*, xiii and 1.

37 Anderson and Foley, *Mighty Stories*, 40.

38 We have seen that, although perhaps in a different way now than in the time of Jesus, suffering still isolates a person from their communities (Chapter 8).

39 Morrill, *Divine Worship and Human Healing*, 93. In this regard Charles Jeffrey Helman's description of healing is instructive: "Healing is more than physical cure or forgiveness that cleans the soul. Healing in its fullest definition means wholeness and salvation. The ecclesial community must then be concerned with the 'whole' person with regard to health and well-being of mind, body and spirit. More importantly, the Church needs to be concerned with the wellness of the community as the reconciling community in the world." And further along he writes: "Physical healing cannot be ruled out, but the root meaning of healing is salvation and wholeness and it is to this salvific reality that we address our healing prayers to God through our sacerdotal means." Charles Jeffrey Helman, *The Emergent Revival of Sacramental Healing: An Incarnational Theology* (unpublished dissertation, 2007), 77, 128.

40 Morrill, *Divine Worship and Human Healing*, 94.

41 Ibid., 95. Note again how the human and divine are bound up with each other in Morrill's view.

42 Lukken, *Rituals in Abundance*, 535.

43 Marjorie Procter-Smith, "'Reorganizing Victimization': The Intersection between Liturgy and Domestic Violence," in *Violence against Women and Children*, ed. Carol J. Adams and Marie M. Fortune (New York: Continuum, 1995), 429.

44 D.H. Tripp, "Liturgy and Pastoral Service," in *The Study of Liturgy*, revised edition (London and New York: SPCK and Oxford University Press, 1992), 584.

45 Fretheim, *The Suffering of God*, 136.

46 Perham, *New Handbook of Pastoral Liturgy*, 9.

47 Morrill, *Divine Worship and Human Healing*, 111.

48 Ibid., 94.

49 Ibid., 111.

50 Ibid., 116. The reference to Chauvet is *The Sacraments: The Word of God at the Mercy of the Body* (Collegeville, PA: Liturgical Press, 2001), 39.

51 Critique on the liturgy that calls for change and more authentic storytelling comes especially from marginalized groups. Examples are liberation theology, feminist theology, or voices from disabled people. Cf. Gustavo Gutierrez, *A Theology of Liberation: History, Politics, and Salvation*, trans. Caridad Inda and John Eagleson, revised edn (Maryknoll, NY: Orbis Books, 1988); James B. Nickoloff, ed., *Gustavo Gutierrez: Essential Writings* (Maryknoll, NY: Orbis Books, 1996); Chopp, *Saving*

Work; Procter-Smith, *In Her Own Rite*; Eiesland and Saliers, *Human Disability and the Service of God*. The call for telling the story of God's insistence on justice comes, for example, from political theology. Cf. Metz, *Faith in History and Society*; Morrill, *Anamnesis as Dangerous Memory*.
52 *Common Worship*, 189.
53 Ibid., 200.
54 Ibid., 180.
55 Swinton, *Raging with Compassion*, 125.
56 Ibid., 124. He applies this to lamenting in small groups, which is not relevant for our discussion here but which connects well with the discussion of lament we had earlier. "In lamenting together, people take that which has been fragmented by the experience of evil and draw together the broken pieces, welding them into wholeness with the tears of God's people in the power of the Holy Spirit." Ibid.
57 Thus, 'Holy Communion' is an apt and layered phrase.
58 Fortune, Marie M., "The Transformation of Suffering: A Biblical and Theological Perspective," in *Violence against Women and Children*, 87–88.

10 A communal and liturgical spirituality of reconciliation

In Part II of this book we have been looking for an answer to the question of how Anglican liturgy *can* address and connect to narratives of suffering. The present chapter concludes our search in this part. Our starting point came from Anderson and Foley. After having shown several polarities at work in ritual and narrative, and how these polarities are expressions of an underlying 'paradox of faithful living,' they say that such paradoxical faithful living is embedded in a spirituality of reconciliation. In order to direct our discussion to the topic of suffering, we drew on the connection between human tears and divine tears as proposed by Wolterstorff. We then deepened the discussion of the narrative, theological and liturgical concept of remembrance. This concept formed the basis of the next chapter, which investigated the possibilities of storytelling on the part of God and of suffering people. We then elaborated on the possibility of healing when two story worlds come together. With the present chapter we wrap up these discussions by returning to a spirituality of reconciliation. We will argue for the need of a communal and liturgical spirituality of reconciliation in order to address suffering in liturgy. First, we will set the stage for a spirituality of reconciliation by addressing a number of aspects of this spirituality. We will then focus our attention on the liturgy within the context of a spirituality of reconciliation, explicitly picking up the discussions of the present chapter. The importance of community for a spirituality of reconciliation will be underlined in the following section. Finally, we will address the relation between liturgy and pastoral care that is a consequence of a spirituality of reconciliation and is implicit in the theme of our research, before concluding this chapter.

Aspects of a spirituality of reconciliation

A spirituality of reconciliation is a most apt spirituality for a liturgical community that wants to address suffering and connect to broken people. One may wonder why we propose a spirituality of reconciliation. After all, reconciliation is not necessarily the most obvious word in relation to the stories of suffering that informed our empirical research. There is a formal answer to that, and an answer that lies in the spirituality of reconciliation itself. First, the formal reason is that it comes with the method we have been using. We have drawn much from the narrative–ritual theory of Anderson and Foley, and their proposal of the polarities. They themselves find such a spirituality most apt to weave together the divine and human stories, as well as to weave together pastoral care and ritual. Second, and also more formal, reconciliation is a process that names the suffering but also stretches out to healing. Robert Schreiter, whose concept of reconciliation underlies Anderson and Foley's proposal for a spirituality of reconciliation, likens the process towards reconciliation to healing.[1] Naming suffering and the hope for healing are key to our research, and therefore make it appropriate to draw further on Schreiter's insights. Third, the content and aspects of a spirituality of reconciliation are similar, if not the same, as the key ingredients for answering our research question. Key words include community, remembrance, suffering, narrative, transformation and others, as our discussions below will make clear.

On pp. 85–89 we summarized the contours of a spirituality of reconciliation on the basis of Anderson and Foley's work. Such a spirituality is marked by embracing contradictions, honouring the other, hospitality to the stranger and the courage to be surprised by grace. Anderson and Foley in turn borrow heavily from Robert Schreiter, and we will base our discussion here also on his explanation of reconciliation.[2] While Schreiter writes from the perspective of reconciliation of the social orders in broken societies – for example, after civil wars, apartheid, or dictatorship, his theory is applicable in other situations of suffering as well. He claims this already in his 1992 book, but it is even more evident in his book from 1998 in which he focuses less on the reconciliation of social order and has often other forms of suffering in view.[3] In the latter book he points out how the resurrection appearances of Jesus are moments of reconciliation for the disciples. Many of these reflections are often readily applicable in the context of this book as well.

Schreiter outlines several theological points that are central to a Christian understanding of reconciliation, based on a reading of St. Paul.[4] One point which is most relevant here is that reconciliation is a spirituality rather than a strategy. It requires a certain disposition rather than technical skills. "The process cannot be reduced to a technical, problem-solving rationality .... Thus, reconciliation becomes a way of life, not just a set of discrete tasks to be performed and completed."[5] At the same time, certain 'steps' in the process can be identified. Building on his analysis of the resurrection appearances of Jesus, Schreiter identifies four steps.[6] These steps all resonate with what we have found already in this chapter, and pastoral caregivers will recognize these steps in the counselling process.[7]

The first step is accompaniment. It is being patiently present with the one who suffers or is in the process of reconstructing his life. It is sitting together on the mourning bench, in Wolterstorff's terms. If the cause of suffering is still there, it is holding on together in solidarity with the one who suffers. We referred briefly to the incarnation as theological basis for weaving together the human and divine stories before. Here we add that the incarnation is also the christological basis for accompaniment. The incarnation shows God's solidarity with suffering humankind. Becoming human is the divine act of being present with those who suffer.[8]

The second step is hospitality. A hospitable environment creates an atmosphere marked by trust, kindness and safety. Victims of violence have been lacking such an environment, Schreiter says. Most stories in our research project do not include violence (although some include aspects of spiritual and/or psychological abuse), but trust, kindness and safety resonate also with these stories. Safety is an issue in the experience of worship for more than half of the participants in our project. Situations of suffering are often, if not always, marked by chaos in life. An atmosphere of trust, kindness and safety can create a hospitable environment for people to tell their story. With Schreiter we can conclude: "Hospitality, then, is central to the ministry of reconciliation."[9]

The steps of accompaniment and hospitality require positive experiences with the community one is in. The stories of the participants in our project reveal that community is a major theme in relating liturgy to suffering. Neil Pembroke comments: "Unless we judge that there is a strong bond of love in the body of worshipers, we simply will not have the confidence to tell the truth about ourselves. The tasks of helping each other to nurture hope and of building community are indissolubly linked."[10] However, creating a level of trust in a safe community is one thing. It is yet another thing for the community to help people finding their way into the story of salvation, as Peterson says. He argues that people can enter the story in different ways. He discusses the story of Ruth, and argues that Naomi got into the story by complaining, Ruth by asking for what she wanted and Boaz by taking up responsibilities.[11] These are all valid ways to enter the story of salvation – in other words, to enter into (liturgical) prayer. According to Peterson, by listening to people's stories, the pastoral care-giver can help find an entry point into the story for this particular person. "The pastor begins this work, then, not so much as a storyteller, but as one who believes that there is a story to be told."[12] Part of the attitude of hospitable communities ought to be that these communities believe that everyone, including those who suffer, has a story to tell.

Schreiter remarks that human beings play an important part in these first two steps and can take the initiative for accompaniment and hospitality. The third and fourth step, making connections and commissioning respectively, are hardly due to the agency of people, but are "very much the work of God."[13] Often one discovers to be reconnected and to be commissioned, rather than having chosen it oneself.[14] The third step, making connections, is the opposite of isolation. We have seen already that suffering isolates and therefore silences. This can work itself out in different ways. The isolation may be isolation from a social group, or from one's health, or through the narrative of the lie of oppressive regimes from one's past. Making connections is being restored to one's self, to one's story and therefore identity, to one's body. Note that restoration in this sense is not going back to a previous state, but will always be to a new state, since the suffering cannot be forgotten and often scars remain.

But making connections can also happen in a somewhat different manner. Schreiter gives two examples. One is of a couple who lost their only child. They closed in on themselves, until they realized that their son was outgoing and very involved in church and society. They realized that their withdrawal was not what their son would have wished. The couple was thus able to reconnect to church and society, but also to connect differently to the story of their son's death. The facts remained the same, but the story got a whole new twist. The second example is from Jesus' meeting with the disciples on the road to Emmaus. They had all the words right, but made the wrong connections to the event of Jesus' death.[15] Reconnecting implies a change of perspective.[16]

The fourth step is commissioning. Often those who have been victims and have found reconciliation become reconcilers themselves. The commissioning perhaps implies the opposite of the suffering one has been through. Reflecting on the story of Jesus commissioning Peter, Schreiter comments that the three times of denial find their counterpart in Jesus commissioning Peter three times to care for Jesus' flock. The question for a liturgical community that remembers suffering is how it can creatively use this suffering to move to action. Schreiter stresses several times that there is nothing noble or redemptive in suffering itself. However, it can be used to become redemptive – for example, when a terminally ill patient uses this time to discover the meaning of life.

> Suffering becomes redemptive suffering, then, when it does not isolate us from those around us, but becomes a way to bind us to them in new and deeply human ways. One sometimes sees this when a terminally ill parent can work reconciliation among estranged members of the family, or when someone who is ill is able to bring a community together in a new way.[17]

This step is first and foremost the work of God, but it also takes us back to the first two steps in which human beings have more agency. Accompaniment and hospitalities are antidotes against isolation, and thus create a setting in which reconnection and commissioning can take place.[18]

Storytelling in a communal and liturgical spirituality of reconciliation

Storytelling is at the heart of a narrative understanding of liturgy as proposed in this book, and it is crucial for connecting the divine and human in liturgy. Storytelling also underlies the spirituality of reconciliation as outlined by Schreiter, and by Anderson and Foley. Schreiter points out, using narrative concepts, what happens to suffering persons:[19]

> Suffering is the human struggle with and against pain. It is the experience of the breakdown of our systems of meaning and our stories about ourselves, and the struggle to restore those senses of safety and selfhood. Suffering in itself is neither noble nor redeeming. It is essentially an

> erosion of meaning. It is an interruption and destruction of those funda-
> mental senses of safety and selfhood without which we cannot survive as
> individuals and as societies. Suffering only becomes redemptive or enno-
> bling when we struggle against these corroding powers and rebuild our
> selves in spite of the pain we are experiencing. And ... that is most likely
> to happen when we are able to link our narrative to other, larger narratives.
> Such a linkage does not happen automatically.[20]

This description of what suffering is fits well with the narrative framework of this book. Suffering is the breakdown of a person's meaning-making framework. When people experience major negative life events, they start looking for the meaning of these events within their larger understanding of reality.[21]

Schreiter affirms our argument that meaning is found in the meeting of another story (cf. Chapter 9). When safety and selfhood (i.e. identity) can be found, the process of erosion of meaning is stopped and turned around. Then suffering is transformed, and one can move from despair to hope. Both the empirical findings in Part I of this book and the liturgical–theological reflections in the present part have demonstrated the many possibilities liturgy has for facilitating this process. Liturgically, this process finds its climax or condensed expression in the Eucharist. Here the suffering, death and resurrection are remembered in a most profound way. The Eucharist is the liturgical expression of one of the fundamental theological points that mark a spirituality or reconciliation: "The process of reconciliation that creates the new humanity is to be found in the story of the passion, death, and resurrection of Jesus Christ."[22] Schreiter sees the rituals of the Church as an important resource for reconciliation. He singles out the Eucharist:

> Gathering around the eucharistic table, the broken, damaged, and abused
> bodies of individual victims and the broken body of the church are taken
> up into the body of Christ. Christ's body has known torture; it has known
> shame. In his complete solidarity with victims, he has gone to the limits of
> violent death. And so his body becomes a holy medicine to heal those
> broken bodies of today.[23]

As we drink the cup of Jesus' death, we also drink the cup of his resurrection. The process of death and resurrection, of suffering and healing, of despair and hope, enters physically our bodies. The Eucharist is the liturgical embodiment of transformation.

When two worlds come together, this leads to transformation. Schreiter argues that the process of reconciliation leads to a new place. The outcome of a process of reconciliation can never be predicted. It will never be restoration of the old situation, since the suffering has become part of the memory. "The suffering is not forgotten, but the memory of it is transformed and remembered in a different way so that, its story taken up in the story of the Lord's own suffering and death, it can be made into something life-giving for others."[24]

The new place, where reconciliation leads us to, is a place where perspectives are changed (cf. the step of reconnection). Schreiter says that it is possible "that we shall never quite see, but are asked instead to deepen our trust and confidence in Christ so that we might become more fully human and more conformed to him." He continues: "It is in this way that the cup of suffering is turned into the cup of hope."[25] So transformation is not the annihilation of suffering, but to see it in a new light, and bringing the suffering person (and the community) to a new place.

An expression Schreiter uses several times is "to regain our humanity". Suffering, especially when it involves violence, destroys our memories, identities and therefore our humanity. Reconciliation is to regain our humanity. In a sense, this is true for all suffering and healing processes, because all these processes involve meaning-making. Ultimately, true meaning and our true humanity is discovered in realizing that we are created in the image of God, and in Christ as the image of God. So our story world needs to "find other narratives that can pick up the fragments of our own and piece them back together."[26] We are reminded of the image that liturgist Al used: in the liturgy we are all in a process of grafting our own stories on to the story of Jesus Christ. We are also back to the argument that liturgy needs to incorporate both the story of God and the stories of human beings. If these stories are fragmented because the experience of suffering has destroyed their coherence, then these fragments may find a place in the story of God who also suffered and still mourns with those who mourn. A liturgy that allows narrative space for God to suffer with people, and for suffering people is likely to be a liturgy of reconciliation. Probably such a liturgy is an inductive liturgy.

A spirituality of reconciliation calls for liturgical communities that are hospitable places where stories can be told, where truth-telling is allowed, and where suffering in all its ugliness can be remembered. It calls for liturgies that allow for silence and for lament. A liturgical spirituality of reconciliation can find a place in the liturgy of the Church of England. We have emphasized the dynamic of virtually endless liturgical flexibility combined with a small core of fixed texts that marks the liturgical renewal behind *Common Worship*. Even within a liturgical celebration that is largely 'by the book' there is a good number of occasions for improvisation. It requires creativity on the part of the liturgical ministers, and also willingness on the part of the liturgical community, to address suffering and let the liturgy be one that reconciles.[27] The default text, *Order One*, contains neither many references to God's suffering *with* people nor to suffering as major negative life events on the part of the participants. The discussions in the previous chapters make us critical of this absence. It will not be easy to make the anaphora of the Eucharistic prayers sound as prayers of lament rather than *eucharistia* (see p. 92). Yet given the flexibility allowed for in other parts of the liturgy, it should be possible to incorporate narrative space for God and people to tell their stories of suffering and solidarity.

Community

One significant finding of our research is the correlation between the experience of liturgy and the experience of community. With few exceptions the rule is that when the community is experienced positively, so is the liturgy, and when the community is experienced negatively, so is the liturgy. Liturgy is central in the life of the Church, but it is not the only thing, as was also noted by some participants. Our research has revealed many possibilities for liturgy to address suffering. A communal and liturgical spirituality of reconciliation, as we propose here, acknowledges that these possibilities of the liturgy will be most fruitful when the liturgy is celebrated within a community that bears the characteristics of a spirituality of reconciliation.

Schreiter holds that communities of reconciliation have three important aspects.[28] First, they are "communities of safety, zones in which victims can examine and explore their wounds."[29] Safety is the basis for regaining trust. We are once more reminded of the importance safety has for the participants in our project. Safety is given by the structure of the liturgy and even by the mere fact of the liturgy being there from week to week, month to month, year to year. The experience of safety can come through the building itself, or just being part of the liturgical community, or a consistent message and consistent people. It is noteworthy that when the liturgy was not experienced as safe, it was because the community did not accept or did not know how to handle the struggles of the sufferer. All of this rings true with the spirituality of reconciliation as outlined above, especially with the steps of accompaniment and hospitality.

The second aspect of a community of reconciliation is that they are communities of memory. Such communities are places where truth can be learned and told. Such communities are hospitable to suffering people to tell their stories over and over again. It is in telling stories, and therefore in remembering, that the narrator slowly discovers a new perspective (cf. the step of reconnection). We have seen that remembrance is foundational for narrative, for understanding the Scriptures and for liturgy. In the previous chapters we have built our search for the narrative space for God and human beings largely on the concept of remembrance. With Schreiter's statement that a community of reconciliation is a community of remembrance, we come full circle.

Third, communities of reconciliation are communities of hope. When stories are told and memories get healed, it becomes possible to imagine a just world. Schreiter notes that people who experience violence live on a day-to-day basis. They try to endure and to survive. This is not only true for the experience of violence. Suffering in general robs people of hope. It is significant to note this, for we have seen that people construct their life stories not only on the basis of the past, but also of the future. Both memory and imagination are important in finding meaning. When imagination is not possible any more, one's future is jeopardized. A community of hope, on the contrary, takes people beyond endurance and survival. This point makes clear why reconciliation is a spirituality rather than a strategy. It is not possible to enforce hope on people (and even if it could, it would repeat the act of violence). But communities which are able to accompany those who suffer and to offer hospitality, and which are zones of safety and truth-telling, such communities are likely to foster hope. And even when someone cannot hope, the community can hope on behalf of the one who suffers.[30]

In our introduction of a spirituality of reconciliation (pp. 85–89) we noted that another mark of a community of reconciliation is that it mourns. Its members stand in solidarity with those who suffer, and follow Jesus' invitation to become mourners themselves. Swain comments that suffering has a rippling effect because human beings are interdependent and interconnected. "What hurts you pains me also."[31] The community joins those who sit on the mourning bench. A liturgical community of reconciliation turns its pews into mourning benches.

A community that welcomes in solidarity those who suffer does recognize its own brokenness. This is another mark of a community of reconciliation. It is not as if the people who temporarily do not suffer 'help' those who suffer in a relationship of giving and receiving. As a matter of fact, both the sufferer and the other give and receive. A community of reconciliation is made up by people who are all inherently vulnerable. Jesse Perillo makes this clear in his proposal for an ethic of compassion, an ethic which resonates with a spirituality of reconciliation. Part of such an ethic is the language of vulnerability. It is important for all in the community to recognize their own vulnerability. Only if this is recognized as part of our existence, and therefore taken as normative, will a person be able to hear the vulnerability and suffering of another. "To speak and live a language of vulnerability is to be transformed into a people that listens and pays attention to the other's elaboration of their painful experiences."[32] All are vulnerable, all are broken.

The recognition that all are broken shows a different perspective on the world. Swinton calls this an epistemology of the broken body. This epistemology starts by looking at the cross. "In the broken body of Christ we discover a new way of interpreting and understanding the world."[33] It shows that evil should not be repaid with evil. It also shows that hope is found in the midst of suffering. "God's power is revealed *in the midst of* suffering and evil, not as a triumphalistic conquering power that strives to annihilate evil, but rather as suffering presence that transforms evil not with force and might, but with the practice of persistent, vulnerable love."[34] The cross furthermore demonstrates that God suffers on behalf of people but also with people, says Swinton on the basis of Dietrich Bonhoeffer's theology. With that notion we are back to an important discussion in this part of our book – i.e. to what extent the liturgy gives narrative space to God's story of suffering *with* people. A community of reconciliation that holds on to an epistemology of the broken body will be able to provide this narrative space.

At the heart of the Christian story is the broken body of Christ. This is also the heart of the liturgy. Wolterstorff calls the Eucharist "that sacrament of God's participation in our brokenness."[35] It is a broken symbol itself, as Don Saliers argues. He describes the moment in Leonard Bernstein's *Mass* at which the young priest in an act of desperation takes the vessels from the altar and

> smashes them into a million pieces on the floor. That iconoclastic act of breaking open the symbol requires breaking the symbols. And after a stunned silence he [the priest] sings, 'Things get broken.' Suddenly, in a flash, before me and this well-dressed concert-going audience, there it was, the central symbol of liturgy in its starkest form. For at the heart of Christian liturgy is a broken symbol. Or rather, unless we break open the symbols by bringing our life to them, taking into account human pathos, they will remain inaccessible.[36]

The Christian story is paradoxical. It does contain myth and parable. How is it that hope is found in the midst of suffering? How is it that at the heart of the liturgy is a broken symbol? In the end this is mystery, a mystery that is celebrated every time in when the body of Christ is broken, and his blood poured out, and we do that in remembrance of him. Saliers points to the fact that the Eucharistic celebration should never be an automatism. We need to bring our lives into the symbol, including our pathos, our suffering. This points once more to the need for inductive liturgy which weaves together the divine and human stories. The pastoral need for this is made clear by Wolterstorff in his *Lament for a Son*:

> I tried to jog and could not. It was too life-affirming. I rode along with friends to go swimming and found myself paralyzed. I tried music. But why is this music all so affirmative? Has it always been like that? Perhaps then a requiem, that glorious *German Requiem* of Brahms. I have to turn it off. There's too little brokenness in it. Is there no music that speaks of our terrible brokenness? That's not what I mean. I mean: Is there no music that *fits* our brokenness? The music that speaks *about* our brokenness is not itself broken. Is there no broken music?[37]

These questions are a cry of lament. They defy an answer, because the answer would not be broken enough. Rather, it makes us question our liturgical celebrations, the rituals we have, the way we remember in the Eucharist. Are the cries of lament heard? Is the community capable of crying out in solidarity with those who suffer? Is there broken liturgy?

There are no clear-cut answers to these questions. In the previous chapters we have discussed several salient issues. The present chapter argues that a communal and liturgical spirituality of reconciliation is likely to at least provide the narrative space to voice the lament and eventually to find transformation in situations of suffering. The community is a community of safety, memory and hope. To these aspects we added mourning and brokenness as marks of a community of reconciliation. Brokenness is a way of looking at the world, and gives an important perspective for critically evaluating our liturgies. Liturgy that is embedded in such a community has a good chance to become a liturgy of reconciliation.

Pastoral care and liturgy

Wolterstorff's lament brings out the pastoral interest of the central question this book poses. The question how liturgy can address and connect to narratives of suffering people has a pastoral edge. Anderson and Foley try to connect liturgy and pastoral care in their book, and so it is appropriate to conclude our proposal for a communal and liturgical spirituality of reconciliation with a few reflections on this relationship.

Anderson and Foley emphasize the need of ritual and pastoral care for each other.[38] Rituals, and especially public worship, have a tendency to focus on the communal and the divine stories. Pastoral care is particularly attentive to the individual narratives. The challenge is to bring these together. Pastoral care helps to find new meaning in life, but to find this fully one needs community. At the same time the question for liturgy is how it incorporates the human stories – a question which is at the heart of our research.

Anderson and Foley also state that for "many centuries, a principle mode of care was found in the rituals of the church."[39] This was strengthened by the fact that the presider in liturgy was also the one who had pastoral oversight.[40] Also, today often the person presiding in the worship service is the one who is responsible for pastoral care in that community, as was certainly the case in the churches in our research project. If the primary caregiver in a community is the same one as the primary liturgical presider, it raises the chances for a 'pastoral liturgy.' We have noted a couple of times the importance of the liturgical presider's role. She is the one who selects a good part of the liturgical script, and therefore of the stories that will be told. When she is also the one who is responsible for pastoral care in the community, the stories of the people can inform her selections. In the context of the rite of anointing in the sacrament of the Pastoral Care to the Sick, Bruce Morrill remarks that it is important to discern when the sacrament is needed. "Such discernment is central to the pastoral process of the sacrament."[41] This is a specific context and the focus of our research is not on occasional liturgies but on regular worship services. Yet Morrill's observation is an important one for liturgical and pastoral ministers. With thoughtful discernment also regular liturgies can become occasions for healing.

Having said this, it is also widely recognized that pastoral care for the community does not rest with the clergy alone. Instead, members in the community itself care for each other.[42] This might be in home groups, prayer groups, or other occasions, or even in less formal occasions. The practice of accompanying suffering people, and providing a hospitable environment in which stories can be told, starts with friendship.[43] Not surprisingly, then, in the themes that surfaced from the stories of suffering people in our research, both community and the role of the clergy were important, while community was deemed even more important than the role of clergy. This brings us back to the previous paragraph. A spirituality of reconciliation is liturgical and communal. Even if the liturgical presider has a prominent role, the spirituality needs to be one that is embraced by the community as a whole.[44]

Just as storytelling is important in liturgy, so it is in pastoral care. David Hogue writes: "If we *are* the stories we tell, and if we belong to each other and to God through the stories we share, then retelling those stories for ourselves as well as for others is key to the pastoral task."[45] Identity is formed and meaning is found by telling stories, both in liturgy and in pastoral care.

These notions on the relation between liturgy and pastoral care are very brief. The focus in this book is on liturgy, not on pastoral care. This paragraph, however, shows that the relationship between the two ought not be overlooked. Within the limits of the present work we cannot do justice to both sides of this relationship. Further work needs to be done. This paragraph has brought out some important connections between liturgy and pastoral care that resonate with some important themes in our research. Pastoral care and liturgy need each other, both emphasizing certain aspects of relating the divine and human story, yet these stories are inherent in both. A narrative understanding of both liturgy and pastoral care helps to see the interrelatedness of both. Furthermore, the liturgical presider has an important part to play in a pastoral liturgy. However, the importance of community for pastoral care underlines the need for a communal and liturgical spirituality of reconciliation.

Conclusion

Liturgy that seeks to do justice to stories of suffering needs to be embedded in a communal and liturgical spirituality of reconciliation. This spirituality is marked by several features. It will be a community that provides a zone of safety. It is a community of memory and hope. Such a community embraces otherness and is hospitable to what is strange, only to be surprised by grace. It takes the initiative to accompany people and provides space for storytelling, to discover the divine work of making connections and commissioning. A community that embraces such a spirituality of reconciliation will see, in the brokenness of the liturgy, the Eucharistic sacrament and the cross, a God who suffers with people and takes their suffering and transforms it.

Notes

1 Schreiter, *Reconciliation*, 71.
2 We do so on the basis of Schreiter, *Reconciliation*; and Robert J. Schreiter, *The Ministry of Reconciliation: Spirituality & Strategies* (Maryknoll, NY: Orbis Books, 1998).
3 For example, Schreiter, *Reconciliation*, 3, cf. 36–37; Schreiter, *The Ministry of Reconciliation*, 19–22.
4 Schreiter, *Reconciliation*, 59–62; Schreiter, *The Ministry of Reconciliation*, 13–19.
5 Schreiter, *Reconciliation*, 60.

6 Schreiter, *The Ministry of Reconciliation*, 94–96.
7 For example, before we referred to the pastoral theory of Storm Swain. Her first two 'moments' in the counselling process, holding/earth-making and suffering/pain-bearing, correspond to Schreiter's first two steps of accompaniment and hospitality. Storm's third moment, transforming/life-giving, corresponds to Schreiter's final steps of making connections and being commissioned.
8 We have come across this first step in previous chapters with other scholars already. Johnston-Barrett wonders how a community in which people care for each other in suffering can be achieved (esp. 334–337). She finds that in the concept of paying attention (Simone Weil), and in churches that create safe spaces for sufferers to tell their stories, which can be in home groups or worship services. Telling stories of suffering from the Bible helps sufferers to find their voice and enables them with language to express their suffering, as well as helping them to see that they are not alone in their situation. Johnston-Barrett's reflections fit well with a spirituality of reconciliation that is marked by its openness to others and embracing that which is strange; concepts that resonate with the awkwardness and therefore social isolation suffering brings. Johnston-Barrett, "Making Space: Silence, Voice, and Suffering." Also John Swinton emphasizes the need to listen, including the need to listen to the silence of suffering. This begins with friendship. Swinton, *Raging with Compassion*, 101–103, 116–118. See also the paragraph on community below.
9 Schreiter, *The Ministry of Reconciliation*, 89. The importance of hospitality is mentioned by other scholars whom we referred to as well in previous chapters. According to John Swinton, hospitality is one of the four core practices of a practical theodicy. These four practices fit very well the spirituality of reconciliation proposed by Schreiter and by Anderson and Foley, and also in the present chapter. These practices are: lament, forgiveness, thoughtfulness and hospitality. These practices are based on the concept of friendship. Swinton, *Raging with Compassion*. Don Saliers wonders how liturgy forms and expresses spirituality, and he suggests four ways: first, liturgy is a school for gratitude; second, it should shape us in truth-telling; third, it should form a hospitable attitude; and fourth, it is a school for compassion. Especially the third and the fourth ways resonate with our project, and the second as well as it advocates the use of lament in liturgy. About the third way Saliers writes: "When liturgy lacks hospitality, it forfeits its right to speak to the world in healing and prophecy. We need that hospitable space and time where the stories can be heard and told and life shared deeply in the singing and in the rites. Without that we are all diminished." Don E. Saliers, "Toward a Spirituality of Inclusiveness," in *Human Disability and the Service of God*, 27.
10 Pembroke, *Pastoral Care in Worship*, 101. He elaborates on the aspect of community in Chapters 7 and 8 of his book.
11 Peterson, *Five Smooth Stones for Pastoral Work*, 97–105.
12 Ibid., 88.
13 Schreiter, *The Ministry of Reconciliation*, 95.
14 Ibid., 96.
15 Ibid., 45–51.
16 Several stories in our research contain such moments of reconnection – for example, when a participant eventually accepted that she was mentally ill, after a long period of denial. Clear examples are the two men who told about their struggles with being gay and their faith.
17 Schreiter, *The Ministry of Reconciliation*, 81. A powerful example of the latter is found in the story of Eric, someone who suffered from HIV/AIDS, and through whom a whole church community was transformed (also liturgically) into a community reaching out to those who, for all sorts of reasons, are marginalized. Parnell, "Risking Redemption."

144 *Liturgical theology*

18 It is worthwhile to refer to Swain once more, and to quote her at length, in order to show how her trauma theory and pastoral method reinforce our argument for how a communal and liturgical spirituality of reconciliation might be shaped: "Paying attention in pastoral care to what is life giving means attending to those seemingly elusive but often powerful aspects of transformation. Unlike a sense of holding, which can be intentionally created and practiced, these aspects of life, a little like the Spirit that may inspire them, 'blow where they will' (cf. John 3:8). It is as subtle and profound as the difference between surviving and living, between reacting and acting, between 'self-care' and the Self's care. As we can see in the chaplain's narratives,. these are moments that can be discovered, captured, and delighted in but not manufactured. However, what can be created are the conditions that can contribute to this, even in the midst of a disaster site." Swain, *Trauma and Transformation at Ground Zero*, 177.
19 Again, Schreiter writes from the context of violence, but his reflections on suffering are applicable in other contexts of suffering as well.
20 Schreiter, *Reconciliation*, 33–34.
21 Note that Schreiter, just like Morrill, does not define healing ('rebuilding our selves') in physical terms.
22 Schreiter, *The Ministry of Reconciliation*, 18.
23 Schreiter, *Reconciliation*, 75–76.
24 Schreiter, *The Ministry of Reconciliation*, 99.
25 Ibid., 81.
26 Schreiter, *Reconciliation*, 37.
27 One liturgist who participated in our research remarked that the congregation easily connected to different symbolisms and rituals, something which not every community is able to do.
28 Schreiter, *The Ministry of Reconciliation*, 94–95.
29 Ibid., 94.
30 Cf. Swinton, *Raging with Compassion*, 222. Here and at other places Swinton relates this to the story of the four friends who let their friend on a matress through the roof of the house, in order for Jesus to heal their friend. Swinton recalls when a friend, named George, called him when George's daughter had died. "George was paralyzed with pain and grief, but his friends were able to drop his suffering down through the roof of the pain house and ask for Jesus' healing touch. Friends can hope for one another even when all hope seems to be gone. Without friendship and a hopeful place to express real pain and suffering, the practice of lament can never flourish."
31 Swain, *Trauma and Transformation at Ground Zero*, 111.
32 Jesse Perillo, "The Destructive Nature of Suffering and the Liturgical Refashioning of the Person" (Ph.D., Loyola University Chicago, 2011), 173.
33 Swinton, *Raging with Compassion*, 164.
34 Ibid., 165–166.
35 Wolterstorff, *Lament for a Son*, 39.
36 Saliers, "Toward a Spirituality of Inclusiveness," 28.
37 Wolterstorff, *Lament for a Son*, 52.
38 Anderson and Foley, *Mighty Stories*, Chap. 3.
39 Ibid., 46. See also William A. Clebsch and Charles R. Jaekle, *Pastoral Care in Historical Perspective*, 1st edn (Englewood Cliffs, NJ: Prentice-Hall, 1964); Peterson, *Five Smooth Stones for Pastoral Work* esp. pp. 17–20. Peterson refers to the use of the *Megilloth* (the books of Song of Songs, Ruth, Lamentations, Ecclesiastes and Esther) in Judaic worship. Peterson demonstrates the pastoral implications of these books for worship. He claims that pastoral work has its origin in worship and cannot do without it, one of the reasons being the communal setting of worship.

40 Weil, *A Theology of Worship*, 33, 38. Weil refers for his argument to Justin Martyr, *First Apology*, Chap. 65.
41 Morrill, *Divine Worship and Human Healing*, 159.
42 Billman and Migliore, *Rachel's Cry*, 136.
43 Swinton, *Raging with Compassion*, Chap. 8.
44 Pamela Cooper-White underlines the importance of community in the same vein as we do here. She also stresses the importance of regular worship and the celebration of the Eucharist as hugely healing. Special liturgies of healing have a place as well, although she warns to be cautious with them. Pamela Cooper-White, *The Cry of Tamar: Violence Against Women and the Church's Response*, 2nd edn (Minneapolis, MN: Fortress Press, 2012), 246–250.
45 Hogue, *Remembering*, 104.

11 Conclusion

In this last chapter we will conclude first with answers to the central question of this book. We will also point to some areas of research that deserve further attention. We then wish to show the import of this book, not only for the four churches that participated in our project, but for the wider Church of England and for other Churches as well. We will briefly evaluate the narrative approach to liturgy which we have used. Finally, we will conclude with a narrative description of a liturgy that fully includes suffering.

Answers and further questions

The question that has been leading our project is: How does or can Anglican liturgy (in the archdeaconry of North West Europe in the Church of England's diocese in Europe) address and connect to people with regard to their narratives of serious negative life events? The empirical part of the answer to the research questions rests on the analysis and interpretation of four data sources: the liturgical text (*Common Worship, Order One*), interviews with people who have experienced a major negative life event, interviews with clergy and readers and the observation of worship services. The answer to our research question from the empirical point of view was given in Chapter 5. Part II engaged with the academic liturgical–theological discourse and provided an answer from that point of view. That part deepened our understanding (also our narrative understanding) of what happens in liturgy. We will now draw conclusions from the empirical findings and the liturgical–theological chapter.

1   The liturgy has myriad of authors, narrators and audiences coming together. The main characters are God and the people. The liturgical presider has a huge role in bringing together the story of God and the stories of the people. Furthermore, in the background are the authors of the liturgical text and the authorizing body. Other authors may be singled out, such as the musicians, the choir, readers and intercessors.
2   It is a striking fact that the main narrators, God and people, have the least opportunity to adapt the liturgical script for their purposes. In other words, they have least narrative space.

3 The main storylines or themes of the liturgical text are the state and process towards wholeness, glory of God and living a particular lifestyle. Suffering as a theme comes most to the fore in the storylines wholeness, which also gives most opportunities to address suffering.
4 Liturgy focuses on sin rather than on suffering. The concept of sin might include involuntarily suffering, but the main body of the liturgical text does not have suffering as major negative life experiences on the part of people in view.
5 Suffering is at the heart of liturgy, so the liturgists and the liturgical literature claim. This suffering, however, is for the better part the suffering of God in Christ *because of* and *for* the people. God's suffering *with* people is much less emphasized.
6 Nevertheless, most participants (and also liturgists) in this research, if not all, can point to a number of elements in the liturgy that connect with their situation of suffering. Most often mentioned are community, Eucharist, liturgy as a safe place, the role of clergy, experiences of God, readings, sermon and intercessions. The diversity of points of connection shows that no blueprint can be given for addressing suffering in liturgy.
7 The liturgical–theological reflection on narrative, liturgy and suffering suggested that the connection between the divine and human stories – in other words, between liturgy and people who suffer – can be enhanced by enlarging the narrative space of both people and God. Remembrance is a foundational concept, together with its counterpart 'imagination.' The narrative space of God is enlarged by remembering not only his suffering because of and for, but also his suffering with people. Remembering the suffering of people leads to the language of lament, which helps to find new meaning and hope in the face of suffering.
8 The liturgical renewal of the last decades in the Church of England has moved from a rather monolithic liturgy to a small core of fixed texts on one hand and an invitation to be virtually limitlessly creative for other parts. Even if the liturgy is taken straight from the book, the liturgy contains many instances where pastoral and liturgical sensitivity on the part of the liturgical minister is called for. These instances are obvious places to address suffering and connect the human and divine stories.
9 When both God's story and the stories of people can be authentically related in liturgy, two worlds come together. Then transformation happens and healing may occur. An inductive liturgy gives the best opportunities to include the stories of suffering people.
10 Both the empirical findings and the liturgical discourse point to the fact that liturgy is part of the wider life of the Church. Addressing suffering and connecting the divine and human does not happen in liturgical isolation, but requires a liturgical community that has a spirituality of reconciliation in its DNA.

From our project we can point to a couple of areas that deserve further research. First, we have touched on the relationship between narrative and ritual.

Our research has focused on narrative, although a ritual understanding of liturgy has been in the background. Further research is necessary in order to take into account a more explicit ritual view on liturgy. Second, it is clear that the empirical findings gave much more input for liturgical–theological reflection than we could deal with within the limits of this book. Further research and writing that elaborates on the various themes is needed. Third, we started the research with a pastoral interest. The theme of addressing suffering is a pastoral one in itself. Anderson and Foley bring out the relation between liturgy and pastoral care in their book. This book has demonstrated that addressing suffering is not something that happens, or even can happen, in the liturgy alone. More research is needed in the area of liturgy and pastoral care.

Importance for a broader context

The research that underpins this book was limited to four Anglican churches in the Benelux. Strictly speaking, the conclusions of this research, especially those drawn from the empirical part of this book, are valid only for those four churches. After all, we focused on one particular liturgical text, *Common Worship*; the interviews were with *those* particular people, and with the priests and liturgical ministers of *those* particular churches; we observed *those* particular worship services; and all of this within the particular archdeaconry of North West Europe, which is an expatriate context.

Nevertheless, in a number of ways this book is relevant for a much wider audience, in the first place for the wider Church of England and the Anglican Communion, but also for other churches.[1] The churches that participated in this project were by no means atypical, or it should be the fact that they are international, expatriate communities. But the expatriate factor did not prove to be of major influence for the question of addressing suffering in worship. These four churches are full of people like you and me; they have priests and lay ministers like most other churches; they are communities bringing their stories to worship on Sunday and grafting their stories on to the story of God. It is not hard to identify with these faith communities.

Furthermore, the topic of suffering resonates in virtually all contexts, even outside the church context, for suffering is part of life. The resonance of the topic with many people and in many contexts has become clear to me during the years that I have been working on this project. People respond to the topic easily and have often affirmed the importance of it, and also sometimes told me how it resonated with them personally.

Finally, liturgy is the central act of public worship in any church, whether Anglican or from a different denomination. Many churches do have a written down liturgical order, often including suggested or mandatory texts. *Common Worship* has a set of fixed core texts, but aims for a high level of flexibility in other parts of the liturgy. Most churches, especially those within an established liturgical tradition, will have a similar blend of flexible and fixed parts of their liturgies.

Apart from the likelihood that the reader will be able to identify with the churches in this book and with the topic of suffering, many, if not all, of the conclusions we listed in the previous paragraph are applicable to other church contexts. Here we highlight some additional salient issues that arose from Parts I and II, but the list is by no means exhaustive.

The first issue concerns style. The participants in our project mentioned many points of connection between the liturgy and their situation of suffering. The points mentioned were more or less the same in all four churches, even though their liturgies range from informal to formal. Apparently, style does not matter as much as content or the atmosphere of the community.

Second, the most important theme mentioned by participants and liturgists is that of community. In our theological reflections we have given due attention to this by arguing for a communal and liturgical spirituality of reconciliation. Such a spirituality is not the prerogative of Anglicans and the argument pertains to all liturgical communities.

The theme of community is immediately followed in importance by Holy Communion. This lies at the heart of the liturgy and also at the heart of the experiences of suffering people. It is remarkable, however, that the participants do point to many other aspects of the Eucharist than only the theological meaning of Christ's suffering, death and resurrection. The way that Holy Communion is celebrated is important, for it gives many a sense of community and being drawn into the community. We saw that much happens to people during this time of Communion. The call to the churches in our project is to think clearly about this rite. This call is also relevant for other Anglican churches and other churches in general.

The liturgy, and especially the liturgical text of *Common Worship, Order One*, focuses on sin rather than on suffering. It can be expected that this is the case in other liturgies and liturgical texts as well, given the liturgical renewal of the last century, in which churches have sought more liturgical unity and have taken into account ancient liturgies when rewriting their own. Any church can benefit from auditing its own liturgy with regard to the question of how both sin and suffering get a place.

Related to the previous point, one might analyse the liturgy in terms of God's suffering because of, for and with people. Given the widespread complaints about the lack of addressing suffering in liturgy, we suspect that most liturgies will not have God's suffering *with* people at their core but rather God's suffering *on behalf of* people.[2]

Finally, in many churches the liturgical presider plays a significant part. In Anglican liturgy, where the narrative space of the liturgical presider is still somewhat limited by the liturgical text and the rubrics, it is important to realize the responsibility and opportunities the liturgical presider has for connecting the human and divine stories. In churches where the narrative space for the liturgical presider is even bigger, the responsibility grows, as well as the opportunities.

In conclusion, this book might focus on Anglicans and Anglican liturgy, but as a matter of fact, it is about anyone on a spiritual journey who walks into any given church on any given Sunday. The universality of suffering and the central place of liturgy in the life of the church make the results of our study relevant for a wide range of settings, both within academic and church communities.

The narrative approach revisited

Narrative approaches to the study of liturgy are relatively new. Having appropriated one particular narrative theory and method, and having applied these to Anglican liturgy, we are now in the position to evaluate the usefulness and potential caveats of a narrative understanding of liturgy.[3]

We have argued for taking a narrative approach to liturgy. Especially the discussions in Part II have reinforced our claim that liturgy is inherently narrative. The search for a narrative theory and methodology for understanding liturgy follows logically. The discussions in Part II also pointed to a concept that is key to both liturgy and narrative – i.e. the concept of remembrance. As remembering in storytelling brings together past, present and future, so *anamnesis* spans liturgical time. Furthermore, this book has greatly benefited from a narrative approach, as people's stories of suffering are narrative in nature as well. Finally, a major contribution of a narrative understanding of liturgy is the discussion of who the authors, narrators and audiences are.

Several issues that come with a narrative approach point to both limits and possibilities. First, the empirical research revealed that the narrative method of Ganzevoort, which we used, was not fully applicable to one particular data source. In order to do justice to all six elements in the narrative method, the interaction with other data sources is necessary. For example, the observation of liturgical celebrations does not fully account for the experiences of the participants. On one hand, this may be seen as a limit of the method. On the other hand, however, it points to fact that liturgy is multifaceted and therefore requires the inclusion of various data sources.

Second, the narrative method that we used in this work points to the multilayered nature of liturgy. The difficulty is to make sure that the perspectives and interpretation of different data sources do not conflate where that is not appropriate. However, much more than posing a methodological difficulty, the various perspectives and data sources offer the opportunity for arriving at a rich understanding of liturgy. Here it is true that the whole is greater than the sum of the parts. The liturgical text, the experiences of participants, the views of liturgists and the actual celebrations gain meaning in the light of each other.

Third, the narrative researcher should reflect on the narrative categories or dimensions he wishes and needs to include in the project. In our study we have adhered closely to Ganzevoort's method, although at a couple of points we have adapted the method for our purposes – for example, the inclusion of 'atmosphere' in the observation of worship services. Furthermore, we have integrated Anderson and Foley's work in the overall methodology for the project. The particular method of Ganzevoort might benefit from further methodological reflection of relating the four-step reading method to formulating and answering the research questions of each individual project.

Finally, we have pointed several times to other disciplines in which narrative informs theory and method – e.g. in trauma theory, psychology and sociology. By approaching liturgy narratively, liturgical scholars can critically interact with and also learn from these approaches. Again, this adds to a richer understanding of liturgy.

In sum, a narrative approach to liturgy follows logically from the inherent narrative nature of liturgy. This study has found the narrative approach of Ganzevoort, set within a wider narrative–ritual methodology, useful for understanding liturgy in relation to stories of suffering people, and the project has proven the value of such an approach. A narrative theory and methodology contribute to a deeper understanding of liturgy and participants experiences thereof.

A narrative liturgy

"When we gather for worship, we come for the purpose of storytelling and story listening at least as much as for any other reason."[4] Our research has shown the truth in this statement by David Hogue. Underlying this book is a narrative understanding of liturgy. In this concluding paragraph we will 'take a walk' through the liturgy and show what is going on narratively.[5] We do so on the basis of the findings of our research and give special attention to suffering. By doing so, many discussions in this book find a place in this brief and narrative rendering of liturgy. In a sense, this 'tour' through the liturgy answers our central question in a somewhat different framework than the previous paragraphs. The structure follows *Common Worship, Order One*. To give the tour a more real touch, we will imagine that Anna and Kate, the girls from the story at the beginning of Chapter 1, participate. The tour will show the many opportunities a church has to connect to Anna and Kate in their grief over their lost friends in the car accident.

First, we look at the setting of the scene. The liturgy is there, always there, and as such it gives safety for Anna and Kate. Furthermore, the more structured the worship service is, the more structure it gives in the chaos of Anna and Kate's situation.

Anna and Kate are two of the many characters in the liturgical performance. The Liturgical Commission has drafted the script and the General Synod has approved it. But Anna and Kate have not come to meet with the Liturgical Commission or the members of synod, but with God and their fellow believers. As a matter of fact, God and the people are the primary narrators in the liturgical performance. The performance is led by the liturgical presider, who has (perhaps) also selected the specific texts and songs for today. Other participants include the choir, readers, a member of the congregation who leads the prayers of intercession and perhaps someone at the door welcoming people in.

152 *Liturgical theology*

Having set the scene, we now find Anna and Kate sitting in the pews. Depending on the kind of church, there is a gentle buzz of people talking with each other or a devout silence in preparation for the service. In each case, Anna and Kate now find themselves in the community. Here they feel safe because it is a community that is hospitable, interested in their stories, and its members have shown many signs of compassion. This is a community that sits beside them on their mourning benches. Being part of this community and sitting here alongside its members is already breaking through the isolation that their suffering tries to impart on them.

The organ starts playing the opening hymn and the procession of liturgical ministers and clergy enters in, while all people stand. Now, if there was a feminist joining the worship service, she would perhaps question the practice of standing while the procession enters the liturgical space. Relationships are acted out in the procession; it tells a tale that evokes certain power relationships. Especially if her experiences with clergy in her previous church were negative, the act of standing while the procession enters in may be threatening for her.[6]

The opening hymn is a gathering song. All kinds of people are mentioned as well as all kinds of situations. The song recognizes all individual situations but at the same time unites the congregation in their desire to meet with God. Perhaps the song acknowledges the utter similarity of all people: all of us are created in the image of God, and all of us are vulnerable. At least the song does not exclude anyone but invites and welcomes and includes. Anna and Kate feel welcome too.

Now the presider turns to the people and opens the liturgy in the name of the Trinity. It sets the relationship between God and people. The liturgy is in the name of God, not in the name of the people. The greeting that follows underlines the inequality of the relationship, but, as we have noted in Chapter 2, the greater party is benevolent towards the lesser party. Narratively, this constellation of relationships explains an image that we came across several times: the fragments of Anna and Kate's stories are picked up and mended by the greater story of God; another image is that of grafting our stories on to the story of Jesus.

At this point the presider may add words of welcome and introduce the theme of the service, which is often related to the time in the liturgical year. This is a great opportunity to use liturgical inductive strategies. Particular moments in life may be singled out insofar as that is pastorally sensitive and appropriate. This point in the liturgy can create narrative space for suffering people, to recognize their stories in what is said and done. Here, Anna and Kate may recognize that the coming together of the divine and human stories includes their suffering.

After these words of welcome, the rite of confession starts. The relationship with the greater party will be renegotiated. The people acknowledge their sinfulness and God expresses his will to forgive. In the absolution at the end of the rite the relationship is righted. At its best, suffering people will recognize their brokenness in this rite, but the prayers as such point much more to the people as sinful beings in the sense of personal wrongdoing. Pastorally, this might help people – some need to hear that they can get on with life. But the rite may also be quite unhelpful – for example, when a victim has false feelings of guilt and a victimiser is too easily forgiven. Furthermore, sin defined as personal wrongdoing highlights only one of the meanings of sin, even though an important one. Liturgists may wish to draw on other (authorized) texts for the rite of confession and absolution; texts that emphasize brokenness and suffering on the part of people, Christ's presence with those who suffer and the healing touch of God. Thus, the rite of confession may become a great occasion of recognition for Anna and Kate.

By now the three storylines of the liturgy have been introduced: wholeness, glory of God and living a particular lifestyle. Suffering and healing are particularly prone to be present in the storyline of wholeness, although we have seen that the liturgical text does not emphasize these aspects of wholeness. Nevertheless, the potential to address suffering is most present in this storyline. Again, it needs pastoral sensitivity to draw out the possibilities to connect to narratives of suffering.

The next element in the liturgy, the Gloria, may connect to people who suffer. The emphasis is on the glory of God, which might relate to situations of suffering already, because it points to something beyond ourselves and therefore also beyond the story of suffering. Moreover, Jesus is glorified as the Lamb of God who takes away the sin of the world. If suffering is included in 'the sin of the world,' then the prayer to 'have mercy on us' might be a cry from the depths of suffering.

After the Gloria, a period of silence may follow, before the Collect is said. Suffering silences. Compassion does not always need words. The silent prayer of this moment is an opportunity to be silent with those who are silenced by their suffering. It should be noted, however, that the liturgy is at a high point with saying or singing the Gloria, and therefore it is not self-evident to use this time of silent prayer as a time of silent lament. The Collect can also include a reference to suffering, but this is not necessarily so.

The liturgy moves on with the Liturgy of the Word, starting with the readings and a sermon, while in between the readings a psalm or canticle or song may be recited or sung. The readings tell the story of God, and the Gospel reading particularly tells the Jesus story. It is quite likely that the divine and human stories intersect. Even when this is not self-evident, the sermon is the occasion *par excellence* to draw out the points of connections between the stories, and Anna and Kate may find their own stories in the story of God. This part of the liturgy also provides the opportunity for psalms and songs of lament. Psalms of lament may even be prescribed by the lectionary.[7]

Following the sermon, the Creed is said. It renders succinctly the story of God in relation to people as Christians have believed it for many centuries already. Reciting the Creed is an act of remembrance. It remembers the mighty deeds of God, but it also remembers the faith of all ages and places, and therefore connects Anna and Kate with the larger faith community. The Creed does not mention suffering as major negative life experiences on the part of people, but it does mention the suffering of Jesus. The Creed provides the grand narrative in which Anna and Kate can find a place for their story.

Understanding the Creed in this way provides a seemly context for the prayers of intercession, which now follow. In these prayers the community cries out to God, together with Anna and Kate and others who suffer. Here, the lament may be uttered full force. In any case, this is one of the most obvious places to tell the human story of suffering and bring that into the liturgy.

The liturgy now moves on with the Liturgy of the Sacrament. The liturgist might like to use "a suitable sentence," and then say the peace. This suitable sentence might connect the peace to the prayers of intercession. It might address Anna and Kate in their situation. If used sensitively, the peace might be exchanged in the sense of *shalom*, denoting wholeness. The liturgy of the Sacrament starts with a great opportunity to connect the wholeness that comes from God with those who long for it.

The table is prepared while a hymn or song may be sung, and a collection might be taken at this point. This is a moment in the liturgy that moves towards remembering the suffering of God in Christ. This becomes visible in bringing forward the bread and wine. If the intercessions were used to bring out the suffering of people, and the exchange of peace has picked up on that, the moment of preparing the table may mark the transition from the stories of suffering people to the story of the suffering God (although in neither story is the other absent). The transition may be highlighted by an appropriate hymn or song, or maybe by other things, such as a poem, a video clip, or silence. Because this is a moment of transition from one story to the other, the connection between the two might be emphasized. The flexibility of the liturgy, as proposed by *Common Worship*, invites to creatively think about the possibilities for making connections.

The Eucharistic prayer highlights the suffering of Christ. His death and resurrection are primarily interpreted as those acts that reconciled sinners unto God. Sometimes the text points to the interpretation of healing and wholeness for those who suffer, but that is not the main thrust of the Eucharistic prayers, although in some more than in others.

Jesus' identification with those who suffer is most visible in the breaking of the bread and the pouring out of the wine. When Anna and Kate take the bread and the wine, God's suffering and Anna and Kate's suffering intersect in a metaphorical and physical way. In terms of the four steps a community takes to foster reconciliation, here the third step of making connections happens (cf. Chapter 10). The prayer after communion, which is said by all, reflects the fourth step of commissioning:

> May we who share Christ's body live his risen life;
> we who drink his cup bring life to others;
> we whom the Spirit lights give light to the world.

This version of the post-communion offers a number of points for Anna and Kate to identify with in their situation, especially if they have experienced the hope of the suffering, death and resurrection of Christ that has been expressed powerfully in the Eucharist.

As the Creed remembers the grand story of the mighty deeds of God, so the Eucharist remembers God's suffering in Christ for humankind. The Creed connected Anna and Kate with the grand story of God and with the faith community; the Eucharist connects their story firmly with the Jesus story. That story tells them that God is with them in their suffering, though the liturgical text could express this much more strongly than it does. That story also gives hope because Jesus has overcome suffering and death. The Eucharist is not only an act of remembrance. It is also an act of imagination. It expresses the possibility of another world, although myth and parable are both present in the story. In the liturgy, and in the Eucharist, the story world of God and the story worlds of Anna and Kate meet, and transformation can take place. Perhaps transformation happens only over time and after many liturgical performances in which the human and the divine stories are told over and over again. But every act of liturgical storytelling hints at the possibility of reconciliation, and every act of storytelling allows Anna and Kate to imagine the possibility of a better world.

Finally, the people are dismissed. The minister chooses a suitable blessing, perhaps one that connects God's blessing to the imagined better world. The blessing makes clear that the divine and human narratives remain connected, also after the liturgical performance is done. To paraphrase the blessing given in the text: 'The peace of God keeps Anna and Kate's hearts and minds in the knowledge and love of God.' The liturgy has proved this knowledge and love to be one that accompanies Anna and Kate in their suffering and that it creates a safe zone that allows them to tell their story (cf. the first and second step of a spirituality of reconciliation, see Chapter 10).

Not only does the blessing of God go with Anna and Kate. A communal and liturgical spirituality of reconciliation does not leave suffering people alone, for this is a spirituality, not a strategy or technique. The liturgy is embedded in the community and the wider life of the church. So the final commissioning does not send Anna and Kate away all by themselves but keeps them in the community. And so, finally, the people are commissioned to go in the peace of Christ. Hopefully, the liturgy has brought Anna and Kate to a place where they can join the response: "Thanks be to God."

Notes

1 For the methodological underpinning of generalization from the type of research in this book, see Jennifer Mason, *Qualitative Researching* (London, Thousand Oaks, CA, New Delhi: SAGE Publications, 2002), 194–200; John Swinton and Harriet Mowat, *Practical Theology and Qualitative Research* (London: SCM Press, 2006), 46–49.
2 I claim this point only for churches in a Western context.
3 See also van Ommen, "A Narrative Understanding."

4 Hogue, *Remembering*, 99.
5 For a similar 'tour' through the liturgy, see James K.A. Smith, *Desiring the Kingdom: Worship, Worldview, and Cultural Formation* (Grand Rapids, MI: Baker Academic, 2009), Chap. 5. Smith gives an ethnographic 'thick' description of liturgy in which narrative has an important role, cf. p. 63–71. Extensive commentary on the different parts of the Eucharistic liturgies in *Common Worship* can be found in Bradshaw *et al.*, "Holy Communion"; and Perham, *New Handbook of Pastoral Liturgy*, Pt 3. Bradshaw *et al.* show how the rites in *Common Worship* relate to previous liturgical revisions and to ancient liturgies. Perham gives general comments and practical advice.
6 Procter-Smith, *In Her. Own Rite*, 67–71. The purpose of our description of liturgy is not to advance a feminist critique on liturgy; the important thing to note here is that all actions, including the lay out of the liturgical space, communicate a lot, even before anything is said verbally. Especially when suffering persons are present, and that is usually the case, sensitivity is necessary.
7 However, Lester Meyer has demonstrated that lament psalms are relatively underrepresented by most lectionaries. See "A Lack of Laments in the Church's Use of the Psalter"; cf. Billman and Migliore, *Rachel's Cry*, 13.

Bibliography

Abernethy, Alexis D., ed. *Worship That Changes Lives: Multidisciplinary and Congregational Perspectives on Spiritual Transformation*. Grand Rapids, MI: Baker Academic, 2008.
Allen, Leslie C. "Zkr I." *New International Dictionary of Old Testament Theology and Exegesis*. Carlisle: Paternoster Press, 1997.
Allman, Mark J. "Eucharist, Ritual & Narrative: Formation of Individual and Communal Moral Character." *Journal of Ritual Studies*, 14(1) (1 January 2000): 60–68.
Anderson, E. Byron. "Memory, Tradition, and the Re-Membering of Suffering." *Religious Education*, 105(2) (1 March 2010): 124–139.
Anderson, Herbert, and Edward Foley. *Mighty Stories, Dangerous Rituals: Weaving Together the Human and Divine*. San Francisco, CA: Jossey-Bass, 1998.
"A Time to Heal: A Report for the House of Bishops on the Healing Ministry." London: Church House Publishing, 2000.
Balentine, Samuel E. "Enthroned on the Praises and Laments of Israel." In *The Lord's Prayer: Perspectives for Reclaiming Christian Prayer*, 20–35. Grand Rapids, MI: William B. Eerdmans, 1993.
Baptism, Eucharist and Ministry. Faith and Order Paper 111. Geneva: World Council of Churches, 1982.
Barentsen, Jack. *Emerging Leadership in the Pauline Mission: A Social Identity Perspective on Local Leadership Development in Corinth and Ephesus*. Eugene, OR: Wipf and Stock Publishers, 2011.
Barnard, Marcel, Johan Cilliers, and Cas Wepener. "Worship in the Network Culture: Liturgical Ritual Studies. Fields and Methods, Concepts and Metaphors." *Liturgia Condenda*, 28. Leuven: Peeters, 2014.
Bartels, K.H. and C. Brown. "Remember, Remembrance." *New International Dictionary of New Testament Theology*. Carlisle: Paternoster Press, 1992.
Bates, J. Barrington. "Expressing What Christians Believe: Anglican Principles for Liturgical Revision." *Anglican Theological Review*, 92(3) (June 1, 2010): 455–480.
Bearden, Ronald O. and Richard K. Olsen. "Narrative Prayer, Identity and Community." *Asbury Theological Journal*, 60(1) (1 March 2005): 55–66.
Betenbaugh, Helen and Marjorie Procter-Smith. "Disabling the Lie: Prayers of Truth and Transformation." In *Human Disability and the Service of God: Reassessing Religious Practice*, edited by Nancy L. Eiesland and Don E. Saliers, 281–303. Nashville, TN: Abingdon Press, 1998.
Billman, Kathleen D. and Daniel L. Migliore. *Rachel's Cry: Prayer of Lament and Rebirth of Hope*. Eugene, OR: Wipf and Stock Publishers, 1999.

Bohlmeijer, Ernst. *De Verhalen Die We Leven: Narratieve Psychologie Als Methode.* Amsterdam: Boom, 2007.
Botha, Cynthia. "Worship and Anglican Identity – a Résumé." In *Anglican Liturgical Identity: Papers from the Prague Meeting of the International Anglican Liturgical Consultation*, edited by Christopher Irvine, 12–19. Joint Liturgical Studies, 65. Norwich: SCM-Canterbury Press, 2008.
Bradshaw, Paul. "Anamnesis in Modern Eucharistic Debate." In *Memory and History in Christianity and Judaism*, 73–84. Notre Dame, IN: University of Notre Dame Press, 2001.
———. "Services and Service Books." In *Companion to Common Worship*, edited by Paul Bradshaw, 1:1–21. Alcuin Club Collections 78. London: SPCK, 2001.
Bradshaw, Paul, Gordon Giles, and Simon Kershaw. "Holy Communion." In *Companion to Common Worship*, edited by Paul Bradshaw, 1:98–147. Alcuin Club Collections 78. London: SPCK, 2001.
Brown, Sally A. and Patrick D. Miller. *Lament: Reclaiming Practices in Pulpit, Pew, and Public Square.* Louisville, KY: Westminster John Knox Press, 2005.
Brueggemann, Walter. "Formfulness of Grief." *Interpretation*, 31(3) (1 July 1977): 263–275.
———. *The Message of the Psalms.* Minneapolis, MN: Augsburg Press, 1984.
Buchanan, Colin, ed. *Anglican Eucharistic Liturgies 1985–2010: The Authorized Rites of the Anglican Communion.* London: Canterbury Press Norwich, 2011.
Chauvet, Louis-Marie. *The Sacraments: The Word of God at the Mercy of the Body.* Collegeville, PA: Liturgical Press, 2001.
Cherry, Constance M. *The Worship Architect: A Blueprint for Designing Culturally Relevant and Biblically Faithful Services.* Grand Rapids, MI: Baker Academic, 2010.
Childs, Brevard S. *Memory and Tradition in Israel.* Chatham: W. & J. MacKay, 1962.
Chopp, Rebecca S. *Saving Work: Feminist Practices of Theological Education.* Louisville, KY: Westminster John Knox Press, 1995.
Clebsch, William A. and Charles R. Jaekle. *Pastoral Care in Historical Perspective.* 1st edn. Englewood Cliffs, NJ: Prentice-Hall, 1964.
Common Worship: Services and Prayers for the Church of England. Church House Publishing, 2000.
Cooper-White, Pamela. "Suffering." In *The Wiley-Blackwell Companion to Practical Theology*, edited by Bonnie J. Miller-McLemore, 1st edn, 23–31. Malden: Wiley-Blackwell, 2012.
———. *The Cry of Tamar: Violence Against Women and the Church's Response.* 2nd edn. Minneapolis, MN: Fortress Press, 2012.
Crites, Stephen D. "The Narrative Quality of Experience." *Journal of the American Academy of Religion*, 39(3) (1 September 1971): 291–311.
Crossan, John Dominic. *The Dark Interval: Towards a Theology of Story.* Sonoma, CA: Polebridge Press, 1994.
Dahl, Nils Alstrup. *Jesus in the Memory of the Early Church: Essays.* Minneapolis, MN: Augsburg Pub. House, 1976.
Daniel, Alastair K. *Storytelling across the Primary Curriculum.* London: Routledge, 2012.
Dawn, Marva J. *Reaching Out without Dumbing Down: A Theology of Worship for the Turn-of-the-Century Culture.* Grand Rapids, MI: William B. Eerdmans, 1995.
Day, Juliette J. *Reading the Liturgy: An Exploration of Texts in Christian Worship.* London and New York: Bloomsbury, 2014.
Dijk, Denise and Joke Bruinsma-de Beer. "Sprekende Vrouwen: Narrativiteit in de Liturgie Vanuit Feministisch Perspectief." In *De Praxis Als Verhaal: Narrativiteit En*

Praktische Theologie, edited by Reinder Ruard Ganzevoort. Kampen Studies. Kampen: Kok, 1998.
Dillard, Annie. *Teaching a Stone to Talk: Expeditions and Encounters*. New York: HarperCollins, 1982.
Earey, Mark and Gilly Myers, eds. *Common Worship Today: An Illustrated Guide to Common Worship*. London: HarperCollins, 2001.
Eiesland, Nancy L. and Don E. Saliers, eds. *Human Disability and the Service of God: Reassessing Religious Practice*. Nashville, TN: Abingdon Press, 1998.
Farwell, James W. *This is the Night: Suffering, Salvation, and the Liturgies of Holy Week*. New York and London: T&T Clark, 2004.
Fortune, Marie M. "The Transformation of Suffering: A Biblical and Theological Perspective." In *Violence against Women and Children: A Christian Theological Sourcebook*, edited by Carol J. Adams and Marie M. Fortune, 85–91. New York: Continuum, 1995.
Fretheim, Terence E. *God and World in the Old Testament: A Relational Theology of Creation*. Nashville, TN: Abingdon Press, 2005.
———. *The Suffering of God: An Old Testament Perspective*. Overtures to Biblical Theology. Philadelphia, PA: Fortress Press, 1984.
Gandolfo, Elizabeth O'Donnell. "Remembering the Massacre at El Mozote: A Case for the Dangerous Memory of Suffering as Christian Formation in Hope." *International Journal of Practical Theology*, 17(1) (1 January 2013): 62–87.
Ganzevoort, R. Ruard. "Familiaal Geweld Tegen Kinderen: Theologisch-Pastorale Reflecties." In *Wanneer "Liefde" Toeslaat: Over Geweld En Onrecht in Gezinnen*, edited by A. Dillen, Roger Burggraeve, Johan De Tavernier, Jo Hanssens, and Didier Pollefeyt, 120–132. Leuven: Davidsfonds, 2006.
———. "God Voor Schuldigen?" In *Vergeef Me … Verzoening Tussen Mensen En God*, edited by W. Smouter and C. Blom, 84–96. Zoetermeer: Boekencentrum, 2001.
———. "Narrative Approaches." In *The Wiley-Blackwell Companion to Practical Theology*, edited by B. Miller-McLemore, 1st edn, 214–223. Malden: Wiley-Blackwell, 2012.
———. "Reading by the Lines: Proposal for a Narrative Analytical Technique in Empirical Theology." *Journal of Empirical Theology*, 11(2) (1998): 23–40.
———. "Religious Coping Reconsidered. Part Two: A Narrative Reformulation." *Journal of Psychology and Theology*, 26(3) (1998): 276–286.
Ganzevoort, R. Ruard and Jan Visser. *Zorg Voor Het Verhaal: Achtergrond, Methode En Inhoud van Pastorale Begeleiding*. Zoetermeer: Meinema, 2007.
Ganzevoort, Ruard. "De Praxis Als Verhaal: Introductie Op Een Narratief Perspectief." In *De Praxis Als Verhaal: Narrativiteit En Praktische Theologie*, edited by Reinder Ruard Ganzevoort, 7–27. Kampen Studies. Kampen: Kok, 1998.
———. "Hoe Leest Gij? Een Narratief Model." In *De Praxis Als Verhaal: Narrativiteit En Praktische Theologie*, edited by Reinder Ruard Ganzevoort, 71–90. Kampen Studies. Kampen: Kok, 1998.
Gergen, Kenneth J. *Realities and Relationships: Soundings in Social Construction*. Reprint edition. Cambridge, MA: Harvard University Press, 1997.
Gerkin, Charles V. *The Living Human Document: Re-Visioning Pastoral Counseling in a Hermeneutical Mode*. Nashville, TN: Abingdon Press, 1984.
Gibaut, John St H. "The Narrative Nature of Liturgy." *Theoforum*, 32(3) (1 October 2001): 341–365.
Gittoes, Julie. *Anamnesis and the Eucharist: Contemporary Anglican Approaches*. Aldershot: Ashgate, 2008.

Bibliography

Goffman, Erving. "Footing." In *Forms of Talk*, 124–159. Oxford: Basil Blackwell, 1981.

Gordon-Taylor, Benjamin. "Liturgy." In *The Study of Liturgy and Worship: An Alcuin Guide*, edited by Juliette Day and Benjamin Gordon-Taylor, 12–20. An Alcuin Guide. London: SPCK, 2013.

Graham, Elaine, Heather Walton, and Frances Ward. *Theological Reflection: Methods*. London: SCM Press, 2005.

Grimes, Ronald L. "Infelicitious Performances and Ritual Criticism." *Semeia*, 41 (1 January 1988): 103–122.

Groves, Phil and Angharad Parry Jones. *Living Reconciliation*. Cincinnati, OH: Forward Movement, 2014.

Gschwandtner, Crina. "Toward a Ricoeurian Hermeneutics of Liturgy." *Worship*, 86(6), (2012): 482–505.

Gutierrez, Gustavo. *A Theology of Liberation: History, Politics, and Salvation*. Translated by Caridad Inda and John Eagleson. Revised edn. Maryknoll, NY: Orbis Books, 1988.

Harasta, Eva and Brian Brock, eds. *Evoking Lament: A Theological Discussion*. London: T&T Clark, 2009.

Helman, Charles Jeffrey. "The Emergent Revival of Sacramental Healing: An Incarnational Theology", unpublished dissertation, 2007.

Hoffman, Lawrence A. "Does God Remember? A Liturigcal Theology of Memory." In *Memory and History in Christianity and Judaism*, 41–72. Notre Dame, IN: University of Notre Dame Press, 2001.

Hogue, David A. *Remembering the Future, Imagining the Past: Story, Ritual, and the Human Brain*. Eugene, OR: Wipf and Stock Publishers, 2003.

Irvine, Christopher, ed. *Anglican Liturgical Identity: Papers from the Prague Meeting of the International Anglican Liturgical Consultation*. Joint Liturgical Studies, 65. Norwich: SCM-Canterbury Press, 2008.

———. "Introduction: Anglican Liturgical Identity." In *Anglican Liturgical Identity: Papers from the Prague Meeting of the International Anglican Liturgical Consultation*, edited by Christopher Irvine, 3–11. Joint Liturgical Studies 65. Norwich: SCM-Canterbury Press, 2008.

Johnston-Barrett, Melissa. "Making Space: Silence, Voice, and Suffering." *Word & World*, 25(3) (1 June 2005): 328–337.

Keane, Webb. "Religious Language." *Annual Review of Anthropology*, 26 (1997): 47–71.

Kelleher, Margaret Mary. "Liturgical Theology: A Task and a Method." *Worship*, 62(1) (1 January 1988): 2–25.

Ladrière, Jean. "The Performativity of Liturgical Language." *Concilium New Series*, 2(9) (1973): 50–62.

Lange, Dirk G. *Trauma Recalled: Liturgy, Disruption, and Theology*. Minneapolis, MN: Fortress Press, 2010.

Lloyd, Trevor. "Liturgy Unbound by the Book." In *Anglican Liturgical Identity: Papers from the Prague Meeting of the International Anglican Liturgical Consultation*, edited by Christopher Irvine, 20–30. Joint Liturgical Studies, 65. Norwich: SCM-Canterbury Press, 2008.

Lukken, Gerard. *Rituals in Abundance: Critical Reflections on the Place, Form and Identity of Christian Ritual in Our Culture*. Leuven and Dudley: Peeters, 2005.

Mason, Jennifer. *Qualitative Researching*. London, Thousand Oaks, CA, New Delhi: SAGE Publications, 2002.

Metz, Johann Baptist. *Faith in History and Society: Toward a Practical Fundamental Theology*. New York: The Crossroad Publishing Company, 2007.

———. *Glaube in Geschichte Und Gesellschaft. Studien Zu Einer Praktischen Fundamentaltheologie*. 5th edn. Mainz: Matthias Grünewald Verlag, 1992.
Meyer, Lester. "A Lack of Laments in the Church's Use of the Psalter." *Lutheran Quarterly*, 7(1) (1993): 67–78.
Meyers, Ruth A. "Mission." In *The Study of Liturgy and Worship*, edited by Juliette Day and Benjamin Gordon-Taylor, 202–211. An Alcuin Guide. London: SPCK, 2013.
Mitchell, Leonel L. "Essential Worship." *Anglican Theological Review*, 79(4) (1 September 1997): 494–505.
Morrill, Bruce T. *Anamnesis as Dangerous Memory: Political and Liturgical Theology in Dialogue*. Collegeville, MN: Pueblo Books, 2000.
———. *Divine Worship and Human Healing: Liturgical Theology at the Margins of Life and Death*. Collegeville, MN: Liturgical Press, 2009.
Nichols, Bridget. "Scripture, Time and Narrative in the Proper Prefaces of the Church of England's 'Common Worship.'" *Studia Liturgica*, 39(1) (1 January 2009): 122–128.
Nickoloff, James B., ed. *Gustavo Gutierrez: Essential Writings*. Maryknoll, NY: Orbis Books, 1996.
Noonan, Daphne. "The Ripple Effect: A Story of the Transformational Nature of Narrative Care." In *Storying Later Life: Issues, Investigations, and Interventions in Narrative Gerontology*, edited by Gary Kenyon, Ernst Bohlmeijer and William L. Randall, 354–365. New York: Oxford University Press, 2011.
Osmer, Richard. *Practical Theology: An Introduction*. Grand Rapids, MI: William B. Eerdmans, 2008.
———. *The Teaching Ministry of Congregations*. Louisville, KY: Westminster John Knox Press, 2005.
Pargament, Kenneth I. "Patterns of Positive and Negative Religious Coping with Major Life Stressors." *Journal for the Scientific Study of Religion*, 37(4) (December 1998): 710–724.
———. *The Psychology of Religion and Coping: Theory, Research, Practice*. 1st edn. New York: The Guilford Press, 1997.
Pargament, Kenneth I., G. Koenig, and Lisa M. Perez. "The Many Methods of Religious Coping: Development and Initial Validation of the RCOPE." *Journal of Clinical Psychology*, 56(4) (2000): 519–543.
Park, C.L. and S. Folkman. "Meaning in the Context of Stress and Coping." *Review of General Psychology*, 1(2) (1997): 115–144.
Park, Crystal L. "Making Sense of the Meaning Literature: An Integrative Review of Meaning Making and its Effects on Adjustment to Stressful Life Events." *Psychological Bulletin*, 136(2) (2010): 257–301.
Parnell, Vereene. "Risking Redemption: A Case Study in HIV/AIDS and the Healing of Christian Liturgy." In *Human Disability and the Service of God: Reassessing Religious Practice*, edited by Nancy L. Eiesland and Don E. Saliers, 249–266. Nashville, TN: Abingdon Press, 1998.
"Patterns for Worship: A Report by the Liturgical Commission of the General Synod of the Church of England." Church House Publishing, 1989.
Pembroke, Neil. *Pastoral Care in Worship: Liturgy and Psychology in Dialogue*. London: T&T Clark, 2010.
Perham, Michael. "Liturgical Revision 1981–2000." In *Companion to Common Worship*, edited by Paul Bradshaw, 1: 22–37. Alcuin Club Collections 78. London: SPCK, 2001.
———. *New Handbook of Pastoral Liturgy*. London: SPCK, 2000.
———., ed. *The Renewal of Common Prayer: Unity and Diversity in Church of England Worship*. London: SPCK and Church House Publishing, 1993.

Perillo, Jesse. "The Destructive Nature of Suffering and the Liturgical Refashioning of the Person." Ph.D., Loyola University Chicago, 2011.

Peterson, Eugene H. *Five Smooth Stones for Pastoral Work*. Reprint edn. Grand Rapids, MI: William B. Eerdmans, 1992.

Power, David N. *The Eucharistic Mystery: Revitalizing the Tradition*. New York: Crossroad Publishing Company, 1992.

Procter-Smith, Marjorie. *In Her Own Rite: Constructing Feminist Liturgical Tradition*. Order of Saint Luke Publications, 2000.

———. *Praying with Our Eyes Open: Engendering Feminist Liturgical Prayer*. Nashville, TN: Abingdon Press, 1995.

———. "'Reorganizing Victimization': The Intersection between Liturgy and Domestic Violence." In *Violence against Women and Children*, edited by Carol J. Adams and Fortune, Marie M., 428–443. New York: Continuum, 1995.

Ramshaw, Elaine. *Ritual and Pastoral Care*. Philadelphia, PA: Fortress Press, 1987.

Ramshaw, Gail. "A Look at New Anglican Eucharistic Prayers." *Worship*, 86(2) (1 March 2012): 161–167.

———. *Reviving Sacred Speech: The Meaning of Liturgical Language: Second Thoughts on Christ in Sacred Speech*. Order of Saint Luke Publishing, 2000.

———. "The Place of Lament Within Praise: Theses for Discussion." *Worship*, 61 (1987): 317–322.

Ricoeur, Paul. "The Language of Faith." In *The Philosophy of Paul Ricoeur: An Anthology of His Work*, edited by Charles E. Reagan and David Stewart, 223–238. Boston, MA: Beacon Press, 1978.

Rienstra, Debra and Ron Rienstra. *Worship Words: Discipling Language for Faithful Ministry*. Grand Rapids, MI: Baker Academic, 2009.

Riessman, Catherine Kohler. *Narrative Methods for the Human Sciences*. Los Angeles, CA, London, New Delhi, Singapore: SAGE Publications, 2008.

Saldana, Johnny. *Thinking Qualitatively: Methods of Mind*. Thousand Oaks, CA: SAGE Publications, 2015.

Saliers, Don E. "Liturgy and Ethics: Some New Beginnings." In *Liturgy and the Moral Self: Humanity at Full Stretch Before God*, edited by E. Byron Anderson and Bruce T. Morrill, 15–35. Collegeville, PA: The Liturgical Press, 1998.

———. "Toward a Spirituality of Inclusiveness." In *Human Disability and the Service of God: Reassessing Religious Practice*, edited by Nancy L. Eiesland and Don E. Saliers, 19–31. Nashville, TN: Abingdon Press, 1998.

———. *Worship as Theology: Foretaste of Glory Divine*. Nashville, TN: Abingdon Press, 1994.

Scarry, Elaine. *The Body in Pain: The Making and Unmaking of the World*. New York: Oxford University Press, 1985.

Schaller, Joseph J. "Performative Language Theory: An Exercise in the Analysis of Ritual." *Worship*, 62(5) (1 September 1988): 415–432.

Schattauer, Thomas H. "Liturgical Studies: Disciplines, Perspectives, Teaching." *International Journal of Practical Theology*, 11(1) (April 2007): 106–137.

Schreiter, Robert J. *Reconciliation: Mission and Ministry in a Changing Social Order*. Maryknoll, NY; Cambridge, MA: Orbis Books, 1992.

———. *The Ministry of Reconciliation: Spirituality & Strategies*. Maryknoll, NY: Orbis Books, 1998.

Senn, Frank C. *The People's Work: A Social History of the Liturgy*. Minneapolis, MN: Fortress Press, 2006.

Smith, James K.A. *Desiring the Kingdom: Worship, Worldview, and Cultural Formation*. Grand Rapids, MI: Baker Academic, 2009.
Smith, James K.A. *Imagining the Kingdom: How Worship Works. Vol. 2. Cultural Liturgies*. Grand Rapids, MI.: Baker Academic, 2013.
Smith, Susan Marie. "The Scandal of Particularity Writ Small: Principles for Indigenizing Liturgy in the Local Context." *Anglican Theological Review*, 88(3) (1 June 2006): 375–396.
Stosur, David A. "Liturgy and (post) Modernity: A Narrative Response to Guardini's Challenge." *Worship*, 77(1) (1 January 2003): 22–41.
Swain, Storm. *Trauma and Transformation at Ground Zero: A Pastoral Theology*. Minneapolis, MN: Fortress Press, 2011.
Swinton, John. *Raging with Compassion: Pastoral Responses to the Problem of Evil*. Grand Rapids, MI: William B. Eerdmans, 2007.
Swinton, John and Harriet Mowat. *Practical Theology and Qualitative Research*. London: SCM Press, 2006.
Tamez, Elsa. "Job: Dat Is Onrechtvaardig, Roep Ik, Maar Niemand Gaat Erop In!" *Concilium*, 5 (1997): 63–71.
"Transforming Worship: Living the New Creation: A Report by the Liturgical Commission," 2007.
Tripp, D.H. "Liturgy and Pastoral Service." In *The Study of Liturgy*, revised edn, 565–590. London and New York: SPCK and Oxford University Press, 1992.
Van Dusseldorp, Kees. *Preken Tussen de Verhalen: Een Homiletische Doordenking van Narrativiteit*. Kampen: Kok, 2012.
van Ommen, A.L. "Anglican Liturgy and Community: The Influence of the Experience of Community on the Experience of Liturgy as a Challenge for Liturgical Renewal and Formation." *Studia Liturgica*, 45(2) (2015): 221–234.
van Ommen, Léon. "A Narrative Understanding of Anglican Liturgy in Times of Suffering: The Narrative Approach of Ruard Ganzevoort Applied to Common Worship." *Questions Liturgiques/Studies in Liturgy*, 1–2 (2015): 64–81.
Volf, Miroslav. *Exclusion and Embrace: A Theological Exploration of Identity, Otherness, and Reconciliation*. Nashville, TN: Abingdon Press, 1996.
———. *The End of Memory: Remembering Rightly in a Violent World*. Grand Rapids, MI and Cambridge: William B. Eerdmans, 2006.
Walton, Heather. "Speaking in Signs: Narrative and Trauma in Pastoral Theology." *Scottish Journal of Healthcare Chaplaincy*, 5(2) (2002): 2–5.
Walton, Janet R. "The Missing Element of Women's Experience." In *Changing Face of Jewish and Christian Worship in North America*, edited by Bradshaw, Paul F. and Hoffman, Lawrence A., 199–217. Notre Dame, IN: University of Notre Dame Press, 1991.
Wegman, H.A.J. *Riten En Mythen: Liturgie in de Geschiedenis van Het Christendom*. Kampen: Kok, 1991.
Weil, Louis. *A Theology of Worship*. Lanham, MD: Cowley, 2002.
———. "'Remembering the Future': Reflections on Liturgy and Ecclesiology." In *Anglican Liturgical Identity: Papers from the Prague Meeting of the International Anglican Liturgical Consultation*, edited by Christopher Irvine, 31–45. Joint Liturgical Studies, 65. Norwich: SCM-Canterbury Press, 2008.
Wengraf, Tom. *Qualitative Research Interviewing: Biographic Narrative and Semi-Structured Methods*. London, Thousand Oaks, CA, New Delhi: SAGE Publications, 2001.
Westermann, Claus. "The Role of the Lament in the Theology of the Old Testament." *Interpretation*, 28 (1974): 20–38.

Willimon, William H. *Worship as Pastoral Care*. Nashville, TN: Abingdon Press, 1979.

Witvliet, John D. *Worship Seeking Understanding: Windows into Christian Practice*. Grand Rapids, MI: Baker Academic, 2003.

Wolterstorff, Nicholas. *Lament for a Son*. Grand Rapids, MI: William B. Eerdmans, 1987.

———. "Liturgy, Justice, and Tears." *Worship*, 62(5) (1 September 1988): 386–403.

Zimmerman, Joyce Ann. *Liturgy and Hermeneutics: American Essays in Liturgy*. Collegeville, PA: The Liturgical Press, 1999.

———. *Liturgy as Language of Faith: A Liturgical Methodology in the Mode of Paul Ricoeur's Textual Hermeneutics*. Lanham, MD: University Press of America, 1988.

———. *Liturgy as Living Faith: A Liturgical Spirituality*. Scranton, PA: University of Scranton Press, 1993.

Index

Abernethy, Alexis 3–4
absence of God 89
absolution 28, 66–7
accompaniment 133–4
addressing suffering through liturgy 57–68
after-liturgy 57
agency 26, 100, 109, 134
Allen, Leslie 97, 99
Allman, Mark 14, 27
allowing mourning 1–20; approach to liturgy 12–14; churches and participants 14–16; status quaestionis 3–4; tension between liturgy and suffering 2–3
Alternative Service Book 7–10
Amalorpavadass 10
ambiguity 86
analysis of liturgy 21–82; empirical perspectives 69–82; lens of narrative–ritual polarities 46–56; narrative analysis of liturgy 23–45; themes in addressing suffering through liturgy 57–68
anamnesis 13, 98–9, 106–7, 127, 150
Anderson, E. Byron 95, 113
Anderson, Herbert 35, 46–8, 51–9, 79–80, 85–93, 106–7, 118–24, 132–5, 141–2, 148–51
Anglican liturgy 2, 5–11, 76–80
appropriation 119–20
ASB *see Alternative Service Book*
aspects of spirituality of reconciliation 132–5
atmosphere 36–7, 150
audiences 25, 28–30, 42–3, 78; *see also* authors/audiences
authenticity 64, 95
authors/audiences 25–30, 76–7; audiences 28–30; storytellers 25–8

Balentine, Samuel 108
Bartels, K.H. 98–9
Bates, J. Barrington 7
Beauty and the Beast 47
Benelux 3, 62, 148
Bernstein, Leonard 140
beyond liturgical remembering 99–100
biblical concept of remembering 97–8
Billman, Kathleen 3, 108–9, 111
Boisen, Anton 11
Bonhoeffer, Dietrich 139
Book of Common Prayer 2, 7–8, 10, 35–6
Botha, Cynthia 9
Brock, Brian 4
brokenness 57–61, 66–7, 86, 121, 124, 139–41
Brueggemann, Walter 110

Calvin, John 92
celebrating Eucharist 8–9, 14, 27–32, 35–42, 49–55, 58–9, 62, 69–77, 80–82, 91–2, 95–107, 125–7, 136–40
Chauvet, Louis-Marie 125–6
Childs, Brevard C. 97–8
Chopp, Rebecca 100, 117
Christ's healing 123–8, 153
Christ's suffering 64–5, 70, 81, 105, 126–8, 136–7, 147–9, 154–5
churches participating 14–16
Civil Rights Movement 128
clergy awareness 60–61
commissioning 135
Common Worship 2–14, 25–8, 31, 50, 57–8, 70–71, 78, 126, 137, 146–51
communal lament 111
communal meanings of liturgy 51–2
communal spirituality of reconciliation 132–45

Index

communities' suffering 107–14
community 57–8, 138–41, 151–2
comparison of narrative elements 34–43; audience 42–3; experience/genre 36–7; perspective 35–6; relational positioning 40–42; role assignment 38–40; structure 34–5
compassion 92, 106, 139, 152–3
competence 42–3, 77, 81
concealing 49–50
connections 85–94, 134–5; human tears, divine tears 89–93; weaving together human and divine stories 85–9
contrast between churches 62
Cooper-White, Pamela 11
covenantal theology 97–8
Cranmer, Thomas 10
Crites, Stephen 75
Crossan, John Dominic 46

dangerous memory 96, 99–100, 111–14
Daniel, Alastair 76, 120
The Dark Interval 46
Day, Juliette J. 29–30, 34, 36–7, 52–3, 75–6
dealing with tragedy 1–2
deductive liturgy 123
defining liturgy 6
delusion 117–18
denominational unity 7
der Ganz Andere 88
dialogue with God 29
Dillard, Annie 41
Diocese in Europe 76
disastrous liturgy 122
disconnection 4
distancing self from self 119
distinguishing polarities 55
divine stories 85–9
doing justice to stories 142

Eiesland, Nancy L. 3
El Mozote massacre 96
emancipation 73–4
embedded liturgy 53–4, 75, 80, 99, 132, 141–2, 155
empathy 87, 106–7
empirical approach to liturgy 12–14
empirical perspectives on suffering 69–82; central question 69–76; conclusion 76–82
empowerment 118
erosion of meaning 136
ethics of foot-washing 11

Eucharist 8–9, 14, 27–32, 35–42, 49–55, 58–9, 62, 69–77, 80–82, 91–2, 95–107, 125–7, 136–40; and remembering 98–9
eucharistia 92–3, 107, 137
exclusion 86–7
Exodus 89–90, 97, 106
expatriate settings 62–3
experience of community 57–8, 138–41
experience of God 61–2, 89–90; *see also* relationship with God
experience of liturgy in suffering times 69–70
experience of narrative 24, 36–7
experiences other than liturgy 64

Faith in the City 8
fall of Adam and Eve 66
Farwell, James 3
Foley, Edward 35, 46–8, 51–9, 79–80, 85–93, 106–7, 118–24, 132–5, 141–2, 148–51
forgiveness 38, 66–7
Fortune, Marie 128
Fresh Expressions 2–3
Fretheim, Terence 103–5, 107–8, 125
Funk, Robert 46

Gandolfo, Elizabeth O'Donnell 96
Ganzevoort, R. Ruard 14, 23–36, 42–6, 66, 77–9, 95–6, 150–51
General Synod viii–8, 36, 50, 58, 151
genre 24, 36–7
genuine encounters 99
Gerkin, Charles 11
Gibaut, John 13–14
glory of God 30–31, 33–4, 37–9, 43, 64, 78, 147, 153
God's narrative space 103–7
Goffman, Erving 29
grace of imagination 119
grafting 27, 57, 60, 73, 75, 82, 118, 137, 147, 152
Gschwandtner, Crina 119–20

half-truths 122
Harasta, Eva 4
healing 12, 63–4, 82, 89–91, 117–31; in Christ 123–8
heart of narrative understanding 135–7
Hogue, David 113, 117–18, 121, 142, 151
Holy Communion 7, 10, 50–54, 58–9, 62–3, 67, 74, 82, 92, 98–9, 126–8, 148–9, 154–5
Holy Spirit 12, 27, 32, 37, 40, 120, 123

Index

Holy Trinity 32, 152
Holy Week 3
hospitality 134, 141
House of Bishops 12
how liturgists address suffering 70
human tears/divine tears 85–94

iconoclasm 140
identity 38–40, 52, 74–6, 96, 100–101, 113–14
impassibility of God 103
incarnation 123–4, 133–4
indigenized liturgy 10
individual meanings of liturgy 51–2
inductive liturgy 73, 78, 121–4, 128, 137, 140, 147
International Anglican Liturgical Consultation 9
intertextuality 75–6
Irvine, Christopher 8–9

Johnston-Barrett, Melissa 87, 109
journey of suffering 78

Keane, Webb 26, 29
kyrie eleison 90

Lamb of God 126, 153
lament 3, 37, 89–92, 104–5, 108–13, 153; and silence 108–113
Lange, Dirk 3
language of lament 89–90, 107–14, 153
Last Supper 13, 99, 106
lens of narrative–ritual polarities 46–56; concealing and revealing 49–50; conclusion 55; individual and communal 51–2; moment and process 52–3; myth and parable 48–9; other polarities 53–5; private, public, official 50–51
Léon-Dufour, Xavier 106
Liturgical Commission viii, 6, 8, 36, 50, 58, 78, 151
liturgical professions 50
liturgical remembering 99–100
liturgical spirituality of reconciliation 132–45
liturgical theology 83–156; conclusion 146–56; connections 85–94; remembering 95–102; remembering suffering 103–16; spirituality of reconciliation 132–45; when stories meet 117–31
liturgy causing suffering 65
"Liturgy, Justice, and Tears" 89–93

Liturgy of the Sacrament 154–5
liturgy as safe place 59–60, 82
liturgy through narrative–ritual polarities 46–56
living storyline 51
Lloyd, Trevor 9
Lord's Prayer 9, 31–2
Lukken, Gerard 122–3
Luther, Martin 3

meaning-making 52, 74–6, 96, 100–101, 110–11, 113–14
meeting of liturgy and suffering 72–3
memory 95, 138; *see also* remembering
metanoia 118
Metz, Johann Baptist vii, 96, 98–100, 111
Migliore, Daniel 3, 108–9, 111
Mitchell, Leonel 10
moment 52–3
Morrill, Bruce T. 99–100, 106, 122–6, 141
mourning 1–20, 90–92, 104–5, 114, 137, 140–41
"mourning bench" 114, 133, 139, 152
mysticism 100
myth 48–9, 79–80, 86

narrative agency 100
narrative analysis of liturgy 23–45; authors and audiences 25–30; comparison of narrative elements 34–43; conclusion 43; storylines in liturgical text 30–34
narrative approach to liturgy 12–14, 150–51; revisiting 150–51
narrative concept of remembering 95–6
narrative elements 34–43, 77–9
narrative of the lie 86
narrative liturgy 151–5
narrative space for God 103–7
narrative space for people 107–14
narrative–ritual polarities 46–56
necessary irritant 65
New Testament 98–9
Nichols, Bridget 52

official meanings of liturgy 50–51
Old Testament 3, 97, 105
Order One see Common Worship
Osmer, Richard 13, 83, 107
Other, the 88, 125–6
other polarities 53–5
overhearing 29–30, 151

parable 48–9, 79–80
paradox of faithful living 53–4, 85, 87–9

168 *Index*

participants in research 14–16
particular disposition 86
paschal mystery 120, 123–6, 128
passion 41
Passover 106
pastoral awareness 60–61
pastoral care 77, 81, 118, 141–2, 148
pastoral oversight 141–2
pastoral sensitivity 152
pathos 107
Patterns for Worship 7–10
Pembroke, Neil 112, 134
Pentecost 32–3, 49, 65, 90, 103
people's suffering 107–14; identity/meaning-making 113–14; silence/lament 108–13
Perham, Michael 8–12, 27, 125
Perillo, Jesse 139
personal trespassing 66
perspective of narrative 23, 35–6
Peterson, Eugene 111, 134
poesies 77
polarities 46–56, 79–80, 82
post-communion 154–5
potential to address suffering 71–3
Power, David 3, 11, 98–9, 112
practical–theological approach to liturgy 12–14
prayers of intercession 74, 146, 151–2
primary theology vii
private meanings of liturgy 50–51
private rituals 48
process 52–3
Procter-Smith, Marjorie 118, 124
psalms of lament 37, 92, 153
psychology in religion 5, 151
public meanings of liturgy 50–51
public rituals 48
putting on a brave face 64, 81

Rachel's Cry 3
Ramshaw, Gail 3, 10
reciting the Creed 153–5
reconciliation 48–9, 79–80, 84–9, 107, 132–45, 147–8
recovery of lament 3
redeeming narrative 86
redemption 32–3, 100, 135
regaining humanity 137
regarding serious negative life events 76–82; authors/audiences 76–7; narrative elements 77–9; polarities 79–80; themes 80–82
relational positioning 24, 38–42, 78, 81

relationship with God 38–42, 61–2, 72–3
relationship of polarities 55
relevance 4–5
remembering 95–102; as biblical concept 97–8; conclusion 100–101; in the Eucharist 98–9; in liturgy and beyond 99–100; as narrative concept 95–6
remembering suffering 103–16; of God 103–7; of people/communities 107–14
remembrance 98–101, 106, 147, 153–4; *see also* remembering
renegotiated meaning 124
research interests 11–12
restoration 134–5
Resurrection 2, 37, 81, 87, 99, 123–5, 136, 149
rethinking liturgy 3
revealing 49–50
revenge 87, 110–11
revisiting narrative approach to liturgy 150–51
Ricoeur, Paul 119–21
Riessman, Catherine Kohler 95
rites of passage 48
ritual honesty 47–8, 51, 55, 79
ritual–liturgical analysis of liturgy 21–82
role assignment 24, 38–40, 78
role of Holy Communion 67
role of remembrance 100–101

Sacrament 8, 30, 38–9, 49, 54, 65, 127, 139–42, 154; *see also* Eucharist
sacred stories 75
sacrifice 33
safety 58–60, 73, 81–2, 134, 138–41, 147
St Paul 87–8, 133
Saliers, Don 3, 11, 13, 107, 140
salvation 27, 30–32, 66–7
Schaller, John 14
Schattauer, Thomas 12–13
Schreiter, Robert 86, 133–8
secondary theology vii
self-construction 95, 113
self-giving 107
self-sufficiency 122
sexual orientation 87
shadows forth 95
shalom 32, 34, 43, 91–2, 154
silence 108–13, 153
sin and suffering 54, 65–7, 81, 149
Smith, James 13
Smith, Susan Mary 10–11
solidarity with sufferers 73–4, 109, 114
spiritual journey 78, 149–50

spirituality of reconciliation 132–45; aspects of 132–5; community 138–41; conclusion 142; pastoral care and liturgy 141–2; storytelling in 135–7
status quaestionis 3–4
stories of suffering 21–82
story worlds meeting 117–23
storylines in liturgical text 30–35
storytellers 25–8
storytelling 14, 25–30, 76, 96, 118–19, 135–7, 142
structure of narrative 23, 30–35, 78
study of liturgy 43
suffering of God 103–7
suffering as theme in *Common Worship* 70
suffering in worship 69–82
Sunday worship vii, 4, 6, 35, 54, 60, 63, 148–50
Swain, Storm 139
Swinton, John 109–12, 117, 127
symbolism 127

Tamez, Elsa 109
Ten Commandments 66
tension between liturgy and suffering 2–3
text vs. context 54
Thanksgiving for the Gift of a Child 58, 60, 74
themes in addressing suffering 57–68, 80–82; clergy and pastoral awareness 60–61; community 57–8; conclusion 67; contrast between churches 62; expatriate settings 62–3; experience of God 61–2; experiences other than liturgy 64; healing 63–4; Holy Communion 58–9; liturgy causing suffering 65; liturgy as safe place 59–60; putting on a brave face 64; sin and suffering 65–7
theory of narrative 43, 46; *see also* Ganzevoort, R. Ruard

A Time to Heal 12
tone 36–7
transformation 46–7, 88, 111, 117–31, 155
Transforming Worship 6
trauma 77, 151
trespassing 37, 66
Tripp, David 124
type of suffering 5–6

ultimate parable 48–9, 79

van Dusseldorp, Kees 13–14
victimization 153
vulnerability 139

Walton, Heather 77
weaving human and divine stories 85–9, 133–4
Weil, Louis 27, 34
Westermann, Claus 90–91, 110
what is said and done 74
when liturgy and suffering meet 72–3
when stories meet 117–31; healing in Christ 123–8; meeting of story worlds 117–23
wholeness 32–4, 38–9, 43, 52, 63–7, 71, 78–81, 86–7, 147
Witvliet, John 3
Wolterstorff, Nicholas 85, 89–93, 103, 105, 107–8, 132–4, 139–41
wrongdoing 66, 80, 105, 153

Yahweh 98

zēkher 98
zikkārôn 97, 99
Zimmerman, Joyce Ann 11, 119

Taylor & Francis eBooks

Helping you to choose the right eBooks for your Library

Add Routledge titles to your library's digital collection today. Taylor and Francis ebooks contains over 50,000 titles in the Humanities, Social Sciences, Behavioural Sciences, Built Environment and Law.

Choose from a range of subject packages or create your own!

Benefits for you
- Free MARC records
- COUNTER-compliant usage statistics
- Flexible purchase and pricing options
- All titles DRM-free.

Benefits for your user
- Off-site, anytime access via Athens or referring URL
- Print or copy pages or chapters
- Full content search
- Bookmark, highlight and annotate text
- Access to thousands of pages of quality research at the click of a button.

REQUEST YOUR **FREE** INSTITUTIONAL TRIAL TODAY

Free Trials Available
We offer free trials to qualifying academic, corporate and government customers.

eCollections – Choose from over 30 subject eCollections, including:

Archaeology	Language Learning
Architecture	Law
Asian Studies	Literature
Business & Management	Media & Communication
Classical Studies	Middle East Studies
Construction	Music
Creative & Media Arts	Philosophy
Criminology & Criminal Justice	Planning
Economics	Politics
Education	Psychology & Mental Health
Energy	Religion
Engineering	Security
English Language & Linguistics	Social Work
Environment & Sustainability	Sociology
Geography	Sport
Health Studies	Theatre & Performance
History	Tourism, Hospitality & Events

For more information, pricing enquiries or to order a free trial, please contact your local sales team:
www.tandfebooks.com/page/sales

 The home of Routledge books

www.tandfebooks.com